THE COMMONWEALTH OF CRICKET

A fan with his heroes. (The author, centre, with Anil Kumble to
his right and Bishan Singh Bedi to his left.)

RAMACHANDRA GUHA

The Commonwealth of Cricket

A Lifelong Love Affair with the Most
Subtle and Sophisticated Game
Known to Humankind

WILLIAM
COLLINS

William Collins
An imprint of HarperCollins*Publishers*
1 London Bridge Street
London SE1 9GF

WilliamCollinsBooks.com

First published in Great Britain in 2020 by William Collins

1

Copyright © 2020 by Ramachandra Guha

Ramachandra Guha asserts the moral right to be identified
as the author of this work in accordance with the
Copyright, Designs and Patents Act 1988

A catalogue record for this book is
available from the British Library

ISBN 978-0-00-842250-9 (Hardback)
ISBN 978-0-00-842251-6 (Trade Paperback)

Typeset in Adobe Garamond Pro
Printed and bound in Great Britain by
CPI Group (UK) Ltd, Croydon

MIX
Paper from
responsible sources
FSC™ C007454

This book is produced from independently certified FSC™ paper
to ensure responsible forest management.

For more information visit: www.harpercollins.co.uk/green

In memory of my father,
who bought me my first cricket books.
And for my son, first reader of this one.

The longer I live, I am pleased to say, the less nationalistic I become. The outcome of a match is interesting but not, on the scales of time, of any great moment. What IS important is whether a particular contest gives to posterity a challenge that is accepted and won, or yields in classical technique an innings or a bowling effort that makes the game richer, so that the devotee can say years afterwards, with joy in his voice, 'I saw that performance.'

Jack Fingleton

CONTENTS

1

Cricket in Paradise

I

I have no memories of the first cricket match I saw. Yet I have heard so much about it since that I can write about it as if I did. The match was played at the cricket ground of the Indian Forest College (IFC) in Dehradun. The field was ringed to the south and the west by stately old beech trees. To the east were rows of probationers' hostels, built in red brick. On the ground's northern side ran a road, beyond which were officers' bungalows built in the style of Lutyens' Delhi. If one bowled or umpired from the southern end (as I often did in later years) one had a magnificent view of the Mussoorie Hills rising to seven thousand feet and beyond.

Dehradun is now the capital of the state of Uttarakhand, and has a million and more residents. When I was born, in 1958, it was a small district town in Uttar Pradesh, notable for its beauty. It was set in a long, low, valley, with the Siwalik Hills to its south and the Himalaya mountains to its north. Its western border was defined by the Yamuna river; its eastern border by the Ganga, which the Yamuna eventually joined, several hundred miles into the plains. The district had large tracts of sal forests, rich in animal and bird life, interspersed with paddy fields and *litchi* orchards and a whole clutch of government institutions. These included the Survey of India, the Indian Military Academy, and the Forest Research Institute (FRI).

At the time I saw my first cricket match, my father was a scientist at the FRI, of which the Indian Forest College was a part. My maternal grandfather also worked at the FRI. His son – my mother's brother – was a legendary local cricketer named N Duraiswami. When Durai was about ten – and himself watching cricket matches at the IFC ground – he fell from a wall and fractured his right arm. The doctor, who was incompetent or drunk, or perhaps both, set the plaster so tightly that Durai lost circulation in his main arm. Forever afterwards it hung limply from his body. He could use it to shake hands, but little else.

My grandfather was the leading wood scientist in India. Unlike his father Durai was an academic duffer, but a terrific sportsman. He played football, hockey, tennis and squash to a decent level. The game he loved most was cricket. After his accident, Durai taught himself to bowl with his left hand, becoming an artful finger-spinner. He was a useful lower-order batsman, and – even with only one good arm – a superb fieldsman.

The first cricket match I watched was played in 1962, when I was four. It was the annual derby between the probationers of the Indian Forest College and the staff of the Forest Research Institute. The captain of the FRI team was my uncle Durai, eligible to play as the son of an officer. Durai had just then completed three years at St Stephen's College in Delhi, where his cricketing mates included K S Indrajitsinhji, later to keep wicket for India, as well as Prem Bhatia, Ramesh Dewan and Bharat Awasthy,* all to enjoy long and successful Ranji Trophy careers. In the 1961–2 college cricket season, Durai had taken the most wickets for his team. The season ended with the final of the inter-college championship, in which St Stephen's played the university's Law college. Law's team included Manmohan Sood, who had just

---

* This and subsequent chapters mention many first-class and Test cricketers I saw, played with, or heard about. Their career records are available online for those who wish to follow up on them.

played his first (and it turned out, last) Test match, as well as Hanumant Singh, an elegant right-handed batsman then making loads of runs in first-class cricket and who a few years thereafter was to score a hundred on his Test debut. The turning point of this inter-college final was when Durai, fielding at deep mid-wicket, caught Manmohan Sood with the one good hand he had.

Delhi was the capital of India, while Dehradun was, in cricketing as much as political terms, a backwater. Durai was well known and widely admired in the town's sporting circles: for what he had done with one arm, and for having so recently played alongside some of the finest young cricketers in the country. (That he was incredibly handsome also helped.)

In the summer of 1962, Durai was sent down from St Stephen's for failing his final examinations. But honour at home could still be redeemed on the cricket field. In November of that year he played a critical part in Dehradun winning, for the first time, the inter-district championship of India's largest state, Uttar Pradesh. With a lanky fast bowler named Jindo, Durai took all the wickets, and with a burly opening batsman named Sheel Vohra, Durai scored all the runs, as Dehradun defeated the fancied teams of Meerut, Aligarh, and Lucknow districts.

In December 1962, my grandfather turned fifty-eight, the age at which government servants then retired. At the end of the month, and year, he would move from Dehradun to the southern city of Bangalore to start a new research institute, funded by the plywood industry. Durai still had one cricket match to play in our hometown, for the FRI against the IFC. While my uncle captained the FRI, the IFC was led by a fast bowler named Prasad, who had already played Ranji Trophy for his home state (Madhya Pradesh, as I recall) before coming to Dehradun as a probationer of the Indian Forest Service.

Playing alongside Durai for the FRI in the first cricket match I watched was my father, Dr Subramaniam Rama Das Guha. He was the captain's last choice, picked ahead of a promising young fast bowler named Manoj Sharma, the son of the Institute's photographer. The decision was controversial. In past years, Dr Guha had used the long handle to good effect, but he was now pushing forty and a liability in the field. Did Durai pick him ahead of Manoj Sharma because he thought he needed more depth in batting? Or because Dr Guha was his brother-in-law?

It was a glorious winter's day in the foothills, crisp and cloudless. I watched from the tiled wooden pavilion beyond mid-wicket, while Durai won the toss and chose to field. He took six wickets as the IFC were bowled out for 132, in small-town cricket not an insubstantial score. Half of Durai's victims were stumped, dragged out of the crease by his curving, alluring flight, the bails adroitly removed by the wicketkeeper, Ram Nath Gideon, the FRI's medical officer who had once hunted in the forests of Kumaun with the famous slayer of man-eating tigers, Jim Corbett.

When FRI went in to bat, the IFC's Prasad made quick inroads with the new ball. Durai, coming in at number four – much higher than he batted for St Stephen's – steadied the ship. While wickets fell around him he marched on, with clips to leg and the odd cover drive. He reached fifty, and the innings passed one hundred. Twenty to win, then ten, and now only five. With FRI's score at 130 for eight, Durai pushed forward to the IFC's off-spinner. The ball went through with the arm and took the outside edge of his bat, to be taken safely at slip.

The last man in was Dr S R D Guha, on weekdays the officer-in-charge of the cellulose and paper branch. He knew how to experiment with chemicals on different kinds of wood and bamboo, and had published dozens of scientific papers. But could he win a cricket match?

Four deliveries remained in the over. Three runs were needed to win. FRI's number eleven swung the first ball he faced lustily towards mid-on. Watching the ball descend towards the fielder was Durai, in the pavilion, his pads still on. Also watching was the team's twelfth man, Manoj Sharma, whose own disappointment at his team's impending defeat was mixed with vindication at witnessing who had caused it. Had a last-minute choice by a nepotistic South Indian captain just handed the match to the enemy?

Mid-on was the IFC's captain, Prasad, also the only first-class cricketer on the field. Surely he would take the catch. But he didn't and the ball popped in and out of his hands. To the next delivery, Dr Guha swung again and connected better. The ball soared high, over Prasad's head and on to the boundary. The match was won. Number eleven had saved his team's and his family's honour. Waving his bat in the air, my father ran towards the pavilion where we sat. My uncle and I stood up to applaud, and I am told our twelfth man did so too.*

Durai's cricketing career in Dehradun having ended on a winning note, he moved with his father to Bangalore. I stayed on, since my father still had many years of service in the Forest Research Institute ahead of him.

II

The Forest Research Institute was spread over fifteen hundred acres, with homes and offices interspersed with patches of forest, containing trees from all over India, on which the scientists experimented. The campus had three full-sized cricket grounds: one belonging to the IFC, a second to the Northern Forest Rangers College, the third open to the Institute's staff and

---

* The case of Prasad is an exception to the preceding footnote. I cannot now recall his first name or initials, so the reader cannot look up his first-class record. My father is dead, and I do not want to ask Durai, since he does not know I am writing this book.

children. It was on this last field (known residually as the 'FRI Ground') that I watched the first match I clearly remember. A team from the town of Saharanpur (on the other side of the Siwaliks, and known for having even better *litchis* than Dehradun) had come to play the FRI. My father – now no longer a playing member – had taken me along to watch. The visiting side had several Sikhs, including its captain, who was also the opening batsman. To a little Tamil boy from a family of scientists, Sikhs signified strength. This fellow certainly did, for, in the first over of the match, he hooked a bouncer ferociously, the ball landing on the road beyond the ground and bouncing away into someone's garden. Shortly afterwards, it began to rain hard. No more play was possible on the day. The first cricket match I actually remember lasted five, perhaps ten, minutes. But I can see that hook shot still.

My uncle was my first cricketing hero, but it was my father who told me my first cricketing stories. As a boy he had lived in the seaside town of Mangalore, then part of the Madras Presidency. A team had come visiting from the great city of Madras, which included Cota Ramaswami, who had played Test cricket as well as Davis Cup tennis for India. Ramaswami was a famous left-handed hitter who batted with his bat held aloft, above his shoulder. That image stuck, and stayed, which is why when it came to his first and his second ball in that FRI *v* IFC match of 1962, my father played the lofted shot both times. It was more or less the only stroke he knew, though Cota Ramaswami had of course played plenty of others.

When he was twelve, my father moved with his family to Bangalore, then merely a middling size cantonment town, not the global metropolis it has since become. The star cricketer here was Benjamin Frank, a working-class Tamil who was making hundreds in local cricket, en route to a distinguished Ranji Trophy career with Mysore and Bengal. Frank, like Ramaswami, dealt mostly in fours and sixes. Watching him play, my father and his brother were inspired to set up a cricket club, which practised in Cubbon Park. After finishing school and college my father went on to do a PhD in chemistry at the Indian Institute of Science. The assistant in his laboratory was Benjamin Frank's father. Hearing of the research student's sporting interests, Frank senior presented him a bat once owned by his son. Years later, it was this willow which sent that ball for four over mid-on's head to help FRI beat IFC in that epic match of 1962.

My father spoke to me occasionally of C Ramaswami and B Frank, and, more often, of Lala Amarnath, unlike the other two a national cricketing hero, rather than a merely regional one. Amarnath was the first Indian to score a Test hundred, against an England Test side led by Douglas Jardine, no less; the first captain of a Test side representing independent India, in Australia in 1947, against a team led by Don Bradman, no less. He was a flamboyant character, known (and generally admired) for his anti-authoritarian streak, for battling against the Maharajas and colonial civil servants who in his time ruled Indian cricket.

In 1941, my father passed his matriculation exam, at the top of his class; as a reward, his parents paid for him to have a week's holiday in Bombay, always the most glamorous city in India, and at the time the country's cricketing capital too. By a happy coincidence, my father's visit coincided with a match played between the winners of the Ranji Trophy (who, that year, were Maharashtra) and a Rest of India side. He went to watch a day's play, in the course of which he saw Lala Amarnath bat, bowl, field, and keep wicket – and captain his side for a brief while too.

Also playing in that match were C K Nayudu, Vinoo Mankad, Syed Mushtaq Ali, and Vijay Hazare – all authentic cricketing greats – as well as a clutch of other Test players. But my father remembered only Lala. He spoke to me often about Amarnath's all-round genius, as manifested before his eyes in the Brabourne

7

Stadium in Bombay. Occasionally, as when he captained the Cellulose and Paper Branch in a friendly match, he put into practice what he had seen as a boy – by batting, bowling (lollilop leg-breaks), fielding (at slip), captaining, and even keeping wicket for a spell. In his own, entirely modest realm, my father would strive to be what Amarnath had once been at the highest levels of the game.

I had an elder sister, whom my father taught to hurdle and long jump. But for me, his only son, the sport of choice was cricket. Our bungalow in the FRI had a spacious lawn, where I played with my father, with a plastic bat and ball to begin with, then a tennis ball, finally graduating to the real thing. One winter, when I was six or seven, my uncle Durai came visiting from Bangalore. He saw me bowl a leg-break, beating my father on the outside edge. The next ball was tossed up higher. My father went to hit it over mid-off, except that it was a googly this time, and bowled him through the gate.

Watching this double act, Durai charted out a career path for me. I could bowl a leg-break, and a googly as well. And I had two legs and two arms. I would become the Test cricketer that he, with his tragic handicap, never could be.

In India, and South India especially, the relationship with one's *mama*, or maternal uncle, is very close. I was Durai's first and favourite nephew, the son of his only sister (he was then unmarried, and was never to have any children of his own). That I became the object of his fantasies was not surprising. I was in any case cricket-mad. I played the game, I watched the game, I heard the game (on the radio), and I had begun reading about the game too. In 1965, I acquired my first *Wisden Cricketers' Almanack*, featuring the Ashes series of the previous year (the *Wisden* was a present from a neighbour's son, Captain Anup Singh Rawat, newly commissioned into the Army, and affection-ately indulgent of my passion). I read the scores in the *Almanack* greedily, though I suppose not all the articles made sense (one, written by Sir Learie Constantine, carried the title: 'Cricket: An Art or a Science?').

By the time I was eight, I was scoring for the FRI in their matches. In the winter sunshine I sat on a bench outside the pavilion; a table in front of me, the instruments of my trade spread out on it – the scoring book, several pens, and an open bottle of Quink's Royal Blue Ink.

III

My hometown, Dehradun, was greatly beloved of the British colonialists for its moderate climate, stunning views, its forests teeming with wildlife, and its rivers abundant in fish. The FRI was one of many institutions the British set up in the valley. Each had its own cricket ground (or, as in the case of FRI, several), each one as charming as the next. The cricket ground of the Survey of India, at Hathibarkala – or the place where elephants once roamed – had the Mussoorie Hills to its north and west, and thick sal forests on the other two sides. The ground of the Rashtriya (formerly Royal) Indian Military College was next to a canal filled with water from the melting snows; and it had a jewel of a pavilion, with lattice work in intricate patterns.

I have been to Lord's and the Adelaide Oval, and to The Parks at Oxford and the county ground at Worcester as well. It's true that no individual ground in Dehradun was quite as beautiful, but what dazzled was the collection, or combination. No town in Australia or England or South Africa has so many lovely sporting fields as Dehradun. And I watched and played cricket on all of them.

The field in the Doon that carried the most cachet was located in the campus of the Indian Military Academy (IMA), where the officers of the country's army were trained. In India – as in any nation new or old – the armed forces had enormous prestige. The cricket ground's status was in part a product of this. That it had the only turf wicket in the district also contributed. Divided into three equal parts, the others devoted to football and hockey, it was a very long field, that extended so far that on a clear day one had a view of the Siwalik Hills that constituted the Valley's southern perimeter.

The campus of the IMA adjoined that of the FRI. The 'gentleman cadets' took their daily run (carrying heavy backpacks) around the magnificent main building of the FRI. Most mornings one was woken up by the bagpipes of the army band. In those pre-terrorist days, one could walk or cycle from one campus to another without being stopped or searched. They were separated by a nine-hole golf course called 'FRIMA', in theory belonging to both institutions but used by the military men alone, the equipment and refreshments subsidised by the taxpayer.

In his years in the Doon, Durai had played or watched much cricket at the IMA. In 1951, he had seen Frank Worrell bat at the IMA for a visiting Commonwealth side. After Worrell was out for a low score, Durai saw him polish his boots and his pads, a lesson in love of one's sporting gear that my uncle never forgot. A decade later, Durai had played at the IMA for a Dehradun XI against the Services team, when, after getting two or three wickets quickly, he was subject to a murderous assault by Major Rai Singh, a fast-bowling all-rounder who had hit a six out of the Melbourne Cricket Ground in the one Test match he played, back in January 1948. On this day, many years later, Rai Singh hit one drive so hard that after striking the boundary wall it rebounded yards back into the ground; and another even harder, such that it split cover point's boots en route to the fence.

Durai's most vivid memory of the IMA ground, however, pertained not to cricket but to hockey. India then ruled the sport; we had won five Olympic hockey tournaments in succession. Before the 1956 Olympics in Melbourne, the Indian team had their pre-tournament camp at the IMA. As part of their training they played a local side, which was captained by a man named Chaturvedi, who had played hockey for India back in the 1930s. He was now sportsmaster at Durai's school, St Joseph's Academy, and chose my uncle to play for his side that day.

Durai's normal position at hockey was right-half. Chaturvedi usually played at left-half. For this match the sportsmaster exchanged places with his student, thinking it unfair to expose the boy to the greatest trio of forwards that ever played this game – Balbir Singh at centre-forward, Udham Singh at inside-left, and Raghubir Singh Bhola at outside-left. Not that it helped. The ageing schoolmaster could not lay a stick to the ball, as it whizzed between Balbir, Udham and Bhola before finding the back of the net.

At half-time the score was 10–0 in favour of the Olympians. Chaturvedi Saab now asked his student to revert to his original place, while he did likewise. The defence improved perceptibly, with only six goals being conceded by the Dehradun XI in the second half.

Some fifty years after this mother of all one-sided sporting contests, I was in Vancouver, where I was to deliver a lecture on Gandhi at the University of British Columbia. Before the lecture began, I was introduced to an elderly but entirely erect Sikh, who had come to listen to me. He was introduced as Balbir Singh, the three-time Olympic gold medallist, then visiting relatives in Canada. I stooped down to touch his feet, to convey my reverence and that of my uncle too. He withdrew several steps backwards, for the egalitarian Sikhs deplore a custom that comes naturally to the deferential Hindu.

IV

While growing up in the FRI, Durai's closest friend, on and off the field, was a boy named Ram Bahadur Chhetri, whose father was a *chaprassi*, or peon, at the Institute. As his surname indicates, Ram Bahadur (always known as 'Ramu') was of Nepali stock, whose ancestors had come to the Valley in the service of the British Army. Together Durai and Ramu started a cricket team named Sporting Youngsters which trained on the FRIMA golf course. After practice they sometimes repaired to Durai's home for tea and snacks. One day, a bottle of Gordon's Dry Gin caught Ramu's eye. My grandfather was a teetotaller; the gin was kept for the Swiss and German scientists who occasionally came to visit him. Ramu liked the bottle's look and smell; and hillmen are partial to a drink anyway. He would take a swig from time to time, after which his friend, the scientist's son, would top up the bottle with water. Durai made sure to make himself scarce the next time his father brought a foreign visitor home.

Ram Bahadur was an even better all-round sportsman than my uncle. The game he liked best was football. Word of his skill reached the Calcutta Maidan, whose talent scouts were sent to the Valley to recruit him. In or around 1956, he joined the celebrated East Bengal Club in Calcutta. He played eleven seasons for them as a midfielder, helping his club win many championship trophies. Ramu represented his country in the Rome Olympics of 1960, and in the Jakarta Asian Games of 1962 as well, when India won the soccer gold medal. Unlike other celebrated Indian (and global) footballers, Ramu never changed his club; since it was East Bengal who picked him up from obscurity, it would always be East Bengal for him. Many years after he had retired, a still grateful East Bengal Club nominated him their 'Midfielder of the Millennium'.

An essay online entitled *Ram Bahadur: The Dehradun Dynamite* has some stirring paragraphs on the footballing skills of my uncle's closest friend. Here is one:

> Ram Bahadur's best performance in the red and gold outfit [of East Bengal] came in 1957 against Mohammedan Sporting. Despite receiving a serious injury on his head after collision with Mohammedan player Salim, Bahadur played the whole game and made around half a dozen goal line clearances. East Bengal ultimately went on to win the match 3–0 with goals from Tapash Bose and Moosah. At the end of the game, Bahadur laid senseless on the ground with his head fully draped in blood. Remarking on Ram Bahadur's gutsy performance, noted Calcutta football personality and East Bengal recruiter, late Jiban Chakraborty said, 'I never saw Ram Bahadur play a bad game in eleven years for the club. Such was his consistency and talent that he was like a wall in the midfield.'

In winter, after the football season had ended, Ram Bahadur would come back to his hometown and resume playing cricket for Sporting Youngsters. One day, at practice, Ramu was regaling his team-mates with stories of the Olympic Village in Rome, of how the Americans spoke and the Japanese dressed. The giggles got so loud and disruptive that Durai asked Ramu to take a round of the field in punishment. The offender set off as ordered by his captain. As he completed his round and came back to the nets, Ramu saw his team-mates huddled around Durai, who was weeping uncontrollably, struck by remorse at having so wantonly humiliated one of India's most famous sportsmen. It was Ramu himself who calmed my uncle down, saying that while he may otherwise be an Olympian, and a colossus on the Calcutta Maidan, in this town and on this field, Durai would always be his captain.

V

In 1966, I travelled with my parents to Bangalore for the summer holidays. We stayed with my maternal grandparents, who then lived in the locality of Malleswaram, in the west of the city, close to the Indian Institute of Science. In the same house lived my bachelor uncle, Durai. He had been in the city now for four years, and was already well known in its cricketing circles. He captained the Friends Union Cricket Club (FUCC), Bangalore's second oldest club, which had one team in the first division and another in the third.

Cricket in Dehradun was distinctly amateurish, played for fun. Most matches were 'friendlies', although once every other year a desultory knockout tournament was played between six or at most eight teams. Bangalore, however, had a population ten times that of my hometown. Mysore (not yet named Karnataka) was then one of the top teams in India's premier domestic tournament, the Ranji Trophy, and its cricket was all centred around the state capital. The Mysore (later Karnataka) State Cricket Association had a five-tiered league, with a dozen teams in each division. Each match was competed for fiercely; the top teams in the division fought furiously each year for the title, with the middling teams equally focused on not being relegated to the division below. Apart from the leagues, there was a prestigious annual knockout tournament for the Y S Ramaswamy Trophy, in which some sixty clubs took part.

Club rivalries in Bangalore were intense; and, so were the ambitions of individual players. In the Doon a batsman got to fifty for the pleasure of a dozen or so spectators; in Bangalore, one scored a century or took five wickets to better one's chances of shifting from a club in the second to the first division; or, if already in the latter, of getting onto the longlist of the selectors of the Mysore Ranji Trophy team.

In that summer of 1966, I became FUCC's youngest member. The club then practised in the grounds of the Malleswaram High School. Every afternoon I would accompany Durai, riding pillion on his scooter. We would bring out the matting from the school's warehouse, roll it towards the nets, and hammer in the nails that held the mat down. The 'we' here is provocatively presumptuous, for, of course I would be merely watching while the adults did the work.

At the FUCC my cricketing pantheon expanded exponentially. To Durai were now added his team-mates. There was P N Satish ('Chitty'), a geologist from the University of Mysore, with a fast bowler's build and a fast bowler's boots, which he tied briskly each day before practice. Chitty was as handsome as my uncle.* And some others were better cricketers too. It was said that my grandfather's move south had prevented Durai from attending the trials for the Uttar Pradesh Ranji team. But this was merely legend. What, in Bangalore in the summer of 1966, I came to know as hard fact was that as many as four members of the FUCC team had once played in the Ranji Trophy for the state of Mysore.

The four first-class cricketers in my club were K L Mahesh, K M Ramprasad, P S Vishwanath and M Navinchandra. Mahesh drove firmly off front foot and back, and was an accurate medium-pacer as well. In his pomp, Prasad was a tearaway fast bowler; now, some years after his last Ranji match, he had made himself into a medium-pace swing bowler, making the ball duck this way and that off a six-step run. Vishu was a superb middle-order batsman; orthodox in his approach, starting slowly but, once set, settling in for the duration. Navin, a doctor by profession, was a

---

* On googling 'P N Satish, Geology', I find that this hero of my childhood was in later life the co-author of a paper entitled 'Effect of paper mill effluents on accumulation of heavy metals in coconut trees near Nanjangud, Mysore district, Karnataka, India', published in 1991 in the journal *Environmental Geology and Water Sciences*.

capable wicketkeeper and an attacking batsman, particularly adept at the hook and the pull.

I admired this quartet, but my favourite FUCC cricketer was V Ramadas. Ramadas bowled sharply turning off-breaks, fielded well and bravely close-in, and was a high-class batsman besides. In the season just concluded he had scored a century against the Indian Telephone Industries, in the course of which he had hit the great Indian off-spinner Erapalli Prasanna for four (or maybe five) sixes. It was said that Ramadas had not yet played in the Ranji Trophy because the captain of Mysore was his brother, the Test player V Subrahmanyam. One version had it that Subbu did not want to be charged with nepotism; another that he feared that if his younger brother was capped for Mysore he would soon surpass him in cricketing renown.

Neither of these stories emanated from the man himself. I heard of those sixes hit by Ramadas off Prasanna from Durai; and of his brother's alleged jealousy from Chitty, who – as the only buyer of books in the club – may have got it from a reading of P G Wodehouse's cricketing stories (where the youngest of the Jackson brothers, Mike, exceeds the siblings who had made their names before him). Ramadas himself was gentle, modest and exceptionally kind. At practice he marked out a line for me, twelve rather than twenty-two yards from the batsman's wicket, so that FUCC's newest member, all of eight years old, could bowl at the nets too.

I returned from that summer a member of the FUCC and a fan of the Mysore cricket team as well. I could see how superior these cricketers were to those I had seen play in front of me in my hometown. Dehradun was marginal to the cricket of its state, Uttar Pradesh; whereas Bangalore was the epicentre of Mysore cricket. UP was the weakest team in the weakest zone of the Ranji Trophy; whereas Mysore had several cricketers playing for India. I had chosen a club to support; and now I had chosen a state with it. I would, hopefully soon, see FUCC win the First

Division, and see Mysore win the Ranji Trophy championship too.

In the winter of 1967–8, the Indian Test team toured Australia. V Subrahmanyam was a member of the touring side, which may be why his brother Ramadas was finally chosen to play for Mysore against Andhra Pradesh in the Ranji Trophy. He scored 33, while another debutant, G R Viswanath, scored 230. Soon afterwards Ramadas joined the Indian Tobacco Company, who posted him to Chirala, in the depths of the Telugu country. His first first-class match was also his last.

VI

Durai had left Dehradun in 1962, but on his own visits to our hometown Ram Bahadur always came to see us. He had played some cricket with my father, while he regarded the sister of his best friend as a sort of sister too. I myself never watched Ramu play football, but carry vivid memories of him in whites. The first time I visited the IMA ground was to watch Ramu turn out for a scratch Dehradun team against the Academy. When the Cadets batted he fielded brilliantly, throwing himself from side to side at cover point. Later, he scored a brisk fifty, each cut and hook accompanied by polite shouts of 'Well played, Sir!' from army officers who would never break bread – or drink gin – with this son of a Nepali peon but who were nonetheless willing to grant him his sporting prowess.

This must have been in 1966 or 1967, and I suppose it was my father who took me to the ground on his scooter. The next time I visited the IMA I went by myself, and by cycle. The year was 1970. One of Durai's young wards at FUCC had just entered the Indian Military Academy. He was a wicketkeeper batsman named Ashok Kumar. Coming home for a meal, he invited me to watch the Cadets play the Officers the following weekend.

The Cadets batted first, and with Ashok Kumar leading the way, posted a total close to 200. In those distant times that pre-dated the Indian Premier League (IPL), five years before even the first cricket World Cup was played, one-day matches were not defined or restricted by overs. If the side batting second did not lose ten wickets or score the required runs by close of play, a draw was declared. Often, in the face of a high score by the team batting first, a draw was all one could hope for.

So it was this day for the Academy's officers. They could not aim to score 200, but they might yet not lose all ten wickets, at least so long as their captain was at the crease. His name was Colonel C V (Chandu) Gadkari, and he had played six Test matches for India. Back in 1952–3, on a tour of the West Indies, Gadkari and Polly Umrigar had won acclaim for their fielding in the covers – never before, and not for a long time thereafter, were Indian cricketers seen to be so swift of foot and so sure of arm.

That was in the early 1950s. However, by the time of which I speak, some two decades later, Chandu Gadkari had developed an ample waistline. He now fielded, placidly, at slip or at mid-on, and no longer bowled (he had once been a handy medium-pacer). But he could still bat, and bat expertly. He knew to farm the strike, patting a ball down past square-leg or short of point off the last ball of an over. And he had not forgotten how to play attacking strokes either. I remember, from a distance of some fifty years, a sizzling off-drive down to the pavilion, and a hook shot played towards the trees, two among the many fours he hit that day.

Wickets fell now and then in the Officers innings, but the former Test player's was not among them. In between balls and overs Gadkari kept up a conversation with the hapless young men fielding around him. When stumps were finally called, only eight wickets were down, and Gadkari was 90-odd not out. I met Ashok Kumar as he walked off the field, shaking his head disgustedly. The Colonel, he said, had been palpably caught behind the wicket by him early on, but the umpire, 'that b——— Gautham', had given him not out. Gautham (also from Bangalore) had been left out of the Cadets XI that day, and Ashok thought he sought to ingratiate himself with Gadkari to get his place back.

I did not share my clubmate's anger. I gloried in Gautham's mistake – whether willed or otherwise. In Bangalore in 1966, the stars of FUCC had shown me what made first-class cricketers different from the club cricketers of the Valley. Now, four years later, Chandu Gadkari had just as emphatically marked out for me the distance between the Ranji player and the true international.

VII

I spent the summer of 1970 in Bangalore, mostly in the nets at the Friends Union Cricket Club. I was now twelve, and could bowl off twenty-two yards. I was no longer a wrist-spinner, but a new-ball bowler. For I had recently read Ralph Barker's *Ten Great Bowlers* and was captivated by its first chapter, on Fred (The Demon) Spofforth, who, when England were set a mere 85 runs to win in the fourth innings of the Oval Test of 1882, had walked up and down the dressing room saying, 'This thing can be done, this thing will be done.' It was, indeed, with the Demon taking seven for 44 (five of them clean bowled) as Australia won by seven runs. *The Sporting Times* thereupon announced the death of English cricket, and the Ashes were born.

Since I was last in Bangalore, my uncle's club, and mine, had undergone some changes of personnel. Among the newcomers were a quartet in their early twenties: the opening batsmen Satyendra and Narayan Raju, one orthodox, the other wilfully cross-batted; the googly-bowling all-rounder K G Padaki; and the middle-order batsman and fine outfielder Sudhakar Rao. There was also a new wicketkeeper, K G Shashidhar, who might have been picked for Mysore ahead of Syed Kirmani except that he was not such a good batsman, and had an engineering degree to finish besides.

Since I was last in Bangalore, Durai had got a promotion in the commercial firm he worked in, which allowed him to exchange his scooter for a car. Meanwhile, the FUCC had moved their nets from Malleswaram High School to St Joseph's Indian High School, in the heart of the Bangalore cantonment (we played where the Mallya Hospital now stands). For the first hour or so each day, I stood well away from the pitch, throwing back balls hit by Sudhakar through cover or by Raju over mid-wicket. But once the main batsmen had done with their practice I got a chance to bowl. On one occasion I got a ball to swing in late, bowling Durai through the gate – until that date my greatest triumph in cricket – which had Shashidhar, behind the stumps, chortling with delight.

Our practice ground shared a wall with the staff quarters of the Indian Tobacco Company. The 'I' in ITC had previously stood for 'Imperial', and residues of the Raj remained, as in the Bangalore tobacco factory's manager, a man named Chris Hardinge, who, one afternoon, walked over and asked whether he could join the club. Durai was open to the idea, for the visitor was from Yorkshire, the land of Len Hutton, whom my uncle, growing up in the early 1950s, regarded as the model captain, so much so that he massively under-bowled himself, placing his faith in his team's Tyson and Statham, since – as the Ashes series of 1954–5 so demonstrably showed – it was fast bowlers who won matches. This Yorkshireman in Bangalore was a decent all-rounder, but he intimidated his team-mates, who – Durai apart – scarcely spoke any English. FUCC's resident wit, a man named A G Mani who had once bowled barefoot for Mysore Schools against Ceylon Schools, was particularly savage behind

Hardinge's back, comparing him to a rhesus monkey (likewise with a red behind). All this changed when FUCC defeated their great rivals BUCC, the winning runs coming from a six over square leg hit by the Yorkshireman.

Each day, after practice ended, we would repair to the nearby Koshy's Parade Café, where the men had coffee and I drank lime juice. Then Durai and I drove back home, for a hot water bucket bath (showers were scarce in the India of the 1970s), followed by dinner. Afterwards, while my parents and grandparents went off to sleep in the apartment's two bedrooms, Durai and I laid down our mattresses on the floor of the living room. There were still cricket stories to hear before I went to sleep. Many of these were about my uncle's greatest hero, Vinoo Mankad, like him a left-hand slow bowler and right-hand attacking batsman. In January 1952, when Durai was just a little older than I was now, Mankad had bowled India to its first Test victory, taking eight wickets in the first innings and four in the second. This match took place in Madras, the other end of the subcontinent from Dehradun. Whether he heard these wickets being taken, live on the radio, or whether he heard about them later from a cousin who was at the ground, I cannot tell – but Durai could remember and recall them all. So I heard now of how Mankad got out England's two best batsmen – of how by varying his angle of delivery he drew Tom Graveney out of his crease and had him stumped, of how he made a ball dip and had Jack Robertson mistime a drive to be caught-and-bowled.

My uncle Durai venerated the great Test players of the past, and of the present. One Sunday, when there was no practice and FUCC themselves did not have a match, he took me to the YMCA ground, to see City Cricketers play the Indian Air Force in an early round of the Y S Ramaswamy Trophy tournament. City Cricketers was captained by Erapalli Prasanna, who had first played for India in 1962. He then took time off to complete his engineering degree, before returning to the Test side in the winter of 1966–7. Prasanna bowled beautifully in Australia and New Zealand the following winter, taking close to fifty wickets in eight Tests.

In the last months of 1969, India and Australia had played a five-Test series, which I followed on the radio and in the newspaper. Australia won the first Test match in Bombay easily; the second in Kanpur was drawn (courtesy of a dazzling hundred on debut by G R Viswanath); India won the third in Delhi, with Bishan Bedi and Prasanna taking eighteen wickets between them; Australia bounced back in Calcutta, winning by ten wickets, powered by Graham McKenzie with the ball and Ian Chappell with the bat.

This had been the most exciting Test series in living memory. The home side came to Madras for the last Test, still hoping to square the series. Australia batted first, and a sublime century by Doug Walters took them to 258. The score was made to look more substantial when India were bowled out for 163. Then, late on the second day, the debutant Mohinder Amarnath cleaned up Stackpole and Chappell with sharp inswingers, leaving the visitors 12 for two at stumps.

That Madras Test had started on 24 December. Christmas Day was a day of rest. My parents in Dehradun were in holiday mood too. On Saturday 27 December, the third day of play, we had planned to go on a riverside picnic. I took a transistor along, gripped with excitement, and joy, as in the first half hour of play, Prasanna bowled the previously unbowlable Bill Lawry, had the magnificent Walters caught by Eknath Solkar at short-leg, and Paul Sheahan stumped. When Brian Taber was caught in the leg trap for a duck, also off Prasanna, Australia were down to 24 for six, effectively 119 for six.

The only recognised batsman left now was Ian Redpath. A match was on, and the series hung in the balance. For Prasanna's next over I held the transistor close, to hear how Redpath came down the wicket, and was beaten in the flight, with no hope of regaining the crease. The ball missed the stumps by a whisker, eluded the wicketkeeper's gloves, and carried on for four byes. Redpath went on to make 63, taking his side to a total of 153. By now the pitch was a dust bowl, and India eventually lost by 77 runs.

The most articulate of the visiting cricketers, Ian Chappell, left India saying Erapalli Prasanna was the finest spin bowler of his generation. Durai agreed with him; now, in the summer of 1970, I was with my uncle in Bangalore, going to watch Prasanna bowl in a club match. We got up early, Durai and I, to get to the ground, taking along a lunch packed by my grandmother. Outside the YMCA was parked a gleaming blue coach, which had come all the way from Jalahalli – then separated from Bangalore by miles and miles of fields – carrying the smartly turned out officer-cricketers of the Indian Air Force.

The YMCA ground was on Nrupathunga Road, adjoining Cubbon Park. I cannot remember now whether it had sightscreens; most likely not. We set ourselves down where a sightscreen should have been, to get the best view of the cricket. The Air Force won the toss and batted. Their captain as well as leading batsman was D D Deshpande, who had played with distinction for Vidarbha and Services, North and Central Zones, and who *Wisden* had told me was (at that point in time) one of only a handful of cricketers to be given out handled the ball in a first-class match.

Memories of three balls that day are everlasting. All were bowled by Prasanna to Deshpande. The first two were slightly short, and were each pulled for four. The third was of the same length, but instead of turning to leg hurried straight through, catching the batsman plumb in front. The main threat disposed of by their captain, City Cricketers won in a canter.

Many years later, I played against D D Deshpande myself. At lunch, I approached him to speak of when I had first seen him bat. It may have been just another club match, but the mark of a Master made it unforgettable, for me the young fan as well as for him the experienced first-class cricketer. For no sooner had I opened my mouth than Deshpande remarked: 'Ah yes, Pras. He made a fool of me that day.'

It was in the same summer of 1970 that I shook hands for the first time with a Test cricketer. One morning, my uncle and I were driving in his Fiat along Nrupathunga Road when he spied a tiny little figure hunched over a scooter. Durai overtook him from the left, shouted out 'Vishy!, Vishy!', and with his shrunken right hand motioned for the man to pull up. He did, we got out of our car, and my uncle introduced me to G R Viswanath, who in the previous winter had scored that dazzling hundred on debut against Australia in Kanpur. That incident says something about the times – which Test cricketer now would drive a scooter? – and everything about the man himself, happy to be brought to a halt by an ordinary club cricketer who wished to introduce him to his starry-eyed little nephew.

VIII

Bangalore was divided then, as it is now, into two parts, the City and the Cantonment, the separation as much sociological as geographical. The City had two major clubs, the eponymous City Cricketers, for whom both Prasanna and the great googly bowler B S Chandrasekhar played, and Bangalore Cricketers, the club of the aforementioned Gundappa Viswanath. Both clubs were manned and followed almost exclusively by Kannada speakers.

The main clubs of the Cantonment were Swastic Union and the Bangalore United Cricket Club. Swastic was closely controlled by a single family, the Patels, businessmen originally from Gujarat; whereas BUCC had among its stalwarts the Parsi coach, Keki Tarapore, and the English-speaking doctor, K Thimmapaiah, who had scored the first Ranji century for Mysore.

Though he admired many of their cricketers, Durai always spoke of Swastic and BUCC with derision. They exercised undue influence over the Mysore (later Karnataka) State Cricket Association, promoting their players at all levels, from the state Under-16 team to the Ranji squad. Players from other clubs, he claimed (and I believe correctly), were regularly discriminated against. The sole reason Mahesh and Ramadas played only one Ranji match, and Ramprasad and Navinchandra only four apiece, was that they were from our club. Had they turned out for BUCC or Swastic they would have played dozens of times for Mysore, and perhaps been selected for South Zone too.

However, there was one distinction the intriguers of BUCC and Swastic could never take away from us. The first Mysore/Karnataka cricketer ever to play an official Test match for India came from the Friends Union Cricket Club. He was the off-break bowler V M Muddiah. Starting out with FUCC and Mysore, Muddiah then joined the Indian Air Force, and so played most of his sixty-one first-class matches for the Services. He toured England with the Indian team in 1959, although his two Test matches were played at home, against Australia in New Delhi in 1959–60 and against Pakistan in Kanpur the following winter, when one of the three wickets he took was that of Hanif Mohammad.

I cannot remember whether V M Muddiah played for Services in the match in Dehradun when Rai Singh smashed Durai around the ground. I know that he and my uncle grew close in the late 1960s, when Muddiah was posted in Bangalore. By this time his cricketing career had come to a premature end, largely through an excess of alcohol. He came occasionally to the FUCC nets, but did not play for the club.

Had Durai two good hands, he might very well have played cricket for India. And joined the army or air force too. He had the physique and temperament of an officer. That Muddiah had both been in uniform and played Test cricket endeared himself greatly to my uncle. Durai and the man he called 'Mudi' had many cricketing conversations, the contents of which were later passed on to me.

V M Muddiah's own hero was the long-time cricket captain of the Services, H R (Hemu) Adhikari, who played twenty-one Test matches for India, captaining his country in one of them. Adhikari was a fine middle-order batsman and an outstanding fielder in the covers, but his chief distinction is that he was the first Indian cricketer to make physical fitness central to his game. Muddiah must have spoken often about him to Durai, since in my uncle's cricket talk 'Mudi says Hemu once said' appeared as often as 'Mudi once told me'. When an off-spinner in the FUCC's 'B' team bowled with a 4–5 field, both he and his captain got a shelling from Durai afterwards, since Hemu had told Mudi that on matting, where the ball always turned sharply, no spin bowler worth his salt bowled with less than six fielders on one side of the wicket – 6–3 or 7–2 for the left-arm spinner, 3–6 or 2–7 for the off-break bowler.

In the winter of 1970–1, Durai came to Dehradun to visit his sister and check on my cricketing progress. He was satisfied by my bowling, less so by my batting, and least of all with my fielding. He went about setting this right, informed by what he thought Hemu Adhikari would have done when confronted with a twelve-year-old boy frightened by a hard leather ball coming at him with speed.

Our bungalow at the FRI was fronted by a porch held up by a solid brick wall, against which Durai now stood his nephew. Around me he placed flower pots, four in front, four on either side. With a bat in his hand, my uncle sent a succession of balls my way at a fearful pace, from about six yards away. Pinned to the wall, surrounded by pots, I had nowhere to duck and run away. I had to try and catch the ball, with both hands.

That neither I, nor even Durai, had met Hemu Adhikari made him an even more palpable presence, and his strictures even more effective. Working via V M Muddiah and my uncle, that winter the former Services and India captain forever banished any fear I had when confronted with a cricket ball – though I still couldn't always be relied upon to catch it.

IX

The most famous institution in Dehradun was the Doon School, founded in 1935 as an Indian version of Eton and Harrow. My grandfather had five sons, and could not afford to send them all here to study. So Durai enrolled at St Joseph's Academy and played cricket (and other sports) there.

I was an only son, and my father was determined to send me to the Doon School. I joined in 1970 and found that, compared to the preparatory school I had previously attended, the cricketing facilities were excellent. There were regular nets for juniors as well as seniors, and four separate cricket fields.

The master in charge of cricket was S K (Sheel) Vohra. While in mufti he taught mathematics, acquiring the nickname 'Bond', after James, secret agent 007, for his ability to catch those who had copied answers from their neighbours. In whites, he was a dogged opening batsman and the finest wicketkeeper I have ever played with or against. Bond was large, over six feet tall, and weighing close to three hundred pounds. But his footwork was sure and his glovework immaculate. Keeping to spin, and down the leg side, he was superior to some recent stumpers of the Indian national team.

Bond played one Ranji match for Uttar Pradesh, as had another master on the staff, Rajinder Pal Devgan. RP was a marvellous attacking batsman, with every shot in the book. He bowled both medium-pace as well as wrist-spin. And he moved beautifully in the field.

Bond had played cricket with Durai, while RP had grown up watching Durai play. Like V Ramadas – my other mentor who had likewise played one first-class match – they were helpful to me because of whose nephew I was. But their kindness had other sources as well: my own manifest obsession with the game, for example. Under the tutelage of these two cricketing schoolmasters I abandoned bowling fast, and took to off-breaks instead. I played two years in the First XI, in the second of which I was the school's leading wicket-taker.

Once, in a Staff *v* Students match, I beat RP in the flight, leaving him stranded in the manner of Redpath to Prasanna in Chepauk in 1969. The parallel did not end there: for here, too, the wicketkeeper missed the ball, which went for four byes. RP smiled, patted the crease, and hit my next ball past mid-off for four. The one following went through mid-wicket; the one after that, to the left of point. RP scored a rapid-fire hundred; even at the receiving end of this pasting, I enjoyed it.

When the First XI played on Sundays, Bond was always one of the umpires. His concentration must have been phenomenal, for he seemed to remember almost every ball bowled and every run scored. We cricketers looked forward to the matches, but we looked forward even more to the reports Bond would write on them. These covered two full foolscap pages of the *Doon School Weekly*. On Tuesdays, Bond would sit on the steps of the pavilion, correcting the proofs. On Thursdays, after lunch, the printed copies were distributed to the boys.

With an almost indescribable sense of anticipation, we school-boy cricketers read what our master and coach had written about us. On good days it went like this: 'Guha started promisingly. In his second over he had Clifford caught behind off a straighter one (47–2). In his fourth over he comprehensively beat and bowled Mr Prasad (58–3).' Or he might have written: 'Guha came in and almost immediately played a handsome cover drive, the ball racing down the slope for four.'

After I wrote the above paragraph I had the good sense to mail the School Archivist for Bond's *Weekly* reports of the First XI's matches. On Sunday 23 April 1972, with me six days short of my fourteenth birthday, we played the Yadavindra Public School, Patiala, the most important match of the year. Bond's report began:

It was our turn to host the annual fixture against YPS this time. Sunday morning has come to be associated with clouds over the past few weeks and that day was no exception. The only thing was it did not rain but made conditions fairly pleasant for cricket. The game itself saw a very tense and exciting finish in which we managed to snatch a thrilling two-wicket victory. The YPS team was dismissed for a none too impressive score of 91. We reached 83 for three without any difficulty but then in a dramatic collapse lost five more wickets before Mukhopadhya and Guha hit the winning runs.

Those who read further would find that I had in fact starred not with the bat, but with the ball. YPS started solidly, and got to 32 for one, whereupon:

Guha was brought on from the other end and he had Harinder caught by Chablani in the slips on his third ball. Reetmohinder, however, pulled and drove him with tremendous force. Chayal defended quite soundly and gave good support to his captain. They took the score to 70 when Guha decided to bowl round the wicket. This move paid off immediately and caused havoc among the batsmen. Chayal and Dang were beaten completely on the back stroke and were lbw while Pathak was well taken by Chablani in the slips and then Lamba gave an easy catch to Arun at mid-on. Reetmohinder was lucky when Senapati dropped a none too difficult chance at deepish mid-on ... A few balls later Reetmohinder tried a big hit and skied the ball to the middle of the pitch and Ranjan made no mistake. The last pair added six runs before Guha clean bowled Jaspal on his faster ball.

The report goes on to describe our own innings, its fine and comfortable start, then the stunning collapse before we scraped through to win. Here is Bond's concluding paragraph:

> I must give full credit to the YPS team for fighting back from a seemingly hopeless position. They fielded aggressively and did not miss any chances. The bowling was just steady and it was spineless batting which was mainly responsible for the quick dismissal of our top order. I could not understand the hurry our batsmen were in and Mukhopadhya showed an ideal temperament in the crisis to carry his team to victory. In the morning, Guha bowled extremely well and for once had a good haul of wickets to show for it. He was very accurate and varied his pace and flight cleverly … The match once again, brought forth the glorious uncertainties of this game and on the day's play, I think we had a definite edge over our opponents.*

X

During the winter holidays of 1972–3 my uncle Durai came on his biennial visit to Dehradun. This time he brought his whites along, to play cricket for the first time in his hometown since he had left for Bangalore a decade previously. He rustled up as many

---

* A note about two of my team-mates who feature in this match report. I forgave Senapati his dropped catch, because his game was really not cricket, but squash, in which he went on to become India's national champion. As for Mukhopadhya, in later years he 'showed an ideal temperament' in the many crises he had to face as India's Ambassador in Syria, Afghanistan, and Myanmar.

of his old Sporting Youngsters team-mates as were still around. They were asked to band together once more to play against a Rest of Dehradun XI, whose captain would be my schoolmaster S K Vohra, 'Bond', who had himself always played for a club other than Sporting Youngsters.

The cricket club that Durai once ran in Dehradun contained three Rams: Ram Bahadur, who we have met already; an all-rounder named Ram Kishan, and an opening batsman named Ram Manohar Mishra. The last two Rams were still based in Dehradun; but the most talented of the ilk, the great footballing-cricketer, had recently taken a job as a security officer in the Assam oilfields of the Oil and Natural Gas Commission (ONGC). My uncle told his team-mates that they need not worry; for in their star player's absence he had brought along a substitute Ram, his nephew, who had recently been taking all those wickets for the Doon School First XI.

So Durai and I played together in a cricket match for the first (and, as it turned out, last) time. Naturally, I remember the day vividly, down to the names and institutional affiliations of my team-mates. Three among this reassembled Sporting Youngsters side worked at the ONGC's Dehradun headquarters; these were Ram Kishan, the fast bowler Jindo and our bits-and-pieces cricketer Lachman Singh Bisht, whose best sport was hockey. Ram Manohar Mishra worked with the FRI; as did the batsmen Vijay Singh and Pramod Rana and the wicketkeeper Mintu Bhattacharya. The off-spinner P K Bose worked with the Survey of India. That, with uncle and nephew, makes ten; lamentably, the last name escapes me.

While I remember many things about this match, for one crucial detail – the date – I had to consult the internet. My uncle would have come to Dehradun in the Christmas break, and so the match must have been played on Sunday 31 December 1972. Bond had requisitioned the Doon School ground for this contest between Sporting Youngsters and the Rest of Dehradun side.

Playing for the latter team were my other cricketing master R P Devgan, some players of Bond's club Aryans (among them a terrific opening batsman named Jagat Kumar Sharma, who taught at Welham Boys School), and several members of the best college cricket side in the Valley, the DAV.

Unlike in Bangalore, where Durai could commandeer the FUCC nets, in the easygoing world of Dehradun cricket there was no place this reconstituted side could practise before the match. The captain had to trust to what he remembered of his old team-mates, and hope that their skills had not unduly diminished over the years. He was most nervous, however, about me, his team's youngest member. So, for a week before the contest, he made me bowl for an hour a day at a lone stump erected in our garden. I had to do this alone, in full concentration, with him making the sudden surprise visit from inside the house, where, I now suspect, he was probably watching me from behind the curtains.

On the day itself, Durai drove me to the Doon School in my father's new old-model Fiat, sold in India under the authentically *swadeshi* name of Premier Padmini. We reached the ground more than an hour early, since in studying my bowling my uncle had discovered that, while I could turn my off-break a mile, I didn't know how to bowl a straighter one. Now, before the match started, his old team-mate P K Bose would teach me this crucial variation in the off-spinner's armoury. So, while Durai and the others caught up on the years, Bose took me to a side of the ground, where he demonstrated how in delivery stride – and not before – one slid one's fingers along the seam to seek to make the ball run straight through. After the lesson had concluded and we walked back to rejoin our team-mates, Bose warned me not to try out my new trick in this match, but to work at it in the nets after school resumed.

Durai lost the toss, and Bond's team batted first. Their innings was held together by a jewel of a half-century by R P Devgan.

His cover driving was majestic. RP could have gone on and on, until he was undone by Bose's straighter one, with me watching in admiration from mid-on. The senior off-spinner got three wickets while Durai got five. Brought on to bowl at the tail, I did not disgrace either captain or mentor, getting the last two wickets to fall.

Rest of Dehradun ended with about 120. In reply, Sporting Youngsters lost wickets steadily. The players were in their late thirties, out of practice, and prone like all small-town cricketers to flash hopefully outside the off-stump or play even more hopefully across the line. Vijay, Mintu, Ram Kishan all played some dashing shots and then fell, to a catch behind the wicket or at mid-on. I cannot recall how many Durai himself scored, or how he got out. But I do clearly recall going out to bat myself, at the fall of the ninth wicket, my teeth chattering partly out of nervousness and partly at the chill as dusk was about to descend. There were fourteen runs still to get. Back in 1962, a sole four was what my father had to hit to save his brother-in-law's honour. He managed that, somehow, but now, ten years later, and with my uncle's pride once more at stake, three boundaries and a bit were altogether beyond me. A tall off-spinner named Bansal had the ball; the first one beat me all ends up, and the next one bowled me middle stump.

By the time felicitations and commiserations were exchanged it was dark. Durai and I drove back in silence to the FRI, both of us close to tears. As we passed the teak forests and the night fell further upon us, in my mind, and surely his, was just this thought – had the best of all our Rams, Ram Bahadur, been available to play for us that day, Sporting Youngsters would never have lost the match.

XI

The last match of my final year in school was played against a team from the hill station of Mussoorie, which included several members based at the mission settlement of Woodstock. We bowled second, I took six wickets, but a bearded white man held out for a draw, blocking my best deliveries. As we walked off the field, honours even, I told the visitor, 'For an American, you play with a straight bat.' He replied in Hindustani: 'Aakhir yaar, cricket mé aur zindagi mé bhi straight bat ké saat hee khelna parta hai' (*My friend, in cricket as much as in life, one must always play with a straight bat*). There were peals of approving laughter all around. I later learnt that the dogged defensive batsman was studying at the Film and Television Institute of India in Puné, and that his name was Tom Alter.*

I left the Doon School in 1973, but for the next decade, so long as my father was working at the FRI, I kept coming back. In summer and winter I would play cricket for a team called Falcons, led by my two schoolmasters, and containing the Afghan aristocrat Aslam Khan, a magnificent all-round sportsman who later became a politician; the Patiala prince Randhir Singh, an Olympic shooter but also a decent cricketer; and Durai's old tormentor Major, now Colonel (retired) Rai Singh, whose batting had declined because of age and the loss of an eye, but who could still keep an immaculate length with old or new ball.

I played with Bond and RP's Falcons all over the Valley; in the

---

* Tom Alter went on to have a long and successful career on stage and in film, but cricket remained his first love. He wrote one book and many articles on the game, played club cricket into his forties, and – most importantly – did the first ever TV interview with Sachin Tendulkar (when Sachin was fourteen). You can watch it here: www.youtube.com/watch?v=oez4TSdZvJI. Tom died of cancer in 2017, aged sixty-seven, having always lived life and played cricket with a straight bat.

Survey of India ground, in our own school's main field, in the three cricket fields of the Forest Research Institute, and in the IMA's gorgeous ground too. Once, Bond and I won a close match against the ONGC. Bond had batted from start to finish; coming in at number ten, I helped with scoring the last ten or fifteen runs. Keeping wicket behind us was Ram Bahadur, who now worked in the head office of the ONGC. I think Ramu would have been happy to catch or stump my teacher, but had I given a chance I am not sure he wouldn't have fluffed it.

I also played once at the grounds of the St Joseph Academy, where Durai had been a star cricketer. A bat manufacturer from Jalandhar had recently given the FRI's Wood Products Laboratory a specimen for testing. For this match at St Joseph's, my father asked me to take this bat along. With it, I hit the sweetest six ever – over the bowler, over the trees, down into the lane that connected Rajpur Road with the Parade Ground. Shortly afterwards I attempted a pull, and the bat came off in my hands. A sound middle, but a disastrous handle – my report was duly passed on to the manufacturer.

In 1982, my father retired from the Forest Research Institute, and my parents now moved down south. Among the farewells I paid was one to Ram Bahadur. He lived in Panditwari, an old settlement – originally of Hindu priests as the name indicates – located just outside the FRI. Ramu was pleased to see Durai's nephew, and excited too, since he had something to show me. My friend the Olympian and Asian Games gold-medallist was now fat and forty-six, but, still, a sportsman. Taking me to an inside room, Ramu took out a new cricket bat, smelling gloriously of linseed oil. 'Pick it up, Ram,' he whispered, 'see how lovely it feels.' I did, and agreed that the balance was perfect. 'I paid one hundred and seventy-five rupees for it,' said Ramu, before adding: 'But I told the Missus it was a gift from the office.' I nodded understandingly, for in the love of cricket surely it was utterly moral to tell one's wife an untruth.

After his wife had given us tea, and I had in turn praised the latest of the dozens of trophies her husband had received over the years, Ramu walked me back to the gate of the FRI. But there was another detour. He had to show me, with the same pride he showed me his bat, the houses he had built for his sisters. There were, as I recall, three homes in all, each free standing, each paid for by the love and sporting success of a brother which had made these children of a peon members of the Indian middle class.

Ram Bahadur had never spoken of his family to me before. I had not known how many siblings he had. Were there any brothers too, I now asked, as we walked down the path that led us from Panditwari to the main road. Ram Bahadur stopped, stood straight, faced me and said: 'Ram, I have only one brother. His name is Duraiswami.'

2

An Eleven of One's Own

I

In cricketing terms, my years in the Doon School were important to me, and to my country. They constituted – to invoke the title of a book by the Bombay writer Raju Bharatan – *Indian Cricket's Vital Phase*. In the first months of 1971, India beat West Indies in a Test series in the Caribbean. I followed the matches via K N Prabhu's reports in the *Times of India*, a copy of whose delayed *dak* edition reached my school library. Later that year, India toured England. In forty years of trying, we had never won a Test in England before. The first Test of the series fell in the school holidays, so I heard every ball on the radio, courtesy of the British Broadcasting Corporation.

That match ended in a thrilling draw. But then the school term resumed, and I went back into boarding. Only those in the senior-most form were allowed access to the common room and its radio. I thus followed the second Test (when rain saved India) and the third and final Test (when B S Chandrasekhar of Bangalore's City Cricketers took six wickets to set up an Indian win) second-hand, live through the bits and pieces conveyed by my kindly house captain, Vivek Bammi, and with a day's delay through K N Prabhu and the *Times of India*.

Meanwhile, my cricketing education also proceeded through the books my father bought me. In a shop in Delhi named Ramkrishna and Sons, he found several books by a writer named A A Thomson. I read them many times over. Thomson had a distinctly English sensibility; asked to list the best ten cricket books of all time, he named John Nyren's *The Cricketer's Tutor*, H S Altham and E W Swanton's *A History of Cricket* and 'any eight of Cardus'.

I had heard of Neville Cardus, of course, but at this stage not had a chance to read his work. Ramkrishna and Sons, which my father visited when on tour in Delhi, apparently had no books by Cardus on their shelves. But Thomson was a handy substitute. He had a charming, free-flowing style, and a fund of anecdotes. He also had an uncle who had taught him all that he knew about cricket, albeit one who had watched rather than played the game. His books were full of stories told to him by this 'Uncle Walter', who seemed more kindly – perhaps I should say more *avuncular* – if just as cricket-mad as my uncle Durai.

The book by A A Thomson I enjoyed most was called *Cricket Bouquet*. This had one chapter on each of the seventeen first-class cricketing counties in England (Durham had not yet become the eighteenth). Their histories were recounted, their greatest players lovingly profiled. Each chapter ended with an All-time XI of that particular county.

In the winter of 1972–3, India played a five-Test series against England, at home. The first Test, played at New Delhi's Feroz Shah Kotla ground, fell in the school holidays. An uncle (not Durai) got me a ticket for all five days. I reached New Delhi a day early, and found that the English side were staying at The Oberoi, the city's newest and grandest hotel. I had learned via A A Thomson of the great line of Kent wicketkeepers, from Huish and Hubble to Les Ames and Godfrey Evans and beyond. I was determined to meet the latest (and greatest) representative of that tradition, Alan Philip Eric Knott. I got his room number from the operator and dialled it. Knott picked up the phone, where-upon I said something about Kent cricket in general and its stumpers in particular. I would like to meet him, I said, adding that it was important. 'Everybody here says it is important,' wailed Knott, and put the phone down.

My ticket was in the western stand, not the best place to follow the swing of Geoff Arnold or the turn of Bhagwat Chandrasekhar (the leading wicket-takers on either side), but the perfect posi-tion to watch the arc of Bishan Bedi's flight. The Sardar was slim and supple, and wore a *patka* of a different colour each day. Before every ball he pushed the *kada* on his right hand back, and set off on his three-step run. His bowling action was smooth, seamless, side-on, and with a strong follow-through. I became a fan for life, discovering during the course of the Test that I had come late to the party. On the second day, Bedi got his one hundredth Test wicket. No sooner was the batsman dismissed than a large red banner came up in the stand opposite mine. It read: SPIN ONE HUNDRED MORE.

In those pre 9/11, pre 26/11 days there was no security as we entered the ground. So it was not just banners that spectators brought with them. One fellow in my stand ran up and down setting off fireworks; another fellow spent all day blowing brightly coloured balloons and releasing them into the sky, from where they fell, one by one, among us and sometimes in the playing arena too. The colour and the noise were intense; but in between watching balloons and hearing crackers I was able to follow the cricket as well.

Two players among the visiting side impressed me greatly. One was Alan Knott, whose dives down the leg-side were so thrilling that I forgave him his pre-Test rudeness. The other was the blond giant, Anthony William Greig, then with a full head of hair. To combat the spin of Bedi and Chandrasekhar, Greig took his stance with his bat held a foot off the ground; some-thing quite common nowadays, but back then a genuine innovation. He scored runs in both innings; and bowled his share of overs too. However, he impressed me most with his fielding.

When the fast bowlers operated, Greig stood in the slips, but as soon as the spinners came on he stationed himself at silly point. The position was new to me, for at school my coach and his coaching manual had acquainted me only with silly mid-off, which is much straighter. That position, I now saw, was appropriate for schoolboys, who would knock the ball up in the air, but not for first-class players. With them, the close-in fielder had to watch out instead for the deflection off bat and pad, which comes squarer. Such indeed were the chances taken by Greig that day, given by Gavaskar and Sardesai, off Underwood both times. In his long vigil at silly point he had his eyes focused on the bat, but his ears were alert to sounds from elsewhere too. When a firecracker burst in the crowd, Greig collapsed to the ground, as if shot. All this while a Test hung in the balance.

England won the match by six wickets. Afterwards, I walked back to the house of my aunt, a nursing officer in the Indian Army who stayed at the Maulana Azad Mess. The roads I passed carried the names of the great leaders of the freedom struggle: Bal Gangadhar Tilak, Rajendra Prasad, Kasturba Gandhi, Motilal Nehru. At fourteen, I was a fervent cricketing patriot, and seeing these names while contemplating my side's defeat deepened the anguish.

Cleaning up a cupboard recently, I found a letter written to me by the editor of *Wisden*. It was in answer to one of mine, sent shortly after that Delhi Test of 1972. It does not carry a date, though the postmark tells me it was sent from London sometime in February 1973. Here is the letter in full:

WISDEN CRICKETERS' ALMANACK
Sporting Handbooks Ltd,
13, Bedford Square,
London, WC1

Dear Mr Guha,

I thank you for your recent letter. I am very busy getting through the final pages of the 1973 Wisden before it is printed in a fortnight's time – hence the delay in reply.

Above you see the monogram used by MCC – just the club's initials.

Glad you enjoyed the first Test at Delhi. Greig certainly played well in that match and he may become a great all-rounder but he has not yet reached that exalted state.

You have some wonderful spin bowlers in Chandra, Bedi, Venkat and Prasanna and I am afraid many of our batsmen have been baffled by them.

By the time this letter reaches you, India may have won the series 3–1 which will be a fine performance.

With best wishes
Yours sincerely
Norman Preston

In fact, the margin was less emphatic than that predicted by the editor, 2–1 rather than 3–1. But India winning the Tests at Calcutta and Madras meant that by winter's end, the patriotic pride dented at Delhi had been entirely restored.*

––––––––––

* Do fourteen-year-old Indians still write to *Wisden*'s editor, I wonder? And does he answer their mails? Unlikely, for England is no longer the centre of world cricket – India is.

II

By the time I had graduated from high school, I knew that playing cricket for India was entirely beyond me. I was a decent enough bowler, who turned the ball sharply on matting, and had good control. However, as a batsman my range of strokes was roughly that of my father's, and I was slow in the field. Besides, I was handicapped by my chronic asthma; there was no telling when I would get a bronchial attack and have to miss practice for a week.

Even a career in the Ranji Trophy was unfeasible. But I still hoped to play cricket for St Stephen's College, as my uncle Durai had done before me. I finished my school-leaving exams in December 1973; the University of Delhi admitted undergraduates only in July. I persuaded my parents to let me spend the interim six months in Bangalore, practising with the FUCC.

In the week or two before I went south I still had some cricket to play in the Valley. Lala Amarnath, once captain of India, was holding a camp for young cricketers in the Rashtriya Indian Military College (RIMC) ground. My teacher, S K Vohra 'Bond', had been asked to assist him. As I have related, back in 1941, after he had finished school, my father had seen Amarnath bat, bowl, and keep wicket in Bombay's Brabourne Stadium, and for ever afterwards regarded him as the complete cricketer. Now, thirty years later, Bond took me along to spend two days in the great man's company. I told Amarnath of where and how my father had seen him play. 'I was the second best wicketkeeper in India,' said Lala, adding with characteristic modesty, 'also the third best seam bowler [after Nissar and Amar Singh] and the best batsman.'

At the time I (so briefly) met him, Lala Amarnath was in his early sixties. He still stood on his head before the nets each day, and dared us to do likewise (I failed). One remark he made strikes me now as extraordinarily prescient. There was no delivery, he said, off which a run could not be scored. The short ball could be pulled and the overpitched ball driven for boundaries, but even the ball of perfect length, pitched in line, could be dropped at one's feet or pushed to the off or the on for a single. This is a belief now put in practice by every cricketing side in the world, but back in 1973 it required a genius to see it.

I bowled in the nets before Lala Amarnath and, after he had departed for Delhi, bowled in a match at the Indian Military Academy. Bond was captaining a team composed mostly of schoolteachers, with the odd local cricketer added on. RP was playing of course, as were two masters who had newly joined the staff of the Doon School. One was a guitar-loving Malayali named Krishna Kumar. The other was called Yogi Durlabhji; from a family of famous jewellers in Jaipur, he had played squash for St Stephen's College and had become a schoolteacher to escape being drafted into the family business.

The cricket field at the IMA was for me a sacred space, for it was where Frank Worrell and C K Nayudu had once played. My own local heroes N Duraiswami and Ram Bahadur had performed here too. It was here that, watching Chandu Gadkari bat, I first learnt what separated the men from the boys. Besides, the sandwiches at lunch were terrific; so were the *barfis* at tea, made from cows freshly milked at the Military Dairy Farm.

The home team batted first. I was brought on early and in my first over induced an edge which Bond, stooping down from his great bulk, took smartly behind the stumps. I had one batsman caught at short-leg and another clean bowled. The wicket I relished most was that of the star Academy batsman, a cadet named Jagtap, who his officers were sure would play for the Services before the year was out. He went to hit me over mid-on, a position the cricket-loving Australian Prime Minister, Sir Robert Menzies, once called the last refuge of mankind. It was normally the place where the team's worst fielder was placed. On this day, however, the position was occupied by our best, RP, placed there to encourage the fifteen-year-old student bowling in his first big match. Jagtap's lofted on-drive, otherwise intended for the boundary, was caught by my teacher, leaping backwards athletically.

I ended with six wickets, and the Malayali musician with three, prompting the witticism that the Academy was done in by a *jugalbandhi* of those two great avatars of Vishnu, Ram and Krishna. As we walked off the field, my teachers Bond and RP converged on Yogi Durlabhji, lately of St Stephen's College. 'Is Ram good enough to play for the College?' they asked anxiously. Yogi's reply was studiedly non-committal. 'He bowls all right,' he said. 'It depends on how he bats and fields.'

III

When I was growing up, Test matches were few and far between, and cricket fans identified strongly with state and county sides. I had read in books written by Australian writers of the intense rivalries between Sheffield Shield teams. Victoria fans apparently never forgave Keith Miller for moving from his home state to New South Wales, while New South Welshmen always held it against Don Bradman that he had abandoned them for South Australia.

The strength and depth of provincial affiliations was most emphatically demonstrated to me via the books of A A Thomson. While he wrote with affection about players from other counties, a special love was reserved for Yorkshire cricketers. Even after Keith Miller had come and gone, even as Garfield Sobers was winning Test matches and Test series more or less on his own, for Thomson the greatest all-rounder in the history of cricket remained a Yorkshireman born in the village of Kirkheaton, a left-hand bowler and right-hand batsman. Only which one he wasn't sure – was it George Hirst, or was it Wilfred Rhodes? And had there ever been a batsman better in a crisis than Maurice Leyland? Or a slip fielder more reliable than John Tunnicliffe? And who was the best player on a sticky wicket? Edgar Oldroyd, of course.

For cricket fans, Oldroyd and Tunnicliffe were obscure names even in the 1960s. Indians who loved the game were scarcely likely to know of Hirst or Leyland either (Rhodes they might have heard of). But to this boy in Dehradun, Thomson had endowed these names with glamour and mystique, while placing them in a particular cricketing tradition, that of the county of Yorkshire.

Reading A A Thomson, I went in search of a state team to follow too. Which would it be? I chose Mysore, for purely pragmatic reasons. My club was located in the capital of that state, my uncle and grandparents lived in that city as well. That several Mysore cricketers were then playing for India may have been a consideration. That one FUCC player was then playing for Mysore certainly was.

This was Sudhakar Rao, the most gifted of the quartet of young cricketers who had joined my club in 1970. 'Sudha', as he was known, had scored a string of fifties and hundreds in league cricket. He had been so prolific and so consistent that even the men of Swastic and BUCC, who ran the State Cricket Association, could not ignore him. Besides, he was an excellent fielder.

In the winter of 1972–3, Sudhakar Rao made his first-class debut for Mysore. Durai was pleased, but not content. The next step was to make him play for South Zone, and then for India as well. I shared my uncle's hopes and fantasies entirely. I could never play cricket for my country, but I might yet have a club-mate who would.

In 1973, the state of Mysore was renamed Karnataka. Early the following year, I travelled to Bangalore for my six-month break between school and college. I cannot remember what I did in February 1974 – attended nets and read books, I suppose – but of eight days in March I have the clearest memories. These were spent watching my home state play in, and win, the quarter-finals and semi-finals of the Ranji Trophy.

In its early years, the Mysore State Cricket Association had played its Ranji matches in the premises of the Rajendra Sinhji Institute. The RSI had a charming cricket field, and it was centrally located, right on Mahatma Gandhi Road. However, in the 1950s a churlish RSI secretary denied permission to hold matches there. These now shifted to the only other turf wicket in Bangalore, owned by the Central College. This was located in the City, close to Kempegowda Road and its row of cinemas.

Hard though it is now to imagine, the Mysore State Cricket Association was then run by a man who was intelligent, upright and with a focus on the game's future. His name was M Chinnaswamy. There was a large, vacant plot at the other end of Mahatma Gandhi Road, opposite St Mark's Cathedral. It was owned by the Army. Chinnaswamy lobbied in Bangalore and in Delhi to have it handed over on a long-term lease to the cricket association.

Once the land was handed over, Chinnaswamy himself chose the contractors, approved the design, allocated the contracts and stood supervising the workers until late at night. Durai venerated him, and with good reason. Chinnaswamy was as principled as my uncle, and as committed to cricket. Because he ran a whole association rather than a mere club, he could do more good too. His one flaw was characteristically male, and characteristically Indian – namely vanity, which led him to be persuaded to have the place named after himself.

IV

In March 1974, the Chinnaswamy Stadium was still in the process of completion. One saw piles of bricks and girders everywhere. However, the playing arena was ready, and so too the pavilion and the ground floors of stands. In the previous season, some Ranji matches had been played at the ground.

India's premier first-class tournament was then organised on the basis of zones. Karnataka played in the South Zone, alongside Hyderabad, Andhra Pradesh, Tamil Nadu, and Kerala. In its early years, only one team from each zone made it to the knockout; through time, this had been increased to two. The tournament was very competitive; the great zonal rivalries included Bihar *v* Bengal in the East Zone and Services *v* Delhi in the North. The matches were most fiercely fought in my own zone, where Hyderabad, Madras (later renamed Tamil Nadu) and Mysore (later Karnataka) competed for the top spot. With so few Test matches played those days, no live cricket on television and the IPL many decades in the future, Ranji Trophy matches in my youth attracted crowds of twenty and even thirty thousand.

Back in the 1940s and 1950s, the knockout rounds were keenly contested too. This was no longer the case; at the upper reaches the tournament had now become extremely one-sided. The last time anyone other than Bombay had won the Ranji Trophy was in 1957–8, before I was born.

In the decade of the 1960s, Bombay's least distant rival was Rajasthan. Their captain, Bhagwatsinhji, the Maharana of Udaipur, recruited Test cricketers from other states (including some Bombay players) in a bid to win the Ranji Trophy. When they did win, said the Maharana, he would take a dip in the holy Ganga at Banaras – an event that might have attracted a large crowd, not so much because of the man's lineage (he claimed to be descended from the Sun God) but because of his size – he weighed in at two hundred kilogrammes, the scale saying (it was rumoured) 'one at a time please'.

That victorious immersion never took place. Between 1961 and 1970, Rajasthan played Bombay in six Ranji finals, and were thrashed each time. Meanwhile, other teams were preparing their own challenge. Hyderabad were led by the country's best cricket brain, M L Jaisimha, under whom the Indian captain, Mansur Ali Khan Pataudi, was happy to play.

My home state thought it had a (long) shot at beating Bombay as well. The Mysore captain through much of the 1960s, my clubmate Ramadas's brother V Subrahmanyam, believed that if they ever got 300 runs on the board the great spin duo of Prasanna and Chandrasekhar would get Bombay out for less than that score. In the winter of 1966–7, this theory was put to the test, when Mysore were drawn to play Bombay in the semi-final of the Ranji Trophy. Subrahmanyam won the toss, and scored a hundred himself in taking his side to an impressive total of 350 plus. To no avail, since, when Bombay replied, the left-handed Ajit Wadekar got 323 off his own bat. The match was drawn; and Bombay went through to the final on the basis of their hefty first-innings lead.

When Yorkshire is strong, England is strong – so A A Thomson had said. It was the same for Bombay and India. When we won in England for the first time in 1971, six players in the winning XI were from the island city. However, two others were from Bangalore, while two more were among the reserves. In my eyes, Karnataka would be to Bombay what India was to England. My national team had just beaten our former rulers in a Test series away from home; I waited for the day when my state team would defeat the national champions in a Ranji match.

In the 1973–4 season, Karnataka qualified from the South Zone. They were drawn to play Delhi in the quarter-finals. If they won, Bombay would be next. V Subrahmanyam had migrated to Australia, and Prasanna was captaining Karnataka in his place. He had with him two other established international stars, Chandrasekhar and G R Viswanath, with a fourth in the making, the wicketkeeper Syed Kirmani. The other members of the team included the experienced all-rounders V S Vijaykumar, B Vijaykrishna and A V Jayaprakash; two young batsmen from Swastic Union, Sanjay Desai and Brijesh Patel; and FUCC's own Sudhakar Rao.

Delhi were led by the great Bishan Bedi. He had with him some rising university players and a few hard-boiled professionals with many years of Ranji cricket behind them. However, Bedi was the only world-class player in the team, as against four of ours.

We were expected to win easily. And we did. A brief flutter occurred on the third day, when, after conceding a first-innings lead of 100 plus, Delhi came back strongly, courtesy of four wickets by Bedi, among them Viswanath, bowled middle stump by an arm ball. Karnataka were wobbling slightly at 100 for four, when Sudhakar Rao, weaned on his club captain's left-arm spin, took the battle to Bedi, driving him past and over cover. Sudha scored 65, Kirmani chipped in with a brisk 38 not out, and Karnataka set Delhi a fourth-innings target in excess of 400, which was well beyond their reach.

The manager of the visiting side was Gulshan Rai, who had played inter-college cricket with Durai in Delhi. On the second day of the match, my uncle persuaded him to come home for dinner, bringing his team's captain with him. Durai had in his apartment a bottle of Scotch whisky, saved for an occasion such as this. Fortunately, there were no playing members of the FUCC who had a liking for alcohol, and even had there been one, he could not, the colour of the liquid being different, have done to Durai's whisky what Ram Bahadur had once done to my grandfather's gin.

There were four people at that dinner: Durai, Gulshan Rai, Bedi and myself. The Sardar did most of the talking, and most of the drinking too. By the end of the evening the bottle was empty. As we escorted the visitors to their car I plucked up the courage to ask Bedi what bowling tips he had for me. 'Spin the ball,' he said. '*Spin* the ball,' vigorously moving the fingers of his left hand.

Indian cricketers are notoriously mingy. The more famous and wealthy, the more they expect favours and freebies. Tiger Pataudi once remarked that Bishan Bedi was the exception, the one cricketer of his acquaintance who spent more money on others than on himself. I can provide confirmatory testimony. Before he left Bangalore, the Delhi captain had asked his manager for my uncle's address, to which he dispatched a signed Gunn and Moore bat. Durai was at work; but I was at home to receive it.

Karnataka played Delhi on the 1–4 March 1974. On the same dates, Bombay were playing Bihar in another quarter-final, the venue the Keenan Stadium in Jamshedpur, a cricket ground named after an American engineer which figures in Sujit Mukherjee's charming *Autobiography of an Unknown Cricketer*. The state of Jharkhand had not yet been created, and undivided Bihar had a good Ranji team, many of its players employed by the Tata Iron and Steel Company for whom John Keenan had once worked.

Bombay were expected to defeat Bihar rather easily, but that turned out not to be the case. Sunil Gavaskar and his opening partner Ramnath Parkar were both dismissed for ducks as Bombay struggled to a first-innings score of 200. Bihar's most experienced batsmen, Tilak Raj and Ramesh Saxena (both exiles from Delhi), got a century and a half-century respectively, taking their side to an impressive lead of over a hundred. Durai and I, listening in to the radio at the Chinnaswamy Stadium, could scarcely contain our excitement, for if Bihar upset Bombay that would make it so much easier for Karnataka.

The match was now in its third day, and Bihar had two fine spin bowlers in the Shukla brothers, Rakesh and Anand. But, as Durai and I well knew, Bombay were always best with their backs to the wall. Parkar and Milind Rege scored fifties, and Gavaskar, Parkar, Ashok Mankad and Wadekar all made useful contributions. They collectively pushed the total up to 283.

Bihar were now set 182 to win. It seemed a modest target, but not against Bombay, who bowled and fielded like tigers. Then there was the question of self-belief; one side always expected to win the trophy, the other had rarely even been the top team in its zone before. The superb slow left-armer Padmakar Shivalkar got four wickets, the leg-spinner Rakesh Tandon three. Parkar and Solkar, the two best fielders in India, took two catches apiece. Bihar fell 59 runs short of their target. With another team unable or unwilling to push Bombay out of the way, Karnataka had now to contend with the champions themselves.

V

There was a ten-day break before the semi-final. I spent some of it at the FUCC nets, and some at the Chinnaswamy Stadium, watching the Karnataka players practise. G R Viswanath at the nets was a revelation. After ten minutes of playing according to the book, he proceeded to have fun, hitting Prasanna and Chandrasekhar over their heads. Some of his shots landed on the top tier of the stadium. I knew that notwithstanding his size Vishy had exquisite timing; but his love of the lofted drive was a surprise. He had never been known to play these shots in a match.

The first Ranji Trophy semi-final ever played at the Chinnaswamy Stadium commenced on Friday 15 March 1974. I was one of some thirty thousand people who had turned up to watch. Karnataka won the toss and chose to bat. Vijaykumar flashed at the first ball, which moved late and away, and caught an edge which was taken safely at slip by Sunil Gavaskar. In came Viswanath, at once the littlest of men and the largest of home-town heroes. We rose to him; the sounds of our shouts and claps must have reached Vidhan Soudha, the State Assembly, half a mile away across Cubbon Park.

Viswanath took guard. The bowler was Abdul Ismail, who, having moved the last ball he bowled away, chose to bring one back this time. Vishy played back and was struck low on the right leg. Even from where I sat I knew that must be plumb lbw. But the umpire thought otherwise, possibly on the theory that one did not give great Test players out first ball. Or perhaps – like every spectator in the stadium – he merely wanted to watch Vishy bat.

Which he did, and from the best position in the ground to boot. For Vishy batted all of that day and part of the next. My memory tells me he hit at least a boundary every over – some firmly past point or to the left of mid-off and the right of mid-on, others delicately, through cuts and glides down behind the wicket. I am certain he never lifted a ball, and stroked everything along the ground. But perhaps I misremember the tempo at which he made his runs, for the match statistics tell me that Karnataka scored at less than three runs an over.

Vishy was eventually dismissed for 162, caught at slip by Gavaskar off Rakesh Tandon. The other main scorer was Brijesh Patel, who got 106. Patel had none of Vishy's grace, and he was not particularly comfortable against the moving or bouncing ball. But, brought up on matting wickets, he was supremely authoritative against spin, the cut and the pull being his main scoring shots.

Karnataka ended with 385 on the board. It was more than we had ever scored against Bombay before. But would it be enough? Of the first six in Bombay's batting order, five had played for India, and the sixth would do so before the year was out. We feared two men in particular: Gavaskar, the greatest batsman the country had ever produced, and his captain, Ajit Wadekar, who had a fantastic record against Prasanna and Chandrasekhar.

The first man out was Ramnath Parkar, with the score at 49. I cannot recall how he was dismissed (caught Vijaykrishna off Prasanna the scorecard tells me, taken at short-leg I presume), but remember vividly how Gavaskar fell. He came down the track to Prasanna, aiming to drive through mid-wicket. However, what he thought was the off-break was in fact the drifter, which floated away at the last minute to take off-stump. Gavaskar applauded Prasanna as he walked off, in a spontaneous salute from one master to another.

Ajit Wadekar was now joined by Ashok Mankad, another prodigious run scorer in the Ranji Trophy, and for whom Durai had a particular soft spot, as the son of Vinoo Mankad. Both were calm, and utterly unhurried, as they played themselves in and took the score along. I remember that Mankad junior hit some lovely square drives, that Wadekar swept effectively, and that neither seemed in the least troubled by either Pras or Chandra.

The partnership between Wadekar and Mankad passed fifty, then a hundred. Bombay had reached 198 for two. Where would a wicket come from? Providence, of course. Mankad played a ball into the off-side; and called for a run. Then, seeing backward point advance swiftly on the ball, he sent his partner back. Wadekar stopped, turned, and slipped. The throw came in, sharp and accurate, and Prasanna took off the bails.

The fielder whose unexpected speed across the turf made Mankad change his mind was Sudhakar Rao of the FUCC. His accuracy of arm had been developed under Durai's close guidance. The Hand of Destiny that swung the match belonged to my club, and hence in some measure to me, too.

The dismissals of Gasvaskar and Wadekar are imprinted in my mind for ever. For the others I shall have to consult the scorecard. This tells me that Bombay ended at 307 all out, with Prasanna getting five wickets and Chandrasekhar four. Their innings finished just before tea on the third day. Any chance

Bombay had of coming back into the game was thwarted by half-centuries from Brijesh Patel and Sudhakar Rao. The match ended in a draw, with Karnataka winning on the first innings. For the first time since I had entered this world, Bombay would not lift the Ranji Trophy.

Once again, Durai and I had our eyes on the match unfolding before us, with our ears to the radio, which was carrying news of the other semi-final being played between Rajasthan and Hyderabad. Jaisimha's side were hot favourites to win. They had even more Test players than Bombay – six, with a seventh capped for India in due course. For the first two days it looked as if Hyderabad would win. They bowled Rajasthan out for 196, and then scored 276 themselves. Rajasthan did somewhat better in their second innings, reaching 246 before being dismissed.

Hyderabad now required 168 runs to reach the final. Their batting line-up included Pataudi, Jaisimha, and Abbas Ali Baig, who had all scored Test centuries against better attacks and in more trying circumstances. But in cricket, each day is different from all the days that precede it. Batsmen who had once mastered Trueman, Statham, Graham McKenzie and Wes Hall were now undone by an obscure off-spinner with a shady action named G S Shaktawat, who took six wickets as Hyderabad collapsed for 155.

Durai and I were over the moon with delight. Jaisimha's Hyderabad would have been far more difficult opponents. They knew our game intimately. In the event, we defeated Rajasthan comfortably in the finals, by a margin of 185 runs. As this match was played in Jaipur, I had to be content with following it on the radio.

It is almost half a century since I watched my first Test match. I have watched at least forty more Tests, and an equal number of one-day internationals as well, among them two epic India–Pakistan World Cup contests. Yet those eight days at the Chinnaswamy Stadium in March 1974 remain the absolute highlight of my life as a cricket fan. Let me end this recollection with one anecdote, and one set of statistics. Commenting on All India Radio during these matches was V M Muddiah. At one point Durai took me to meet him, introducing his nephew as an off-spinner who sought his guidance. Muddiah gestured at the field in front us, pointing directly at the figure of the Karnataka captain. 'Son, there's the master off-spinner,' said the first man from our state to play for India: 'You will learn more from watching him bowl than from hearing me speak.'

The statistics pertain to the bowling figures for the home side in the crucial first innings of these two games. Now the oldest member of the Karnataka team was also, at this level, the least experienced. K Laxman was forty, but had never played in the Ranji Trophy before. He bowled quickish left-arm spin; although he did not turn the ball much, he was extremely accurate. Prasanna had been his team-mate for many years in league cricket, and knew that he was just the man he wanted to close an end up, whenever Chandrasekhar wanted a break. And so it turned out, as these numbers so emphatically reveal:

Karnataka's bowling figures, 1st innings only

Against Delhi
E A S Prasanna: 29–3–74–3
B S Chandrasekhar: 26.2–3–76–7
K Laxman: 12–6–11–0

Against Bombay
E A S Prasanna: 63–21–117–5
B S Chandrasekhar: 44–6–145–4
K Laxman: 17–9–20–0

The crowd at the Chinnaswamy Stadium loved Laxman. We called him *Thatha*, grandfather. The cheers when he handed over his cap to the umpire and wiped his bald pate were loud; those when he came out to bat and played defensively forward, louder still. In our side of present and future stars, he was the under-stated team-man. This may have been his first as well as his last Ranji season. Yet the debt we cricket fans of Karnataka owe him was, and remains, colossal.

VI

In later years, I have often discussed that 1974 semi-final with a devoted follower of Mumbai cricket, the journalist and author Rajdeep Sardesai. He tempers my triumphalism by reminding me that his team won the next three Ranji championships, and have won it quite often thereafter too. At the time of writing, Bombay/Mumbai have a staggering 41 titles. Karnataka are a distant second, with eight titles in all.

Rajdeep's father, Dilip Sardesai, made his Ranji debut in 1958. He retired from first-class cricket in 1973. Sardesai senior was a key member of the Indian side that won Test matches and Test series in West Indies and England in 1971. He also never played in a losing Bombay side, a fact in which his son takes just and proper pride. If I ever speak of the 1974 semi-final which Karnataka won, Rajdeep turns the conversation to the many matches against Bombay which we lost, taking particular pleasure in re-telling the story of the time we scored 350 on the first day and – so he claims – Chinnaswamy had the entire Managing Committee of the Mysore State Cricket Association flown into Bombay the next morning, their hopes dashed when Wadekar and Dilip Sardesai batted the whole day. (I know no one in Bangalore who believes this tale.)

I first met Rajdeep Sardesai in 1992. Over the years, the

arguments have raged back and forth, in conversation, in print and on Twitter. Rajdeep once wrote that 'Guha's sometimes excessive admiration for Karnataka cricketers may cause another Cauvery dispute.' (He was conveying exasperation, even disgust; reading this presumed put-down. I was of course delighted.)

I do not, cannot, deny my partisanship. But I must insist that Karnataka's victory over Bombay in March 1974 was enormously important, not just for me and my side, but for Indian cricket as a whole. For it led to a wholesale decentring of the sport. Bombay had then won the championship fifteen times on the trot. In the fifteen years that followed, Bombay won the title three times, but so did Karnataka. Bishan Bedi's Delhi, now augmented by the Amarnath brothers and Chetan Chauhan, did even better, winning four times in this period. And Hyderabad and Tamil Nadu also won one title apiece.

The next fifteen-year period witnessed a further decentring, with Bengal, Haryana, Punjab, Baroda and the Railways also winning the Ranji Trophy. More recently, Uttar Pradesh, Gujarat, Vidarbha and Saurashtra have won the championship as well. The ending of the domination of Indian cricket by one city, this enlargement of the catchment area of the winning sides, has made cricket in India much more *Indian* than it ever was before.

This decentring may have happened anyway. But two misjudgements hastened it; that which ruled G R Viswanath not out when he was palpably leg-before; and that which led to Ajit Wadekar's run out. The first was the handiwork of an umpire named Ganguli. It is said that when the umpire returned to his native Calcutta and next met the members of the Bengal Ranji Trophy team, he told them: 'I have done what you have been unable to do all these years – make sure that Bombay does not win the Ranji Trophy.'

As for the second misjudgement, years later I met Ajit Wadekar, and, with all the mischief and malice at my command, reminded him of the stumble that led to his dismissal and his team's defeat. Wadekar was known to be a man of few words, and on this occasion restricted himself to just two. 'New shoes,' he remarked, shrugging his shoulders enigmatically. If Ajit Wadekar had been wearing his old shoes while batting that day, Bombay's unbroken run of Ranji championships might have extended not just to fifteen, but to fifty-five.

3

Eavesdropping on Greatness

I

I joined St Stephen's College in the second week of July 1974. The college was in the university campus in North Delhi, but their cricket ground lay at Mori Gate, a mile-and-a-half away, across a wooded hill known as the Ridge. Durai had told me that practice began as soon as term began, so, on my first afternoon at St Stephen's, I dressed up in whites, slung my boots over my shoulder, and set out for Mori Gate. As I walked out of Allnutt Court towards the west gate of the college, I was stopped by a student in sawn-off shorts and with hair much longer than mine.

'Fresher! Where the f—— do you think you are going?'

'For cricket practice, sir,' I replied.

'Can't you see how much it has rained this morning?' said my interlocutor, pointing to the wet ground underfoot. 'There will be no practice today.'

The senior who brought me to my senses was named Arun Lal. He was already a fixture in the college cricket team, and had played for the university too. Because of a freckled face he was known as 'Piggy' (he still is).

Piggy Lal had come to St Stephen's two years before me, from the school known as Doon's rival, Mayo in Ajmer. He was admired for his batsmanship – he had scored two fifties in the last inter-college championship final, in which we beat our bitter rivals, Hindu College – and for his superb fielding close-in. Somehow, he also managed to get a high first-class in his economics degree, to hectically socialise, and to play cards late into the night.

Piggy Lal was the star cricketer in Residence, as the hostel in St Stephen's was quaintly or pompously known. Some cricketers who were day-scholars had an even more impressive record. Two Stephanians had played for Delhi against Karnataka in the Ranji quarter-final that I had watched in Bangalore the previous March. They were Rajeshwar Vats and Praveen Oberoi. Unlike Piggy or myself, Vats came from a plebeian background; he spoke Hindi, and preferably Punjabi, and had studied in a government school in West Delhi. He both opened the bowling and the batting for the college. Oberoi was from a moderately prosperous business family. He bowled quickish left-arm spin, and had captained Indian Schoolboys before entering university.

Vats was, like Piggy, in the final year of his BA; Praveen a year ahead, doing a Master's degree. In the second year of his BA was Piyush Pandey, now an acknowledged guru of Indian advertising, then the St Stephen's College wicketkeeper. Pandey was a makeshift stumper but a first-class batsman; his on-drive was particularly handsome. Meanwhile, the best cricketer in my own year was Rajinder Amarnath, the youngest son of the Lala, and known as 'Johnny' (an English corruption of the Punjabi 'Jaani', or dearest, the pet name that his mother had originally given him). Amarnath had modelled his game on his elder brother, the Test cricketer Mohinder; like him, he batted in the middle order and moved the ball both ways at medium pace. He too had played for Indian Schoolboys, and in any case he possessed one of the most famous surnames in cricket.

In a day or two the rain stopped, and practice began. Every day after lunch we freshmen cricketers walked out of Allnutt

Gate, positioned ourselves at the foot of the Ridge, and thumbed a lift to anywhere near Mori Gate. Male commuters on scooters and motorcycles offered us a ride, one at a time. Collective journeys were rare; although I remember an occasion when a police jeep stopped to take four or five of us to the ground. The driver had been instructed to stop by his boss, riding in the front seat next to him. She was the Deputy Commissioner of Police, Delhi North, Kiran Bedi, who had played tennis for India before becoming the country's first female police officer.

The college hockey and football fields were adjacent to the cricket field, which meant that the trips to and fro were congenial to cultivating friendships. One afternoon, I found myself in the same rickshaw as our football captain, a gentle Parsi named Novy Kapadia. When he heard where I was from, he told me that his boyhood hero was my fellow townsman Ram Bahadur. He had watched Ramu play in the Durand Cup in the early 1960s, and still remembered the precision of his passes and his tireless running up and down the field.

In the monsoon we practised on a cement wicket; and on turf for the rest of the year. Nets ran from three to six in the afternoon; and there were some twenty one-day 'friendly' matches to be played each season, before the inter-college championship began in January. As holders of the trophy, St Stephen's were seeded directly into the quarter-final, which was a three-day affair. The semi-final was played over four days; the final, over a full five days, as in a Test match.

Every day, after practice, we would walk or thumb a ride back to St Stephen's, and head for the college café, which had a large table specially reserved for the cricket team, the scrambled eggs and toast paid for from the games budget. The bearers in the café had been around since Durai's day. One evening, in my first month in college, a bearer named Dolly (short for Daulat Singh) poured me a cup of tea while saying: 'Jo téra Mama ek haath sé karta tha tu do haath sé nahi kar payega.' (*What your uncle did*

61

with one hand on the cricket field, you will never be able to do with two.)

II

At the Doon School, cricket was only played for three months, from February to April; the football season preceded it and the hockey season came after it. At St Stephen's, the game was played for much of the academic year, the season ending only six weeks before the summer exams. Cricket in college was far more competitive as well. Two of my masters in school, Bond and RP, had played one Ranji match apiece for Uttar Pradesh, and then returned contentedly to club cricket. Here, at St Stephen's, several of my team-mates were playing actively for Delhi, while nurturing ambitions of playing for North Zone and perhaps India too.

The Ranji season commenced only in November. Our college nets started as early as July. Because our facilities were excellent, current or former Test players sometimes came to practise with us, brought along by our own Ranji players. I bowled one day at the nets to Mohinder Amarnath, another day to Chetan Chauhan. The former had moved to Delhi from Punjab, the latter from Maharashtra; both in the hope that this would help them fight their way back into the Indian team.

A third visitor to Mori Gate was Ashok Gandotra, who had captained St Stephen's in the 1960s, before playing two Test matches for his country. He had moved from Delhi to play Ranji Trophy for Bengal, and had now moved back again. He made us bowl to him on the main square, with fielders positioned as they would be in a match. Gandotra had a left-hander's natural grace, stroking the ball beautifully through the off-side. But he also flashed and missed rather too often, even against us college bowlers. On the other hand, Mohinder and Chauhan seemed totally in command. Our assessment was accurate: Gandotra's achievements lay in the past, while the other two went on to have long international careers.

One Delhi cricketer who never, so far as I remember, came to Mori Gate was Bishan Bedi. This was probably not by choice but circumstance. Between July and September, if Bedi was not playing for India he was playing for his English county, Northamptonshire. By the time he returned home, the nets were being erected at the Feroz Shah Kotla for the Ranji season.

The summer of 1974 had been a miserable one for Indian cricket. After three successive series wins, our Test team had been thrashed in England. We lost all three Tests, and were dismissed for a mere 42 in the second innings at Lord's. However, Bedi himself had bowled moderately well in the series. His reputation had not been seriously dented. The aura around him had scarcely dimmed.

Or at least not in the St Stephen's College ground at Mori Gate. For while Bishan Bedi did not come to train with us, the best among us went to apprentice under him at the Kotla, bringing back stories about the great man.

One Stephanian cricketer then playing for Delhi under Bedi was Rajeshwar Vats. Burly, with a curving moustache, he was what was known in North India as a *Dada*, a man you didn't want to mess with. In university cricket, Vats terrorised bowlers of opposing sides with his ferocious driving, and their batsmen with his outswingers and sharp bouncers. But no one lived more in terror of him than the freshmen cricketers of his own college. After practice ended, he would sometimes ask one of us, in Punjabi, to stay on and bowl to him. 'Aidhar ayeen, changi khilanyi' (*Come here, and bowl properly to me*) was a call we dreaded, for that meant not only bowling to him until it was so dark that we would have to walk back to college, but also that if he hit a ball a mile – as he could and would – we had to go fetch the ball before he sent another one along for the same treatment.

At our ground in Mori Gate, a low tin shack served as the 'pavilion'. It had string beds on which we sat during a match and the ground staff slept at night. There was a small latrine behind the shack. If, after practice ended, one saw Rajeshwar Vats in the middle distance, the only escape was to make for the loo, and then crawl out under the barbed wire into the road beyond, for if one re-entered the pavilion or exited through the main gate, one would be spotted and subjected to that harshest form of cricketing torture, bowling unwillingly at a bully in the nets.

Word of Vats' university reputation (personal as well as cricketing) had reached Bishan Bedi, who thereafter referred to him sarcastically as *Pehelwan*, a Hindustani word that requires a many-worded translation in English. Perhaps *the village wrestler who remains undefeated, albeit in the village wrestling pit alone* shall do.

One day, when Rajeshwar Vats was away, Praveen Oberoi told a story that delighted us. The previous afternoon, at the Delhi nets at the Kotla, Bedi had caught Vats bowling off about nineteen yards, to make a greater impression on the batsman (and therefore captain as well). Bedi warned him that this was counter-productive, for this might lead to his being no-balled in a match. Later, during fielding practice, Vats dropped a series of easy catches. His captain now asked the offender to bring two bricks from a pile that lay at the edge of the ground. He did as ordered, not knowing why he had been so asked. Bedi told him to carry a brick in each hand, and take a round of the Kotla. 'Bhag, Pehelwan, Bhag,' said the captain. *Go take a round of the ground, my mighty friend.* Vats bravely took up the challenge, but after running about fifty yards sank to the turf, in agony and exhaustion. Try it if you can; not even an Olympic wrestler can run around a large cricket ground holding a brick aloft in either hand.

In my first year in college, Delhi played Karnataka in the semi-finals of the Ranji Trophy. The match was at the Kotla, and courtesy of my FUCC mate Sudhakar Rao – who was playing for the visitors – I got passes for all four days. This time my loyalties were somewhat divided, for Piggy Lal was to make his first-class debut for Delhi in this match. Piggy's first ball in first-class cricket was a fast googly bowled by B S Chandrasekhar; it went from bat to pad, before falling safely to the ground. His second ball was flighted, and fuller in length. Piggy went to drive, but the ball curved inwards in its flight before spinning sharply away to take the off-bail. Piggy did slightly better in the second innings, scoring twelve runs. Karnataka won the match comfortably, by seven wickets.

It was many years before I was to meet Rajdeep Sardesai, but my perhaps excessive love for Karnataka cricketers was already beginning to grate on those around me. In this match Sudhakar Rao made a half-century, but only after playing and missing often. In the bus back to the university, Piyush Pandey teased me: 'So, your clubmate made fifty-four runs, and was beaten fifty-four times!'

III

The winter after I joined St Stephen's, the West Indies visited India for a five-Test series. In these, my growing-up years, the West Indies were the most charismatic side in world cricket. My uncle Durai spoke more often of them than of the Englishmen or the Australians. One of his abiding – and abidingly sad – memories was of watching them play a Test in Delhi in his own first year at St Stephen's. Playing for India was the forty-one-year-old veteran, Vinoo Mankad, the hero of my uncle's youth. Now, the once great slow left-armer was butchered by Kanhai, Sobers, Collie Smith and company, ending with an analysis of 55–12–167–0. To rub it in, India lost by an innings, Mankad got a duck in the second innings, and never played for his country again. Durai told me this story often, quoting Kipling and his Two Impostors as he went.

The first Test series I myself remembered following was in England in 1966, with West Indies winning 3–1. The first match I am certain I heard on the radio was the Lord's Test of that year, when the West Indies captain, Garfield Sobers, and his cousin David Holford scored hundreds to take their team to a draw. Seven years later, allowed entry into the school common room after dinner since I was in the Senior Form, I heard Sobers and Bernard Julien score hundreds as their team comfortably won the Lord's Test.

Garry Sobers retired early in 1974. But Indian cricket fans remained in awe of the West Indians. The Caribbean side that toured the subcontinent was captained by Clive Lloyd. It would play five Tests, and, before the Tests began, some warm-up matches, including one against a Combined Universities side.

Picked to play for the latter were Praveen Oberoi and Rajeshwar Vats of our college, as well as the batsman Hari Gidwani of Hindu. Praveen and Hari and their admirers all sensed that this journey could be the making of them as cricketers. The names of those who had passed through Combined Varsities en route to full Test honours was legion. They included Hemu Adhikari, Pankaj Roy, Polly Umrigar, Ajit Wadekar, even Sunil Gavaskar. A hundred, from Hari's bat, or five wickets to Praveen's name, and they might soon join that company. One of them, perhaps, scarcely both. But which one?

A week later Praveen Oberoi returned, his dream destroyed. Surprisingly (in view of his past record), he had been relegated to twelfth man. In the nets, the Punjab slow left-armer Deepak Chopra had made more of an impression, and there was no room in the playing XI for two of their kind. Hari Gidwani was chosen, and with scores of 39 and 42 did not disgrace himself. But the century was scored by someone else, Anshuman Gaekwad, who, before the season was out, did in fact find himself playing for India against the West Indies.

Praveen did not show up in college for some time, but straight off the train came Rajeshwar Vats. For he had opened the batting at Indore, and lived to tell the tale. In the first knock he went early, but the second time lasted an hour. In vivid Punjabi, he told us of how he negotiated the new ball, jumping out of the way of a bumper and nudging an outswinger past gully for four. With his score at 24, Roy Fredericks came on to bowl his chinamen. The first ball was a slow half-volley. This is what happened next (as rendered, from this distance in time, in my inadequate English): 'I leapt out, and gave it all I had. I thought it was four past cover, but this s...r f...r at silly mid-off blew on his left palm, and then put his hand down, stopping the ball dead at his feet – the way, you know, a short corner push [in hockey] is stopped before it is struck towards goal.' The *Pehelwan* had given it his hardest, and the ball had carried all of three feet. Vats was so unnerved that he walked out to the next delivery, waved his bat in a hopeless fashion, missed, and was stumped.

Some hours previously, when the West Indies batted, it had been Vats' turn to bowl. The openers were on the move, and he had been instructed by his captain, Gaekwad, to keep them quiet. Bowl well outside the off-stump, said the Baroda man. Vats' first ball, at a lively medium pace, was a couple of feet wide, but the batsman stepped across and cracked it past point for four.

Gaekwad walked up to him, hissing, 'Wider, wider.' Vats did as told, and bowled the next ball a couple of feet wider still. But, as he now narrated to us, 'the m...r f...r., just for a change, walked over and hit me against the line, over mid-wicket for six.' Vats was taken off after two overs that cost 19 runs, figures that read respectably beside those of the main bowlers: A Roy, 18–0–95–0; R Chadha, 14–1–61–1; A Zarapkar, 29–3–113–1; and (most consolingly for us) D Chopra, 30–0–125–1.

The s...r f...r at silly mid-off, it can now be revealed, was Vivian Richards, that m...r f...r of a batsman, Gordon

Greenidge. It was their first tour overseas; as it was for that magnificent fast bowler, Andy Roberts. Moving up the ladder of experience, the other batsmen in the side included the Guyanan trio of Roy Fredericks, Alvin Kallicharan and Clive Lloyd himself; while among the bowlers were Vanburn Holder, Bernard Julien, Keith Boyce and the veteran off-spinner Lance Gibbs. Deryck Murray, a former boy prodigy and Cambridge Blue, kept wicket.

Richards, Lloyd, Kallicharan, Roberts, Greenidge, Gibbs – six of the greatest of modern players, their names making music in any order and in any language. They came with their lesser colleagues to India in that winter of 1974–5, to play what must still rank as the most exciting five-Test series ever played on Indian soil. Certainly it seemed that way to me. For I was then sixteen-and-a-half, a full-time cricketer myself, a college boy eavesdropping on greatness, playing with the lads who played with the men who played with the Gods. From me through Arun Lal to Bishan Bedi (his Delhi captain) to Clive Lloyd was but two-and-a-half cricketing steps.

IV

In the past, when there was a five-Test series in India, the matches were played at Delhi, Bombay, Madras, Calcutta and Kanpur. The principle at work was geographical socialism: one for each zone, North, West, South, East, Central. However, for this series against the West Indies, M Chinnaswamy persuaded the Board of Control for Cricket in India to have Bangalore replace Kanpur instead.

So the Chinnaswamy Stadium hosted the first Test against the West Indies. Missing from the Indian side was someone who had been a regular fixture for the past eight years: Bishan Bedi. Bedi had been dropped not on cricketing grounds but because he had in a television interview made some disparaging remarks about those who administered cricket in India. His replacement in the squad was the Haryana left-arm spinner Rajender Goel, who was not however picked in the playing XI.

West Indies won that first Test thanks to the batsmanship of Greenidge, Kallicharan and Lloyd, and some superb fast bowling by Andy Roberts. Roberts' fellow Antiguan Vivian Richards failed with the bat, being dismissed for 4 and 3 respectively, out both times to B S Chandrasekhar.

The second Test was to be played in Delhi. I was desperately keen to watch it, but where would a ticket come from? I had, via my family in Bangalore, made contact with a member of the Indian squad, the reserve wicketkeeper, Syed Kirmani. He lived in the same locality as my grandparents and had studied in the same college as my youngest uncle, Shankar. The evening before the match, I walked over the Ridge to see Kirmani at the Maidens Hotel, where the Indian team was staying. He told me that he had no ticket for the next day, but I could come back the next evening.

Bedi was back for this Test, but meanwhile the captain and vice-captain, Pataudi and Gavaskar respectively, had to sit out because of injuries. On grounds of seniority the wicketkeeper Farokh Engineer should have led India, and at a reception a day before the match started the Board's Vice-President, R P Mehra of Delhi, informed Engineer that he would be captain. However, overnight Mehra was overruled by the President, M A Chidambaram of Madras, who determined that his fellow Tamil S Venkataraghavan would lead India instead. Since Prasanna and Bedi were automatic choices, to accommodate Venkat meant that Viv Richards' nemesis Chandrasekhar had to be dropped from the playing XI.

I followed the first day's play on the television. India were dismissed for 220, and West Indies were 10 for one at stumps. That evening, I went over to the Maidens Hotel, and found Kirmani, who told me that he had nothing to offer me for the second day, but I could come back and try again for the third, or fourth, or fifth. I walked back disconsolately to the college; however, my spirits lifted over dinner, when a classmate told me he had a spare ticket, obtained from a friend of his father, a Joint Secretary in the Education Ministry.

This ticket was for the newly built R P Mehra Block. (The habit of having structures named after living cricket administrators was not restricted to Bangalore. The Madras stadium, Chepauk, had recently been renamed after M A Chidambaram.) The stand was right over the sightscreen, the best view in the ground. I arrived an hour before play; right below me, the Indian captain for the match, S Venkataraghavan, was having fielding practice. A ground boy was throwing balls onto a roller, fast and hard, and Venkat was taking the crazy rebounds left, right and above, the ball always coming to rest in one or other, occasionally both, of those capacious hands. It was a virtuoso display, apparently put on for my benefit only.

When play started it was Bedi from one end, the military medium of Abid Ali from the other. Abid hopefully bounced Greenidge, who hooked him for six over square-leg. I had never seen a hook shot as savage as this – it was hit not up in the air, as would be the case in college cricket, but parallel, the ball's elevation never exceeding eight feet. The ball flew low over the boundary fence, before bouncing on a row of cement steps and up onto the next two rows as well.

Batting with Greenidge was the nightwatchman, a little slow left-armer from St Kitts with an exquisite name, Elquemedo Tonito Willet. Prasanna dismissed both of them in the first hour, bringing together Kallicharan and Richards. The former played some attractive shots, but the latter was studied and cautious, happy that Chandra was not playing but taking no chances nonetheless. The next day's newspaper claimed that Richards edged Venkat to the keeper when his score stood at 5, but was given not out. I have no recollection of this, but do remember Kallicharan's lovely late cuts and leg glides.

When Kalli had reached 44 he went to swing Bedi over mid-wicket. He got a leading edge, and the ball ballooned high into the off-side. 'Brijesh!' yelled the Sardar, his voice reaching out to us in the stands. Patel took the catch, and the West Indies were 123 for four. The door was ajar, to be impatiently closed by the visiting captain. Lloyd came in, all seventy-five inches of him, the slouch and the spectacles masking the most malevolent of intentions. In or about December 1974 he was possibly the most dangerous batsman in world cricket. (The Australian swing bowler Gary Gilmour, asked how he would like to bowl to Lloyd, answered: 'With a helmet on.') In a matter of an hour he turned this game around. Venkat was pulled, and then hoicked for six over mid-wicket. Bedi was square cut, hard, but most brutal of all his shots was a back-foot drive off Prasanna. The ball traced a flaming path over the turf, the stalks of grass bowing their heads, crushed, as the missile sped from the giant's three-pound mace to the boundary.

In between overs Lloyd talked to Richards, putting heart into the novice. His shots then began to unfold, elegant in their classicism. Venkat brought on Abid, in hope, but Richards stroked him twice to the off boundary. When Lloyd was given out, to the most disgraceful of lbw decisions, the balance had already shifted. A lovely off-drive for six off Bedi, almost caressed, and a late cut took Richards to his hundred. He was now being supported first by Bernard Julien, who drove handsomely, and then by Keith Boyce, who swept away to leg. By close of play the West Indies were 378 for six, the match in their command.

As I have said, I can recall little of the first day of the 1974 Delhi Test that I watched on TV, but the minutiae of this second day are with me still. Five sixes, one apiece by Greenidge, Lloyd, Richards, Boyce and Julien. Artful bowling by Prasanna and Bedi. Dreadful fielding in the course of play but, before that, Venkat's dream practice performance put on for two boys and a passing crow. A sight I cannot forget came into view during the tea interval. As I came down for a leak I passed Keith Boyce, standing on the steps of the Willingdon Pavilion, smoking a *beedi*. I looked him up and down, taking in the whites well ironed, the shirt buttons open, the fast bowler's big boots and the fast bowler's beautiful body. And the *beedi*, held askance, in splendid and fateful arrogance.*

V

That evening I had my appointment with Kirmani but did not keep it, knowing by now that nothing would come of it. Other alternatives were explored, and after much scrounging I garnered a ticket for the thirty-rupee stand, bought at a premium of one hundred per cent. By the time the deal was settled and the money raised it was already half-past nine. I reached the Kotla as play began, almost the last person to enter a stand for which others had queued up from four in the morning. All I could find was a berth on the ground, my nose pressed against the barbed wire. After the first over I stood up to stretch myself: 'Abe salle Guha!' came a cry from behind, which continued: 'Idhar aa jaa.' (*You dolt Guha, get up and come here.*) I looked up, and saw my fellow college cricketer, Piyush Pandey, calling me to sit with him up at row fifteen. I scrambled up, and settled into a crowd of rowdy Stephanians. On one side of me sat Pandey; on the other, Chandan Mitra, as I write the editor-printer-publisher of a yellow rag with saffron shades named *The Pioneer*.

It was not the best of views, looking out over wide mid-off, but at least I had a seat. As the sun bore down Richards began to go bananas. Bedi was hit for six, then Prasanna for two more. Venkat put himself on, and Richards drove him straight, breaking the stumps at the other end. Even the captain, the best fielder in the side, would not put his hand in front of that shot. Then Piyush

---

* Keith Boyce was to die in 1996 of a heart attack, having just turned fifty. The *beedi* I saw was probably one of thousands he smoked. Collectively deadly, but how magnificent when viewed one by one!

Pandey issued a prediction. The next one, he said, will go over the Wills Filter hoarding that rose high to the left of the sightscreen. Richards came crashing down the wicket, and aimed for long-off. The ball climbed ever higher, cleared the Wills sign comfortably, and finally came to rest in the Ambedkar football stadium. It had travelled, in effect, from New Delhi to Old Delhi. In this city of kingdoms a new king had announced himself.

Richards finished with 192 not out and his team won easily. Pataudi returned to the Indian side for the third Test in Calcutta; so, more materially, did B S Chandrasekhar. In a marvellously close-fought match India won, their heroes being Gundappa Viswanath (52 and 139), Bedi (four wickets in the first innings) and Chandra (three in the second). In the fourth Test at Madras, Vishy batted brilliantly again (97 not out and 46), and his Karnataka captain Prasanna chipped in with nine wickets.

The teams thus went to Bombay all-square: would India now emulate Bradman's 1936–7 Australians, the only side in cricket history to win a five-Test series after losing the first two matches? On a perfect Brabourne Stadium pitch the toss was vital, and Pataudi lost it. Clive Lloyd scored 242 not out in a score of 608 for six declared, and though Solkar and Vishy battled bravely, India lost late on the fifth day.

A last memory of that West Indies side of 1974–5 is contained in a television clip. On the third evening of the fifth Test, we sat in the college common room watching edited tapes of the second day's play, which took twenty-four hours to reach Delhi. Lloyd had been 64 not out overnight, with the West Indies commandingly placed at 309 for three. Pataudi took the second new ball at the start of play, and Eknath Solkar ran in as fast as he could bowl. It was a leg-stump half-volley, and Lloyd played his celebrated pick-up stroke, depositing the ball into the stands. The umpire signalled six, but the batsman put his palm to his mouth, unsuccessfully stifling a yawn. He was sleepy, having partied all night, but also bored, having to face this apology of an opening bowler. I can see that big mouth open now, wide enough to swallow a cricket ball.

VI

Between 1974 and 1979 – the years I was in college in Delhi – I witnessed a great deal of cricket in the Kotla. For the Test against England in December 1976, I had a ticket for the R P Mehra Stand for all five days, not just one. This was thanks to a girl-friend whose father knew the former India off-spinner Ghulam Ahmed – then the Secretary of the Cricket Board. From these, the best seats in the ground, I saw John Lever demolish India with a devastating spell of left-arm swing bowling, carried out with – or without – the use of Vaseline.

The wicket I remember best was that of S Venkataraghavan. Tamils claimed their state captain to be an all-rounder; a charac-terisation he had adopted as his own, for in Ranji matches he sometimes batted as high as number five. We residents of Karnataka scoffed at this characterisation, thinking – or knowing – this to be a ruse to keep our own Prasanna out of the Indian team. Notably, when playing for India, Venkat merely headed the tail, never batting higher than number eight. Now, in this Delhi Test, he had been sent in by the captain, Bishan Bedi, as nightwatchman late on the second day, to protect the middle order after two early wickets fell. Playing on the batsman's ego, the canny England captain, Tony Greig, placed a silly mid-off and silly mid-on apart from the regulation slips and leg slip. This so offended Venkat that, instead of merely prodding forward and keeping the ball out, he sought to hammer it through the vast vacant spaces on the off-side. The ball was full, swung in late, and crashed into the off-stump even as the batsman was completing a stroke which had begun with an extravagant backlift and carried on with an equally lavish follow-through.

England won that Test easily. Two years later, I saw a West Indies side vastly depleted by Kerry Packer's chequebook saved by rain at the Kotla. My friend whose father knew the Board secretary was no longer my girlfriend, so I was back to scrounging a pass a day at a time, one day over mid-wicket, the next day wide of mid-off. It was from the latter vantage point that I saw Kapil Dev's maiden Test hundred. In the seats next to mine were a doctoral student at the Delhi School of Economics and his wife. Their names must be recorded; they were (the future television entrepreneurs) Prannoy and Radhika Roy.

I also saw a great deal of Ranji cricket at the Kotla. This included another Delhi *v* Karnataka match, played in March 1978, and won (of course) by my side. B S Chandrasekhar took loads of wickets, and G R Viswanath scored a jewel of a hundred, at one stage hitting my college team-mate Praveen Oberoi over extra-cover into the crowd, thus bringing into the playing arena what he otherwise kept only for the nets. The stroke was in the nature of a spanking, for in his previous over the bowler had struck the batsman on the pads. The ball was clearly missing leg-stump, but Oberoi's appeal was so loud and extended, with such an expressive gesture of disgust following its (just) denial, that this great and gentle man thought he must treat the upstart a lesson – with the bat, of course, since Vishy never ever used angry words in person, whether on or off the field.*

---

* Some days after I had written these words, a friend sent me the report of an unidentified, but presumably British, journalist on Kumar Sangakkara's last first-class hundred, for Surrey against Somerset in September 2017. Compare what I have written about Vishy above to this para below: 'To this correspondent, though, the finest moment came a ball after Dom Bess, Somerset's young off-spinner, had turned one sharply past Sangakkara. As if riled by the merest hint of fallibility, Sangakkara took a couple of strides down the wicket to his next delivery and caressed Bess for a straight six. It was a shot that, delicately and beautifully, carried a simple message: Sangakkara is in charge.' https://www.espncricinfo.com/series/8052/report/1068577/day/2/surrey-vs-somerset-specsavers-county-championship-division-one-2017.

I played once at the Feroz Shah Kotla myself, for St Stephen's against a Delhi Under-22 side. I bowled a few overs without reward, but while batting (at number eleven) slogged the left-arm spinner R S Hans (formerly a student of my college, and in a few years to be an India reserve) over mid-wicket for four. My enduring memory of that day is of the Delhi stumper Ravi K Raj, in his build and looks the spitting image of the tennis player Vijay Amritraj, who kept up a continuous series of wisecracks while keeping quite beautifully. Umpiring when my side batted, I had never seen such dazzling glovework at close quarters; and still cannot figure out how this man played only two first-class games in his life.

The reigning deity of the Kotla in those years was, of course, Bishan Bedi. His presence at the ground was marked by his car, a blue Volkswagen Beetle. In those distant, pre-liberalisation days, when there were few cars on the road and fewer foreign ones, the Sardar of Spin owned one of two Beetles in Delhi that we university students knew of. The other was driven by Professor Mrinal Datta Chaudhuri of the Delhi School of Economics, who in his own profession and among his own acolytes carried as much glamour as did India's premier spin bowler.

When, for Ranji or Test match alike – or even to watch the Delhi team practise in the nets – we entered the Kotla, we first looked to see where Bishan Bedi's blue Beetle was. Inside the ground, we looked for the owner. When we were too far away to hear him, his gestures signified what he was saying – as when we saw him send the twelfth man twice in quick succession to the field to chastise a Delhi batsman, crawling in his nineties. On two occasions I actually came within handshaking distance of him: once in the Willingdon Pavilion while chatting to Piggy Lal, once in the Maidens Hotel when searching for the elusive, evasive, Syed Kirmani. But I didn't dare introduce myself, or alert Bedi to when and where we had once met. For me – at least then – he was unapproachable, as heroes of one's youth shall always be.

VII

My years in St Stephen's expanded my knowledge of cricket, and of cricket literature. The college library had a fine collection of books on sport. It was in St Stephen's that I first heard of Ray Robinson and J H Fingleton. I came to prefer these two Australian writers to Thomson and Cardus; they may not have been as lyrical, but they had a far better understanding of cricketing character and technique. I read – and re-read – Robinson's *Between Wickets* and Fingleton's *Masters of Cricket*.

I was also reading Indian writers on the game. For the princely sum of six rupees I picked up Sujit Mukherjee's *The Romance of Indian Cricket*; and for roughly twice that amount, his *Playing for India*. Mukherjee was a few years older than my uncle Durai, and had once played first-class cricket for Bihar. Formerly a professor of English literature (with a PhD from a great American university) he had since become a publisher and translator. The first of his cricket books focused on the heroes of his own youth – C K Nayudu, Amar Singh, Vinoo Mankad, and the like. The second sought to provide a comprehensive record of all who had, until that date, played Test cricket for India. Shades of Cardus hung over the first book, and of Fingleton over the second, but this was in acknowledgement, not emulation. As a cricket writer, Mukherjee had a personality and character of his own.

In 1977, Mukherjee's daughter Rukmini joined St Stephen's. We became friends, and in February 1978 she took me to meet her father at the Pragati Maidan, where the second World Book Fair was being held. Mukherjee presided over the Orient Longman stall; he was tall and erect, and smoked a pipe. A fortnight later I sat next to him while watching my beloved G R Viswanath score the match-winning hundred against Delhi that I have already referred to. When, in a last desperate throw of the dice, Bedi took the new ball, and Vishy cut and drove Mohinder

Amarnath for boundaries, Mukherjee took the pipe out of his mouth and exclaimed: 'Hazare! Only Hazare could play the on-drive like that.'

That day at the Kotla was one of the happiest of my life, mostly because of Vishy's batsmanship but also for the stories that Sujit Mukherjee told me. When, back in the early 1950s, Mukherjee played for Bihar against Holkar, as the youngest and most historically-minded member of his side he was determined to record it for posterity. So he took his cricket bat to the opponents' dressing room, and asked them to sign it, one by one. The first signature solicited for and graciously granted was, of course, that of C K Nayudu. His brother, the googly-bowling all-rounder C S Nayudu, signed next, followed by Mushtaq Ali. Two other Test cricketers, Chandu Sarwate and Khandu Rangnekar, also obliged the young man. Seeing their seniors sign, the lesser Holkar players did likewise.

But one Holkar player politely declined the Bihar player's request. This was the left-arm medium-pacer H G (Ghasu) Gaekwad. Recounting the tale to me decades later, Sujit Mukherjee said he first thought Gaekwad had not signed his bat out of modesty. It later struck him that there might have been another reason – that he was illiterate.

The latter explanation seems more likely. Ghasu Gaekwad was a left-arm medium-pacer who cut rather than swung the ball, in the manner of Bangladesh's Mustafizur Rahman now. Durai, who had watched him bowl and heard stories about him, told me that Ghasu was much more effective on matting than on turf, and that he needed his skipper C K Nayudu to stand at mid-off to tell him what to bowl. Gaekwad was picked for the England tour of 1952 after a productive Ranji season; that Holkar's captain was India's chairman of selectors may have had something to do with his selection. However, in England he could scarcely get a wicket. It was a wet summer, he was bowling on turf rather than matting, and C K Nayudu was not prompting him from mid-off. That he could not read the signs at the ground or hotel or in the railway stations, must have put Ghasu Gaekwad off his game as well.

The World Book Fair of 1978 was memorable for having met Sujit Mukherjee; and for having picked up my first copy of C L R James' *Beyond a Boundary*. I can't remember whether I had borrowed the book from the college library and read it already. But I have a clear recollection of thumbing through books at a second-hand stall in Pragati Maidan, with the *shehnai* of Bismillah Khan playing in the background. The stall was out in the open, with rows of unclassified books in a large barrel. Opposite me was Krishna Kumar, who had just left his job in the Doon School and was en route to the United States. 'Here, this is for you,' said KK, flinging a book across the barrel. It was a paperback edition of *Beyond a Boundary*. I paid four rupees for it. I have that copy still, now bound in leather and with gold lettering on the spine.

VIII

In those years at St Stephen's, watching cricket and reading about cricket, important as they might have been, were subordinated to playing cricket. Four or five hours each day at the nets; twenty or thirty competitive matches every season; it was thus that I most enhanced my knowledge of the game.

There was then a terrific rivalry between St Stephen's and Hindu College, who met every year in the finals of the inter-college championship. In my first year, I played the warm-up matches but was not good enough to be in the XI for the final. A crowd of some twenty thousand had turned up, with live commentary on the match transmitted over All India Radio.

The match was hard fought all the way through. Hindu were set 300-odd to win in the fourth innings. They got to about 30 for no loss, whereupon Rajeshwar Vats abandoned his outswingers in favour of bouncers. One short ball hit Hindu's opening batsman, Surinder Khanna, smack on the head (there were no helmets in those days). He fell to the ground, bleeding profusely. He was carried off, and Hari Gidwani walked in to take his place. Vats bowled another bouncer, which Hari hooked between square-leg and fine-leg for four.

Through that fourth afternoon and through most of the fifth day, Hari Gidwani batted magnificently. He was in his last year in university; in his four previous years Hindu had lost to St Stephen's each time. Gidwani was determined to end on a winning note; just as determined not to let this happen was his exact contemporary, Praveen Oberoi, who had never played in a losing college side before. The rivalry was personal and it was institutional. To this sixteen-year-old watching it unfold, it had an epic quality.

Wickets fell steadily to Praveen and Vats, but Gidwani's was not one of them. He played all round the ground; although it was his cuts and his on-drives that made the most impression. At the fall of the seventh wicket, Surinder Khanna, his wounds stitched and his head heavily bandaged, came out to bat. Vats bounced him again, and Khanna heroically hooked the ball for four. Shortly afterwards Hari fell to a tired shot, mistiming a drive to be caught at cover. He had scored 180. St Stephen's went on to win by 21 runs. Gidwani's innings remains the finest I have ever seen in a losing cause.

The following two years I played in the inter-college cricket final for St Stephen's. Then, in the first year of my Masters, I had a quarrel with the captain, and walked out before our final against Hindu College. This match was won for Hindu by a magical spell of left-arm swing bowling by Sunil Valson. St Stephen's had been set a modest target to win in the fourth innings, just under 200 runs. 'Wallie' started over the wicket and soon shifted his angle of delivery to round the wicket. He bowled sharp inswingers, and at pace. He took six or perhaps seven wickets, two of which I shall replay in my mind as I write. These were of our best batsmen. Arun Lal was trapped on the back foot by one that swung in late and kept low. Kirti Azad got a wicked lifter, which he gloved to gully.

We thought that both Hari Gidwani and Sunil Valson of Hindu College should have played for India. In the event, neither did. Hari somehow never scored when it really mattered – against a touring side, or in the finals of the Ranji or Duleep Trophy. Valson should have gone to England with the Indian team in 1979; but he was seen as Bedi's man, and Bedi's great rival Gavaskar was now captain, so the mediocre Bombay player Suru Nayak went instead. Wallie got partial compensation when picked for the 1983 World Cup; while India won, he however did not play a single match in the tournament. (Another Hindu College player, Surinder Khanna, had kept wicket for India in the previous World Cup.)

While Hari Gidwani and Sunil Valson never played Test cricket for India, two of my Stephanian team-mates did. These were Arun Lal and Kirti Azad. In his university days Piggy Lal was a free-flowing strokemaker, particularly good on the off-side. Later he adopted a square-on stance, and muscled the ball through the on-side. After finishing his Masters he took a job in Calcutta, where he became a much-loved figure at Eden Gardens, especially after he batted Bengal to victory in a Ranji final, his shots accompanied by shouts of 'Lal Salaam' (Salutations to the Red Flag), as the Communists were then in power in the State.

Piggy Lal was first picked for the Indian squad in 1979, against Kim Hughes' Australian side. In the Bangalore Test I saw him come on as a substitute, and take a perfectly judged catch at deep square-leg (when in the playing XI he was normally placed at slip or silly point, but he could field brilliantly anywhere). Over the next decade he played 16 Test matches for his country. I was privileged to watch one of these Tests, at the Kotla in 1988, when against a fine West Indian pace attack Piggy batted well in both innings, in the second throwing away a chance of a Test hundred through an injudicious hook shot.

The last time I saw Piggy Lal bat was for Rest of India against the Ranji Trophy champions (that year, Haryana) in 1991. This was a sort of selection trial, with India due to tour Australia shortly afterwards. I had gone with Sujit Mukherjee to Faridabad to watch the first day's play. Rest of India batted first, but Piggy was out early, caught behind off a medium-pacer. Afterwards, I walked over to the pavilion to seek my old captain out. I found him in the dressing room, sitting alone and utterly disconsolate, since he knew he would never again play for India. He shooed away some young autograph hunters, but was warm and welcoming towards me. His mood brightened as we talked of our days in college. Then some Bengali journalists came by, and Piggy told them of how he had not in fact nicked the ball to which he was given out. The Calcutta press must have had a field day, representing this as the latest of the countless injustices that India had inflicted on Bengal and Bengalis (adopted ones included).

Our other future Test cricketer, Kirti Azad, was three years junior to me in college. He had played cricket for Indian Schoolboys, and his father had been a cabinet minister under Jawaharlal Nehru. Kirti carried a swagger, which St Stephen's took out of him, albeit in an unusual fashion. In his first year, Kirti got into an argument with a boy from Nagaland which led to the cricketer being knocked out cold by a karate chop. He swore revenge, and said he would come to settle accounts the following Sunday. Word got around the university, so that on Sunday morning some two hundred Naga students from across the campus had assembled at the college's Allnutt Court. At eleven sharp Kirti walked in through the Allnutt Gate, accompanied by a sidekick, a Haryana Ranji player named Kultar Dogra who saw himself as something of a *Pehelwan* too. Seeing the crowd that had come to greet them, Kirti and Kultar turned left into the college café, had tea and toast and went back home.

Kirti Azad knew no karate and knew nothing about the Nagas, but he could play cricket. He had come to college as a hard-hitting batsman and new-ball bowler. The strokes he hit grew harder and went longer, but over the course of time he turned to bowling off-breaks. The year after I left college I was giving commentary on All India Radio while he scored a rapid-fire hundred against Hindu, with nine (or maybe ten) sixes, several soaring over the elevated and open studio where I sat. Shortly afterwards Kirti scored his first Ranji hundred, which he reached through three successive sixes, these hit off the wise and experienced Bombay slow left-armer, Padmakar Shivalkar.

I was watching on TV with tens of millions of others when Kirti Azad bowled Ian Botham to set up a famous win in the semi-finals of the 1983 World Cup. He retained his place in the side that won the final, earning my college team-mate a place in cricket history. Shortly afterwards, I saw Kirti bat against the Railways in a Ranji match at the Karnail Singh Stadium in Delhi. He hit some terrific shots en route to a rapid fifty. After Kirti was dismissed I went to the players' tent to seek him out. I found Kirti lying down, having an oil massage, as befitting a *Pehelwan*. He stood up as he saw me enter. 'Ram, kaisa laga?' he asked excitedly. *How did I find his show?* I answered truthfully that I had enjoyed his fireworks, especially a sizzling straight drive that landed just short of the ropes before bounding away into the bushes.

In later years I have met Piggy Lal several times, and followed with interest his nurturing of young cricketers, his deepening love of wildlife, and his brave (and successful) battle with cancer. I bumped into Kirti in an airport once, but otherwise have not met him. He served three terms as a Member of Parliament, elected from Darbhanga in Bihar, although a still untempered tendency to truculence meant that he was never made a Minister.

There may be another reason; that he incurred the hostility of his senior party colleague Arun Jaitley for having so relentlessly focused on the corruption in the Delhi and Districts Cricket Association of which Jaitley was the long-time president.

Piggy and Kirti played Test cricket for India. Of my other college mates, Rajinder Amarnath played some thirty matches for Haryana, scoring two fifties in a quarter-final against a Karnataka side that included an (admittedly ageing) B S Chandrasekhar. Deepak Sharma, who was two years junior to me in college, also played many seasons for Haryana, scoring 199 against Bombay in a Ranji final which his team won.

Deepak Sharma had joined St Stephen's with two disadvantages: he was not articulate in English, and he was not to money or status born. Promising freshmen cricketers in our college announced themselves by their pedigree; they had either come from elite boarding schools such as Mayo College (as had Arun Lal) or from famous English-medium schools in New Delhi such as Modern School (as did Kirti Azad).

This shy new boy came from an unknown school in West Delhi; and he said he had played for Sonnet Club. We Stephanians had not heard of that place either. The Delhi cricket clubs we knew of were Madras Club (captained by the prolific opening batsman Venkat Sundaram), Salwan Club (for whom Praveen Oberoi played), and Rohtak Road Gymkhana (the club of Rajeshwar Vats). So amused were we by the background and demeanour of this freshman from Sonnet that the senior Stephanian cricketers derisively nicknamed him 'Bonnet'.

Later in the season, our knowledge of Sonnet Club expanded by leaps and bounds, and as it did our condescension receded. Until then, our sole cricketing rival was Hindu College. We normally won the early rounds of the inter-college championship by an innings. Then came the main match of the year, the gruelling, close-fought, five-day final against Hindu. However, the year Deepak Sharma came to our nets we were given the fright of our lives in the quarter-final by the previously unknown Pannalal Girdharlal Dayanand Anglo-Vedic (PGDAV) College, whose opening batsman, Raman Lamba, and opening bowler, Randhir Singh, were far better than our own. It was only our greater all-round depth that allowed us to squeak through.

Both Lamba and Randhir came from Sonnet Club, where they were coached by Tarak Sinha, who had just then taken over as PGDAV's coach as well. An account on the internet describes the origins of Sonnet as follows: 'It all started in 1969, when Sinha, then a budding wicketkeeper-batsman at the government-run Birla School in Kamla Nagar, failed to find a place in the final 16 of Delhi's C K Nayudu team – then led by Salman Khurshid, who is now more famous as a Congress leader. That was when the idea of running a training center where children from lower-middle-class families could learn the basics of the game, came to Sinha. "I realised that government school children did not have the basic coaching facilities to rise," he recalls. "I made a vow that I would strive to give the best playing facilities to cricketers from government schools."'

Incidentally, before he became a Congress politician and Union Minister, Salman Khurshid studied at St Stephen's and at Oxford (although he succeeded in playing cricket for neither). The journey of Sonnet Cricket Club therefore represents an emphatic triumph of the subaltern over the elite. The club has since produced a dozen Test cricketers, and hundreds of Ranji players. I am proud to say that I played against the first generation of Sonnet's cricketers and suffered at their hands. In one practice match against us, the future Test cricketer Raman Lamba scored a hundred before lunch. At least sixty of those runs were off me. When it came to the inter-college quarter-final, however, I bowled Lamba, inadvertently, with a grubber that rolled along the ground. Had that off-break bounced as expected, Lamba would surely have pulled it for four, and gone on to score another hundred. The next year, when I opted out of the final against Hindu because of differences with the captain, my replacement was the Sonnet cricketer Deepak Sharma. He took thirteen wickets in the match, and batted better than I could ever have done.

When the next cricket season began, I made my peace with the (new) captain, and resumed going to the nets. This year, my last in college, again found us playing PGDAV in the quarter-final. Our opponents had given us a fright last time; and this time they were even slight favourites. Our ranks had been depleted by the exit of Arun Lal; theirs augmented by the arrival of Rajesh Peter, a fast-bowling all-rounder being spoken of as the new Kapil Dev.

Indeed, the students of PGDAV were so certain their cricketers would win this year that they came en masse across Delhi for the match. As I warmed up on the first day, I saw a caravan of buses arrive at the ground, disgorging hundreds of young (and very vocal) men who had come from their own college campus in the far south of the city. They sat themselves down on one side of the ground, shouting in praise of their cricketers.

It had rained overnight, so when St Stephen's won the toss we put them in. I came on first change, on the grounds that since I was six inches taller than the other (and better) off-spinner in the team – the aforementioned Deepak Sharma – I could get more purchase from the damp. The surmise was correct. Early on, I got a ball to land on a wet patch, and turn and bounce unexpectedly; it took the dreaded Raman Lamba's glove to lob up for an easy catch to short-leg. This was the first of four wickets I took that day. Naturally, I remember them all; while also recalling, more in relief than in pride, a catch I took at deep mid-wicket to dismiss the dangerous Rajesh Peter.

PGDAV were all out for about 180. The next day, with Piyush Pandey batting superbly, St Stephen's had reached 120 for four, and were all set to win on first-innings. At this stage, the disappointed students of PGDAV descended on the ground, forcing the umpires to flee to the pavilion for safety. The match was abandoned, and so, in the event, was the tournament itself, since no umpires were willing to officiate in another match between these two teams. The season ended with a friendly 'mock-final' between us and Hindu, played without any of the competitive edge a proper final carried.

IX

For five years in St Stephen's I lived for cricket, and had it been asked of me I might have died for cricket as well. Never before, and never since, have I poured as much passion and energy into anything. Playing every day with the best college cricketers in the country taught me much more about the game than books or video clips ever could. My immersion became deeper and even more fulfilling by watching the greatest Indian and international cricketers play at the Kotla.

The grounds where the cricketers of St Stephen's played were by no means as lovely as in the Doon, but they were not without their own charm. The college ground in Mori Gate, where we played our practice matches, was located between two structures redolent with history: Kashmiri Gate, the northern entrance to the Old City; and Qudsia Bagh, an eighteenth-century garden where noblemen and noblewomen had once walked and talked. The inter-college matches were played at the University Ground, which had a pretty two-storey pavilion. The ground was ringed by trees all around, except for the southern end, where we had our own version of the Sydney Hill, with barrackers from Hindu College on one side of the sightscreen and barrackers from St Stephen's on the other.

Cricket season coincided with winter, a season which in the Delhi of the 1970s was glorious. The air was then entirely clear (and clean), and with a blue sky overhead and a gentle breeze drifting across the ground the conditions were perfect for cricket. For me, to play on the same ground in the same tournament for the same team against the same rivals as my uncle Durai was to absolutely achieve my childhood ambitions.

However, my own cricketing talents and achievements were unremarkable. In practice matches, and in the early rounds of the inter-college championship (when Praveen Oberoi was away on Ranji duty, playing for Delhi) I took, on occasion, four or five wickets in an innings. But in the two inter-college finals I played against Hindu College, my contributions were negligible. In one, I took a sharp low catch at short mid-wicket, that so surprised the batsman (whose name was Deshpal Singh) that he stood stunned at the crease, since nothing I had ever done before in the field had anticipated this particular event. In another, I was called on to bowl in desperation when a batsman named Deepak Raina looked like he would take his side to a win. I bowled a leg-cutter, the ball took the edge, and the wicketkeeper, Piyush Pandey, somehow clung on to the catch. Praveen Oberoi came back to clean up the tail, and the championship, once more, was ours.

A week after this final ended, I boarded a *Mudrika*, the sole Delhi Transport Corporation bus identified not with a number but by a name, indicating that it circumambulated the entire length of the then newly built Ring Road. I was travelling from one end of the city to another, from Mall Road, next to the university, to the All India Institute of Medical Sciences, near where some cousins of mine lived. The journey took an hour; all the while, a young man standing opposite looked at me with an amused smile. We passed Old Secretariat, Kashmiri Gate, Lal Qila, Rajghat, and ITO; the smirk stayed on his face, but he would not say a word. Through Ashram, Lajpat Nagar, Moolchand, and South Extension his steady and superior gaze never left me. At last, when AIIMS came and I made to get out, the man said: 'Paanch din dhup mein aage peeche bhage, phir bhi ek hi wicket mila.' *For five full days you ran up and down in the sun, and all you had to show for it was a single, solitary, wicket.*

It was a put-down as decisive as Dolly's in the college café. Forget Piggy Lal and Sunil Valson, Hari Gidwani and Kirti Azad, even compared to my uncle Durai I was a most ordinary cricketer. With earnest perseverance and enormous good luck, I just about made the St Stephen's First XI; clinging precariously to my place through four years of spectacularly indifferent performance. That said, this was no mere 'college team' but the best college team in India. I played every day with boys who played (for Delhi) with men who played (for India) with and against the greatest cricketers of the age. What little I know and understand of the game I owe entirely to those years of passionate engagement at the College Cricket Ground in Mori Gate.

4

You Only Live Twice

I

After finishing with St Stephen's I took what is now known as a gap year, in the course of which I considered several career options. I considered publishing, journalism and public service, but ended up rejecting all and choosing to do a PhD in Sociology in Calcutta instead. I became immersed in research, and my interest in cricket receded into the background. I came under the spell of a Marxist teacher, who argued that cricket was a bourgeois deviation from the class struggle. So determined was I to show (to myself above all) that the scholar had superseded the sportsman that I gave away my cricket books to a young journalist in Calcutta. The space vacated on my shelves was quickly filled in by books by sociologists and historians. Max Weber and E P Thompson had replaced Jack Fingleton and A A Thomson in my literary pantheon.

I could not get cricket completely out of my system, though. A Bengali friend took me several times to Eden Gardens, once to watch a veterans' match in commemoration of the Golden Jubilee of the Cricket Association of Bengal. Playing for Indian Veterans was Syed Mushtaq Ali, who danced down the wicket to flay the ball (and bowler) in his seventies as he had in his twenties; playing for World Veterans was Freddie Trueman, at fifty-five possessed still of an abiding hatred for batsmen – his shout for lbw when he struck the pads was heard across the Hooghly in Howrah.

In late 1985, my wife Sujata went to the United States to study, and I soon joined her on a teaching assignment. I arrived in deepest January, with a foot of snow on the ground. That summer India beat England in England for the first time since 1971; that September India and Australia played a tied Test in Chepauk. News of these events might have reached me a week late, via the airmail edition of *The Hindu*, but the fan in me began to stir once more.

Deprived of cricket, I turned to baseball. I watched, on television, all the matches of the 1986 World Series, played between the New York Mets and the Boston Red Sox. New Haven, where we lived, was on the train line between the two great cities where these teams were based. I had to choose one team; but which one? Keith Hernandez of the Mets reminded me of my uncle Durai; likewise left-handed, likewise a leader of men. I was impressed by Darryl Strawberry's hitting and Dwight Gooden's pitching; and Mookie Wilson struck me as a character. So I went for the New York team. They won a close-fought series by the narrowest of margins, 4–3, after an epic fielding error which I recall to this day, committed by a man immortalised in baseball history for this one mistake that blighted and destroyed an otherwise impressive career at the highest levels of the sport.

Watching this fancifully named 'World Series' was interesting, entertaining, but not perhaps uplifting. For baseball was not cricket. The game depended excessively on the pitcher, who could pitch if he wished for nine innings at a stretch. When a pitcher was on song, his side won. In cricket the contest between bat and ball was more even, partly because the batsman did not have to return to the pavilion/dugout after hitting a six/home run. The range of strokes on display was far greater (since the playing circumference ran to the full 360 degrees). In aesthetic terms the bowler was more advantaged too, for he could do things in the air as well as off the pitch. And while the base running and throwing in baseball were thrilling, I was less impressed by the catching, having caught balls at slip without a mitt and at short-leg without any protection at all. My favourite player type was the sinker-ball pitcher, who came in for the eighth or ninth innings to save a match. Plump and balding, in his build he resembled a hero of my youth, Erapalli Prasanna; while in his form of delivery (lower and even lower) he reminded me of Pras' worthy contemporary, Syed Abid Ali.

The New England winter of 1986–7 was brutal. Huddled in our apartment, I became nostalgic for warmer climes and the games that went with them. I bowled off-breaks in the living room, the ball bouncing on the floor and against the wall. A doctoral student (of Buddhist philosophy) who lived below us knocked on our door, and said – very politely – that his wife could not sleep because of my exertions. I put away the tennis ball, and took out pen and paper instead. Over the course of the next few days I made up All Time XIs of Ranji Trophy teams, and jotted down some notes to go with them. They were to become the kernel of my first book on cricket, *Wickets in the East*, an (A A) Thomson-esque study of the cricketing histories of Indian states, with a few (E P) Thompson-esque stabs at analysing the game in social terms.

In the autumn of 1987, Sujata and I returned to Bangalore. We lived in her parental home, off M G Road in the heart of the city. I had got a job at the Indian Institute of Science, some five miles to the west. I rode a moped to work. Durai's company had transferred him to Madras, but FUCC was still active in the KSCA's first division. I contacted the captain, Rajanna – who we called 'Ken' because like the Englishman Ken Barrington he batted in the middle order and bowled leg-breaks – and told him I would come for the nets.

I had previously attended nets at my club in 1966, 1970, and 1974. Now I was no longer a school or college student but an Assistant Professor with wards of my own to attend to. So, on the first day of my fourth stint at the FUCC I drove early to work, to get off in time for practice. The air was crisp, the sky cloudless, the jacarandas in bloom, the roads altogether less crowded than they were to become in later years. A line of the Nobel Prize-winning physicist C V Raman came to mind: 'My greatest discovery was the weather of Bangalore.'

My mood of self-congratulation was interrupted by a Standard Herald that crossed my path briskly from a side road. I braked, and so did the driver of the car. His windows were down, and I saw within the face of Erapalli Prasanna. I collected myself and hastily simulated a curving off-break before enquiring, with uplifted palms, whether he still bowled them. He shook his head and sped on his way.

Although no words were spoken by either party, I read meanings into the meeting. For I bowled off-breaks myself. Surely this chance encounter with the master of the art augured well for the revival of my cricketing career? However, when I left work for the FUCC nets, I found that the skill had deserted me completely. I could still turn the ball, but the control was abysmal. I was now thirty, and had not played any serious cricket since I was twenty-one. The muscles that accurately propel a cricket ball had been out of business too long. After a few weeks at the nets the control improved, but the zip off the wicket I remembered from my youth could not be recaptured. I now realised, shame-facedly, that the message intended by the God of Cricket was the opposite of what I had first taken it to be. If the great Prasanna acknowledged that he had bowled his last off-break, who was I to pretend I could still roll them along? I would never again wear whites, though of course I would continue to watch young men in whites playing for my club, my state, and my country.

II

After a year in Bangalore my wife and I moved to Delhi, where I worked at the Institute of Economic Growth, at the edge of the university campus. I had a corner office, which overlooked the Hindu College ground, where I had once played myself. One morning I looked out to see a match in progress. I recognised the bowler immediately. The slanting run-up, the windmill action, and the big buttocks were unmistakable – they belonged to the Karnataka and India cricketer, Roger Michael Humphrey Binny.

In the year that I lived in Bangalore, working at the Indian Institute of Science, I saw Binny score a hundred 'live', for BUCC against FUCC in the first division league. He was a marvellous striker of the cricket ball, and drove especially well. And he was a fine bowler too, moving the ball away at a brisk pace. Now, watching him from my office window, I put my books away, and walked over to Hindu College. It was a State Bank of India tournament, and Binny had come representing the Bangalore branch, where he worked. When the players broke for lunch, I saw him chatting animatedly with someone from the opposing team. It was that other sturdy all-rounder, Madan Lal. Two stars of the 1983 World Cup had, six years later, returned to playing office tournaments.

In my teens it had been all sport; in my twenties, all scholarship. Now, in my thirties, I was achieving some sort of work-life balance. The 'life' itself consisted of three parts, of which two, family and music, have no place in this book. It is the cricket that I must write about. In those years as an academic in Delhi I often visited the Feroz Shah Kotla. Once I spent five whole days there watching Delhi play Tamil Nadu in a Ranji final. Ajay Sharma (later implicated in a match-fixing scandal) scored a chanceless double-hundred, in which his cover driving was especially fine. The cricket was good, and the chatter even better, for the veterans in the press box had seen Amarnath and Mankad and Sobers and Harvey play on that ground.

In 1989, the Indian Cricket Board organised the Nehru Cup, to commemorate the centenary of the country's first Prime Minister. I saw India play West Indies at the Kotla in an early round of the tournament. It was a low-scoring match. The visitors batted first, and I particularly remember a cameo innings by the fast bowler Malcolm Marshall. In sweeping the off-spinner Arshad Ayub for four, he lost his balance; getting up, he saw his partner Gus Logie approaching him. His left knee was still on the ground, his right leg was extended in a sort of yogic pose. From where he was, Marshall raised his left glove to meet Logie's right glove, in the gesture of triumph and solidarity invented in the Caribbean but now adopted by cricketers of all nationalities.

When India batted, the damage was done not by Marshall or Courtney Walsh but by, of all people, Viv Richards. Back in 1974, I had seen Richards score his first Test hundred at the Kotla; now, fifteen years later, I saw him, with his off-breaks, achieve his best bowling figures in international cricket. He got six wickets, and celebrated each one, none as energetically as that of Kiran More. More was trapped on the back foot by a faster ball that kept low; when he was given out leg before, the bowler showed him the way to the pavilion by pumping his right hand up and down, in a gesture of almost inexpressible vulgarity. Watching with horror and fascination, I concluded that while Richards may have disliked some bowlers, he had, for some reason that perhaps only More and he knew, developed a particularly intense hatred for this Indian wicketkeeper.*

---

* After I wrote these words I read Sanjay Manjrekar's book *Imperfect*, which explained to me the roots of Richards' venomous dislike of More. Earlier in 1989, when the two sides met in the West Indies, the wicketkeeper had successfully appealed for a caught behind when Richards had not nicked it. The match was played in the batsman's native Antigua; and he had been out of form. Now, en route to recovering his touch, a conniving keeper had cheated him of his hundred. In Delhi before my eyes, Richards extracted revenge, getting More out fairly, and telling him about it too.

A last, so to say, West Indian memory may not be out of place here. In October 1990 our son Keshava was born. That night, with my wife still in hospital, I returned home. I took out *Beyond a Boundary* from the bookshelf, and turned to the chapter on the tragically unfulfilled promise of the Trinidadian batsman Wilton St. Hill, who C L R James had venerated. Why I did what I did, I'll leave it to the Freudians or Jungians to answer. I can only relate the facts; when my first child was born, and I had to make sense of fatherhood, I sought to do so by a reading of my favourite book on cricket.

In my years as an academic in Delhi, the Feroz Shah Kotla hosted only one Test match. This was played in March 1993. In twenty years of watching Test cricket, I had never seen India win. Here was my chance, for we were playing the minnows, Zimbabwe. After the home team won the toss and a Vinod Kambli double-hundred took them to a score of 500 plus, it was clear my jinx would be broken. It was, but only after some brave resistance from the Flower brothers, Grant and Andy. Zimbabwe were shot out in a session-and-a-half, and, following-on, needed to bat two days to save the match. After Kevin Arnott and the elegant Alistair Campbell fell early the Flowers came together in an assured partnership. They were a study in contrast: the right-handed Grant playing through the line, determined to bat all the way through; the left-handed Andy more adventurously working the spinners behind square on either side of the wicket. The brothers batted a long time together, for almost four hours. Azharuddin shuffled his three spinners, tried Kapil Dev and Manoj Prabhakar, even Sachin Tendulkar's little wobblies for an over or two. It was a terrific display of concentration on the part of two batsmen whose instincts would tell them to attack anyway. In the end the natural tendency asserted itself. Maninder threw one teasingly up, and Andy Flower wandered hopefully down the wicket. He missed it, and was stumped. Now Anil Kumble returned to get rid of the inferior talents. It was also Kumble who finally dismissed Grant Flower, lbw for 97 after five hours of patiently heroic batsmanship.

Four months before this Test, on 6 December 1992, a medieval mosque in the northern town of Ayodhya was demolished by a mob that claimed it was built on the site of the birthplace of the mythical Hindu God-King, Ram. The demolition was followed by bloody riots across northern and western India, in which thousands of people died. Muslims were the main victims. The vandalism and the violence sent me, brought up as I was on a plural and inclusive idea of India, into a deep depression. I took to my bed, emerging only when, on 10 January 1993, my daughter Ira was born. Even then I could not concentrate on scholarly work. I had research papers to write, but they would not get written. The block was finally overcome by writing about cricket, about the great Indian cricketers of the 1970s in particular. In a furious few weeks in February, I put on paper my memories of watching Gavaskar and Viswanath bat; Bedi, Prasanna and Chandrasekhar bowl; and Syed Kirmani keep wicket. I added a chapter on Kapil Dev, and had the elements of my second book on the game, *Spin and Other Turns.**

Writing on cricket was therapy, and so was watching it. The five days of the India–Zimbabwe Test of March 1993, which I watched in the company of the writer Suresh Menon, completed the healing of my patriotic soul. I could now resume the work-life balance so rudely disturbed by the murderous mobs in Ayodhya.

---

* This book got me my first mention in the *Wisden Cricketers' Almanack*, with Alan Ross briefly mentioning it in his round-up of the year's cricket literature. Ross, a quintessential British liberal, wrote that 'Guha ranges widely over other matters than Indian cricket and his writing has a warmth and perception admirable in one whose early studies and adherences were of Marxism.' Twenty years previously, before I had ever read of Marx and Marxism, I had written a letter to the editor of the *Almanack*; now, having had my phase (and fill) of Marx and Marxism, this notice in the game's Bible confirmed that my return to cricket was complete.

III

I moved back to Bangalore from Delhi in 1995. A year later Durai moved back too, from Madras, and took control of the FUCC once more. I occasionally dropped in at the nets – strictly to watch – and at the matches as well.

Durai had retired early from his job in part because of Friends Union; and in part because he wished to look after his widowed mother. He built an apartment above hers, in Jayamahal Extension. One day in 1996 or 1997 I went to see my grandmother, and after chatting with her for a bit I asked where my sixty-year-old uncle was. 'He is lying down in his room,' she said. 'His team lost a match today. I think he may be crying, just as he did in Dehradun when he was sixteen.'

In the 1960s and 1970s, when Durai himself was a player, my club had never won the first division championship. That day in the 1990s they had just lost a close match, ending their chances for the season. Hence the despair and the disappointment. Fortunately, things began to look up. In the following decade, FUCC won the championship on three separate occasions. They also won the state's premier knockout tournament four times, as well as some T20 tournaments.

If not the best cricket club in Bangalore, FUCC has always been certainly the best run. Every member has always paid his fees on time. The club have never cheated or fixed a match, something many other cricket teams in the city and country are known to have done.

Through his sixties and seventies, and into his eighties too, Durai was at the FUCC nets for several hours a day. And he was present at all matches, even those played twenty or thirty miles outside the city. The club ran three teams; in the first, third and fifth divisions respectively. Durai took youngsters in hand, improved their batting or bowling or both (and always their fielding too), saw them play their first matches in Division Five, and, if they were good and committed enough, had them graduate to Division Three or even Division One. Hundreds of Indians were made better sportsmen and better human beings under his direction.

Under Durai's mentorship, FUCC also produced a fresh crop of Ranji players. The best of these was the all-rounder Balchandra Akhil, who played some forty matches for the state. As I write this, Akhil is forty-two himself, and still playing for the club. He was – is – a forceful striker of the cricket ball, a handy medium-pace bowler, and a magnificent fieldsman anywhere. Tall and lissom, he looks every part an athlete, and he has a ready smile too.

Other members of my club who have played for Karnataka in recent years include the off-spinner H Surendra, the batsmen Shyam Ponappa and A R Mahesh, and the all-rounder Sunil Raju, son of Narayan. Then there is Kunal Kapoor, an orthodox middle-order batsman who in 2012 scored a hundred in each innings in a Ranji Trophy match against Haryana. He was the first Karnataka batsman to achieve the feat. To put it another way, an FUCC player did what even G R Viswanath and Rahul Dravid could not.

If my uncle had one disppointment, it was not having produced a Test player, either as FUCC's captain or its coach. Sudhakar Rao came closest, when he was picked to tour West Indies and New Zealand in the winter of 1975–6. Sudha did not represent India in a Test, though he did play a one-day international. Also an FUCC 'international' is C K Nandan, who has umpired several one-day and T20 matches between countries. Nandan excelled in club cricket as a wicketkeeper batsman. However, since his playing career overlapped with Syed Kirmani to begin with and with Sadanand Viswanath later on, he played just two Ranji matches for Karnataka. Durai urged him to move to another state, which he refused to do.

Now, as a senior umpire on the domestic circuit, he moves between states all the time.

IV

Durai played and watched cricket, and he trained and guided cricketers. He was a teacher and practitioner, not a theorist or raconteur. A new friend in Bangalore was. His name was T G Vaidyanathan, and he taught English at Bangalore University. Although better known as a film critic (Satyajit Ray once said TGV was the only Indian writer on the subject he had time for), he also had a serious interest in sport. In his youth (he was some thirty years older than myself) he had played first-division cricket in Madras. He had read widely about the game, and wrote often about it, publishing essays on players past and present in the city newspaper, *Deccan Herald*, and in the *Illustrated Weekly of India*.

I lived in a large, free-standing house in the heart of the city; TGV in a tiny, one-bedroom flat in the suburb of Rajaji Nagar. In the late 1990s, I would go see him every other Sunday, by moped to begin with, by car as my professional fortunes rose. We spoke of subjects other than cricket, of course, but even here the idioms came from our favourite sport. Thus, commenting on a promising sociologist who had since lost his way, TGV compared him to Sachin Tendulkar's gifted and tragically self-destructive contemporary Vinod Kambli. As he put it, 'Ipdi adchaan, apdi adchaan, aproan out.' *A fine stroke here and a fine stroke there, then a slash to a wide ball resulting in a tame catch to the wicketkeeper.*

TGV and I would discuss matches as they came to us on the box, but also cricketers of an older era: especially his heroes Lala Amarnath, Vinoo Mankad, Mushtaq Ali, and Vijay Hazare. He spoke with warmth of foreign cricketers he had seen: of Clyde Walcott's straight drive, and of the leg-breaks and antics of the

Australian Serviceman Cecil Pepper. Sometimes he would pass on recollections of his own time in the field. He had kept wicket for his college and his club, though (like the rest of us) he remembered best his turns with the bat. He once told me of how, as a sixteen-year-old schoolboy, he had faced C R ('Kurmi') Rangachari, a fearsome fast bowler who, in his time as an Indian Test player, had clean bowled George Headley and troubled Don Bradman. Rangachari's first ball reared up off a length and hit the boy on the chest. TGV said the pain went round and round; he felt as if there were bees buzzing inside him. 'And the bugger did not even say sorry. I managed to keep out the other five balls, but the shock had unnerved me. The next over I tried to hit a slow left-armer for six and was stumped.'

By this time TGV was too old to come with me to the Chinnaswamy Stadium. But he did once drag me to a cricket match, played with tennis balls in the dry bed of a temple tank behind his house. The instruments were modest, and the boys only of the locality, but their ambition was anything but small-scale. This was the final of the Cheetah Cup, no less, played under floodlights and with prize money collected from the Rajaji Nagar shopkeepers. There was also running commentary on the match, in confirmation of my friend's thesis that real cricket has first to be heard, not seen. To his delight the boys had taken the names of big-time players: Imran Khan's XI was playing Tony Greig's XI. He was further tickled when the commentary switched from Kannada to English, to the language of metropolitan power whose use helped dignify this otherwise humdrum match.

In 1997, the Indian cricket team toured Sri Lanka. In one of the Tests, Sanath Jayasuriya, blazing away as was his wont, was 290 not out at close of play on the fourth day. The next morning my television went on the blink shortly after Jayasuriya had crossed 300, as only a dozen batsmen had done before him. I asked TGV to keep me up-to-date. He would phone at the end of each over, speaking in that bastard-tongue, cricket-Tamil. 'Cowper *poche*,' was the first message, Bob Cowper's score of 307 has been surpassed. Then, as Jayasuriya moved to 312, 'Simpson Edrich *rendon poche*.' An English and an Australian opening batsman had also slipped down one of the most select of sporting lists. The next two calls were routine, followed, however, by 'Sandham *poche*'. Ten minutes later it was 'Gooch *poche*', and then, after Jayasuriya went from 334 to 338 in one stroke, 'Bradman, Hammond, Hanif *moonon poch*.' A young Sri Lankan had shoved aside three of the greatest batsmen in cricket history, the wonder carried in the voice of an Indian just this side of seventy. TGV was greatly distressed when Jayasuriya got out for 340; he would not be consoled even when I told him that by getting out when he did, he and Mahanama had fallen one run short of the all-time record for a batting partnership, which was held in part by TGV's own boyhood hero, Vijay Hazare.

V

In Bangalore, I resumed following the cricketing fortunes of my club, and naturally of my state as well. Sujata and I lived, as before, at one end of M G Road. At the other end, less than a mile away, was the Chinnaswamy Stadium.

The first Ranji match I remember watching after my return was against Kerala. It was played in January 1996 at the RSI ground, since the Chinnaswamy Stadium was undergoing reno-vation. In past seasons, Karnataka had defeated Kerala easily, often by an innings. This time was different, in part because our best players were away on Test duty. On the last day, the home side needed about 250 to win. They lost early wickets and went to lunch at 90 for four.

I heard the news and walked across M G Road to the RSI. Soon after me arrived a bunch of old Karnataka cricketers. Word had reached them that their team was in trouble. A V Jayaprakash came, followed by Sudhakar Rao, Roger Binny, and, finally, Syed Kirmani. They huddled anxiously in the home tent, contemplating the unthinkable: that Kerala, the lowliest of Ranji teams, would defeat a three-time champion.

Out in the middle a terrific battle was on. The chief protagonists were the bespectacled off-spinner B Ramprakash and the left-handed all-rounder K Jeshwant. Ramprakash had got rid of the top order. But 'Jeshu' stood in the way. He would place a large leg down the pitch and hit away against the spin over mid-on and mid-wicket. At the other end, the team's best batsman, Vjiay Bharadwaj, played in more orthodox fashion. When Bharadwaj fell, to the seam bowler Sunil Oasis, Karnataka were 111 for five. Jeshu was now joined by his fellow left-handed all-rounder, Sunil Joshi. They added eighty, but then Ramprakash got Jeshwant out, and following him, the wicketkeeper A Vaidya as well. There were still twenty-odd runs remaining. Joshi, aided by Dodda Ganesh, took Karnataka over the line with three wickets to spare.

B Ramprakash had bowled unchanged since the morning, taking five for 102 in 49 overs. At the end, as the other players went off, he stood in a daze on the pitch, mutely acknowledging the 'well bowled's from the fans who had strolled onto the middle. His time would come. The next year the two sides met on a sandy track in Palakkad. Ramprakash took 14 wickets in the match, and the unthinkable happened: Kerala defeated Karnataka.

In 1995–6 Karnataka won the Ranji Trophy, defeating Tamil Nadu in the final. The match was played in Madras. Two years later my team entered the final again. Their opponents were Uttar Pradesh, and I would get to see the match, since it was to be played in the now refurbished Chinnaswamy Stadium. I took along my son Keshava, who was then seven. Durai had got us two nice tickets in the pavilion, sitting over mid-off.

For this Ranji final the home team were not at full strength. India were playing a one-day tournament in Dubai, and two of Karnataka's best bowlers, Anil Kumble and Venkatesh Prasad, were on duty there. A third, Javagal Srinath, had opted out because of exhaustion, and was presumably resting at home. When Keshava and I arrived at the Chinnaswamy Stadium to see the players warm up before start of play, Srinath was nowhere to be seen. However, when Karnataka lost the toss and had to field, it was Srinath who took the new ball. He claimed a wicket in each of his first two overs, with UP reeling at 2 for two. The rot was stemmed somewhat by the seventeen-year-old Mohammad Kaif, who batted impressively, getting solidly behind the line, and without a helmet too. Wickets fell steadily at the other end, with the left-arm spinner Sunil Joshi claiming four of them. UP finished on 134 all out, and Karnataka were 34 for no loss at the close.

The next day Keshava had to go to school. I worked at home, following the progress of the Karnataka innings on the radio. Rahul Dravid (then deemed too orthodox to be a regular member of the Indian one-day team) batted all of that day and much of the next. He scored a double-century, and we ended with 600 plus. UP did better in their second innings, with Kaif one of five batsmen to score fifties, but still lost by a wide margin. Srinath had not been seen on the field since the first hour of play, after taking the two early wickets that had more or less sealed the match. The papers reported that the BCCI was cross with Srinath for doing what he did. I wonder what explanation the KSCA offered them. But as a notorious partisan of Karnataka cricket, I was happy to see him place a Ranji Trophy final at home above a *tamasha* one-day international in the Gulf.

VI

Being in Bangalore in the 1990s meant living through and partaking in Karnataka cricket's second glorious phase. My book *Wickets in the East*, published in 1992, had offered this All-Time Karnataka XI:

1. B K Kunderan
2. B Frank
3. G R Viswanath
4. V Subrahmanyam
5. B P Patel
6. P E Palia
7. R M H Binny
8. S M H Kirmani (wicketkeeper)
9. V M Muddiah
10. E A S Prasanna (captain)
11. B S Chandrasekhar
12th man: Sudhakar Rao

By the end of the decade, this XI had to undergo some substantial modifications. Rahul Dravid and Anil Kumble would now be in any all-time India (let alone Karnataka) XI; and Javagal Srinath would surely be in the frame for such a team too, jostling with Zaheer Khan for the privilege of sharing the new ball with Kapil Dev.

Rahul, Sri, and Anil were the three true greats of Karnataka cricket's second glorious phase. But my team had some other superb cricketers too. There was Venkatesh Prasad, who I first heard of when he hit my clubmate C K Nandan on the head in a First Division match, sending our opener to have his head stitched up at the HAL hospital. There was Sunil Joshi, who I first saw hitting three sixes in successive deliveries off my clubmate B T Satish, the last of these striking the top tier of the pavilion. Venky had a lovely smooth action and moved the ball late both ways; when he first played for India, at Sharjah, his bowling deeply impressed Imran Khan, then merely a retired cricketer-turned-television-commentator, not a Pakistan prime minister in the making. Jo was the most classical slow left-armer since Bishan Bedi, and fielded and batted ably as well.

One of the oddities of this second Golden Age was how many new-ball bowlers my state produced. In 1991 or thereabouts, my college team-mate Amrit Mathur, then running the Railway Sports Control Board, invited me to watch a match of the Wills Trophy, being played at the Karnail Stadium. (A major domestic championship named for a brand of cigarettes – inconceivable nowadays, though IPL teams have been named after whisky brands owned by fugitives.) For one or other XI, Board President or Board Secretary or perhaps Wills itself, the new ball was being shared by two promising lads from, to my surprise, Karnataka.

These were Srinath and Venkatesh Prasad. Later that year Sri went to Australia with the Indian team, and Venky got his own international call-up soon afterwards. They were followed in time by four other Kannadigas who opened the bowling for state as well as for country – Dodda Ganesh, David Johnson, Abhimanyu Mithun and R Vinay Kumar.

Despite my veneration for Prasanna and Chandrasekhar, I welcomed this development. I could not, *pace* Francis Thompson, get myself to sing, 'Oh my V S Vijaykumar and my A V Jayaprakash long ago!' Karnataka were winning Ranji championships again, as much through pace as through spin. Why was this so? This may have been because First Division matches were now played on turf, not matting, or because young cricketers were now better paid and had more nourishing diets, and went to the gym, or because when growing up the bowler they saw winning matches for India on the TV was a certain Kapil Dev.

I met and shook hands with Prasanna, Chandrasekhar, and G R Viswanath. Syed Kirmani lived in the same locality as my grandparents, and came home occasionally. These were the heroes of my youth. I had to *look up to them*. The second generation of Karnataka greats were much younger than myself. I had meanwhile written some cricket books of my own, and some books on other subjects too. Cricketing-wise, I admired Anil and Rahul and Sri as much as Pras and Chandra and Vishy. At the personal level, however, I could do something that would have been inconceivable with their predecessors – I could befriend them.

Of this great trio, Javagal Srinath retired first, in 2003. I have met him on about half-a-dozen occasions since. Our longest conversation took place when chance – or fate – placed us on adjoining seats on a flight from Bangalore to Dubai, where he had an International Cricket Council meeting, and I had to catch a connecting flight to a conference in New York. As historians do, I went back to the origins. How did an engineering student from Mysore, I asked, break into a state team dominated so massively by boys from Bangalore? He ascribed it to luck. It so happened, he said, that he had been picked for the Mysore Zone in the 'Pentangular' tournament that helped select the state team. Normally, no Karnataka selector came down to watch such matches. But this time was different – the great G R Viswanath decided to drive down to Mysore to take a look. That day Srinath got six wickets in a single spell, prompting GRV to pitchfork him into bigger things. 'You won't believe me,' said Sri, 'but there were better cricketers than me in Mysore and they just weren't so lucky – when they got centuries or wickets no one was watching.'

Srinath was a rice-eating Kannadiga and (at least when he started out) a vegetarian, but he bowled a lively fast-medium, and brought the ball back wickedly in the air and off the wicket. He had the Indian sign on some high-quality international batsmen; Allan Border and Arjuna Ranatunga were never comfortable playing him, and nor was Michael Atherton. Srinath was a world-class cricketer, who continued to contribute to the game after he retired. He has been a much-admired ICC match referee, and an excellent secretary of the KSCA, where he focused on developing the game in the districts. He has a deep passion, based on both knowledge and experience, for widening the base of cricketing talent. 'If we can have well-run KSCA academies in the districts,' he once told me, 'Karnataka can produce several Tendulkars each year.'

Srinath's closest friend in cricket is his fellow engineer, fellow bowler, and fellow Kannada-speaker, Anil Kumble. Back in 1998, I had written a column in *The Hindu* arguing that when Mohammed Azharuddin retired, Kumble should replace him as captain of the Indian team. He had the intelligence, the character, and the cricketing experience to take over. But it was unlikely that Kumble would succeed Azhar, for there had long been, in India and elsewhere, a prejudice against bowler-captains. Citing the examples of Richie Benaud, Imran Khan and Ray Illingworth, I had said that thinking bowlers could make excellent captains, so long as they were not the main or only strike bowler in the team (which Kapil Dev and Ian Botham, the standard counter-examples, had been). This is how my column ended: 'So long as Srinath is around and bowling well, so long as one does not look to Anil Kumble to get the other side out on his own, the claims of the Karnataka wrist-spinner must be given just consideration when the time comes. Let not these claims be summarily set aside by the dogma that bowlers do not or cannot make effective captains.'

At this stage I had not met Anil Kumble, but had of course watched him bowl many times. I admired his wicket-taking ability while being intrigued by his unorthodox methods, as others were too. In 1995, I was at the immigration counter at Heathrow airport, when an officer, seeing I was Indian, said: 'We have one of your chaps over playing county cricket. He hardly turns the ball [making a suitable gesture with his hand] but takes so many wickets.' In fact, in that season with Northamptonshire, Kumble took more than a hundred wickets in the County Championship, the last cricketer, native or foreign-born, to do so.

Unlike the immigration officer, Anil Kumble knew that to catch or beat the edge one had to turn the ball two inches, not two feet. His variations were subtle, not obvious, made through changes of pace, line, and spin. Kumble's stock ball, the googly, was used alongside one that went straight through and another that turned from leg. With his high action, and brisk pace, Kumble was devastating on a crumbling wicket. He was India's best Test as well as one-day bowler, happy to bowl at the beginning, the middle, and the end of an innings, supremely capable of containing runs and taking wickets at the same time. What Kumble could do with the ball was enhanced by his fine cricketing mind, and the biggest heart in all of cricket.

Alas, when Azharuddin needed to be replaced as India captain it was not by Kumble, but by a batsman, Sachin Tendulkar. Shortly afterwards I met my famous fellow townsman for the first time. India was playing a Test at the Chinnaswamy Stadium, and the day before the match began, the television anchor Rajdeep Sardesai had us both on for a show. It thus fell to a Bombay man to introduce the greatest cricketer ever produced by Karnataka to the state's most devoted and dogmatic cricket fan.

Following Tendulkar, Sourav Ganguly and Rahul Dravid, both also batsmen, were appointed captains of the Indian cricket team. After a successful tour of England in 2007, Dravid surprisingly resigned, whereupon Kumble was nominated in his place. Our next series was in Australia, where the cricketers, the conditions, and the crowds place far heavier burdens on visiting teams than anywhere else. India had never won a series there before.

In that series of 2007–8, India were set to play four Tests Down Under. They were badly beaten in the first Test in Melbourne, but acquitted themselves more creditably in the second, played in Sydney. At one stage the Indian bowlers had the Australians on the ropes, but then the umpire failed to hear an edge, the error allowing the batsman (Andrew Symonds) to go on to make a century.

Anyway, once Symonds had made his ton, India were left to bat the whole of the last day to save the match. This they might still have done, had it not been for more disgraceful umpiring. Dravid was wrongly given out caught at the wicket, and Ganguly was sent packing on the word of an Australian fielder who had scooped the ball up on the half-volley. As those wickets fell – legitimately or illegitimately – Anil Kumble battled for three hours in an unavailing bid to save the match.

After the last wicket was claimed, the Australians celebrated as if a World War had been won. (Their behaviour then, and afterwards, compelled the normally restrained Peter Roebuck to dub them a 'pack of wild dogs'.) Although I shouldn't really have added to Kumble's burdens at this time, I felt compelled to write to him, and I did:

Dear Anil,
I wanted to write immediately the Test ended, to congratulate you on your brave defiance of the Australian bowling. If some of our regular batsmen had shown an iota of your commitment and courage, we would have drawn the Test, regardless of the umpiring. I am glad I did not write rightaway, however, for in the days after the Test you have behaved impeccably. The dignity with which you have comported yourself, and the restrained tone of your remarks, have been in sharp and shining contrast to the public and on-field displays of the other cricketers in this saga. You have brought credit to yourself, to the game of cricket, and to India.

With regards
Ram

A day or two later came this reply:

Dear Ram,
Thanks for your wishes and continued support. I am
confident that our team will be able to put up a better
performance in the remainder [of the] matches and it will be
really nice to read a 2–2 scoreline at the end of this series.

Regards
Anil

Kumble's reply renewed my admiration for his courage, but
opened doubts about his judgement. For the next Test was to be
played at Perth, on a fast, bouncy surface where visiting batsmen
were notoriously vulnerable and the home team's bowlers were,
well, like a pack of wild dogs picking on a defenceless goat.
Australia had not lost a Test at Perth for eighteen years. How did
the Indian captain think *he* could reverse this? Even those with a
hundred Test matches under their belt – such as the members of
Channel 9's commentary team – were as convinced as I that
Perth would see the Australians go three-up in the series. But
somehow, the Indian captain communicated some of his extraordinary self-belief to the members of his team. By batting and
bowling out of their skins, Kumble's men defeated the Australians
by the margin of 72 runs.

Given the horrors of Sydney, and how the Perth pitch has
always behaved, this victory probably counts as the greatest ever
by an Indian cricket team. It is hard to see how it could have
happened had Kumble not been in charge. Only he had the
necessary force of character to lift his men out of the trough, and
make them play in the manner that they did.

A defining moment of that Perth Test was the sight of Sourav
Ganguly fielding at short-leg. That particular position had long
been reserved – in Indian teams at any rate – for the youngest

member of the team. In Sunil Gavaskar's day, or before that in Vinoo Mankad's day, no former captain would be asked to field at short-leg. Even if asked, he would refuse. That a long-time captain and Test veteran would now occupy that position was testimony to the extraordinary regard in which Kumble was held. Four former Indian captains were here playing under him (the others were Tendulkar, Dravid, and Dhoni), and yet giving it their all – only because they so massively and unreservedly respected the man in charge.

Anil Kumble's great contemporary, Shane Warne, did not captain Australia, despite having a fine cricketing brain and the respect of his peers. However, there is another distinction that Kumble carries which his fellow wrist-spinner may envy even more – that of having scored a Test century. Warne won many Test matches for Australia with the ball, and even saved some with the bat. He was not quite a proper batsman, but not a tail-ender either. His style was unorthodox – his favourite shots the slash over slips and the hoick over mid-wicket – but he had a good eye and plenty of guts. Warne scored twelve half-centuries in Test cricket; twice he was dismissed for 86, once he got to 90, and once, God forbid, even to 99 (when, if memory serves, he was caught on the boundary going for a big hit).

If asked to choose between Warne and Kumble as bowlers, one would have to first ask the questioner to specify: against which batsmen, in which country, and on what sort of wicket? To bowl against quick-footed Indians like Sachin Tendulkar, one would choose Kumble over Warne, any time; against leaden-footed South Africans like Daryll Cullinan, Warne over Kumble, every time. On a wearing subcontinental pitch with uneven bounce, one would expect Kumble to run through the opposition quicker than Warne. However, on a first-day wicket in Melbourne or Manchester, Warne would always be our man ahead of Kumble; with his alluring flight and subtle variations, he would in those conditions be far more likely to induce a mistake.

However, if asked to choose between Warne and Kumble as batsmen, one would go with Warne, every time. At Test level, Kumble's defensive technique was suspect, while his main scoring shot was an ugly shovel to leg. Warne, on the other hand, got solidly in line against the fastest bowlers; and he had a fine array of attacking shots. Anyway, in a Test in England during the summer of 2007, Anil Kumble came in late in the order and, with his side comfortably in control, started throwing his bat around with abandon. He soon got to 40, then 60, then 70. At this stage, Ian Chappell, sitting in the commentary box, sent a text message to Shane Warne telling him the news. A panic reply came back: 'Tell Chris [Tremlett, the fast bowler who was Warne's team-mate at Hampshire] to bounce him. He can't take short-pitched stuff.' Either the message was not passed on, or Tremlett was too tired to do as told. When Kumble reached his century, Chappell sent Warne a consolatory SMS. It was not answered.

As with Anil Kumble, I wrote in praise of Rahul Dravid long before I met him. After his impressive debut at Lord's in 1996, Dravid was a fixture in the Test side, but seen as too orthodox and unadventurous to be included in the one-day team. A clever copywriter had named him 'The Wall', an appellation to be upheld if India were playing Tests but to be deplored for the 50-overs game. In August 1998, with a long series of one-day games about to commence, a large hoarding featuring Dravid came down at one of Bangalore's busiest intersections, the corner of Brigade Road and Residency Road. When it became clear that the Karnataka batsman was not part of India's one-day plans, the ad men chose to market somebody or something else. I protested as follows in the pages of *The Hindu*:

Even if Dravid never again lends his face to a product, I would like to raise two cheers for his batsmanship. For the skilled practitioner of tuk-tuk can do more than draw Test matches. He can help win them too. Don Bradman's

Australian team of the Thirties and Forties always had one artful blocker [first Ponsford, then Sid Brown]. In the greatest of modern Test sides, the West Indies as they were between 1977 and 1985, the thunder was stolen by the dashers and bashers, by Greenidge, Richards, Fredericks, Kallicharan and Lloyd, yet they could bat freely only because the now forgotten Larry Gomes kept one end going for long periods.

Why go back so far in time? Think only of February and March of this year [1998], and India's surprising victory over the self-appointed world champions. The batting headlines in that series against Australia were claimed by Sidhu, Azharuddin and, above all, Tendulkar. But their sparkle and fizz was only, so to say, more flower on the Wall. These strokemakers took Dravid's calm solidity for granted. But after Mark Taylor's men went home, the silly season began. The Indian team moved from Sri Lanka to Sharjah, and will soon go on to Canada. There is talk now of squeezing Dravid into the fourteen for [yet another one-day series in] Toronto. Yet it is only when Test cricket resumes later in the year that Dravid will resume his proper place in the playing eleven. The public will learn afresh to spell his name. And, who knows, while coming down Brigade Road at night, my headlights might shine once more on his face.

This was written as a double partisan, of Karnataka and of Test cricket. Yet in so lavishly praising Dravid's batsmanship, I had fallen into stereotyping him. Without ever abandoning the orthodox bedrock on which his game rested, Dravid learned to hit harder and higher. He muscled his way into the one-day squad, showing the selectors (and the ad men) that he could, when the occasion demanded, play across the line and hit sixes too. Besides, he could fill in as a wicketkeeper if the balance of the team so required. As a boy, Dravid had kept wicket for his school team, while his club, BUCC, was also the club of India's greatest ever stumper, Syed Kirmani. Now, he brought out his gloves and his memories, and became an adequate keeper. In the event he was to play more than 300 one-day matches for India, scoring twelve hundreds and as many as eighty-three fifties in them.

If memory serves, I first shook hands with Dravid at a function on the eve of the 2005 Bangalore Test between India and Pakistan. Srinath, who had by now retired, made the main speech, urging the man he called 'a living legend' to give his hometown crowd a century the next day. In the event, Dravid did not oblige – his record at the Chinnaswamy Stadium was as modest as Sachin Tendulkar's at Lord's – but, since he scored plenty of hundreds elsewhere, he has remained our boy always.

For some odd reason, most of my meetings with Dravid have been at airports. Once, when he was captain of Karnataka as well as of India, I berated him (politely) in front of some airline stewards for the state selectors' neglect of a first-rate all-rounder from (where else) the Friends Union Cricket Club. Another time, we met at the check-in counter on a day when a writer we knew had been awarded the Padma Bhushan. Dravid thought it interesting that the recipient had not been awarded a Padma Shri before (something no other Indian cricketer might have noticed).*

That day, we were on the same flight, but while I was in business class, Dravid was in economy – a temporary reversal of fortune, explained by the fact that I was going to address a bunch of company executives, whereas Dravid was travelling with the Karnataka Ranji team. I felt guilty, and as soon as the safety belt sign had been switched off went looking for my lads. I saw the

---

* A Padma Bhushan would be roughly equivalent to a knighthood in the British system; a Padma Shri roughly equivalent to an OBE. In India, it is common for citizens to get one state award, then another slightly higher, and then sometimes one slightly higher still.

fast bowler R Vinay Kumar jumping around in his seat, his ears plugged, listening to rock music. Next to him was the most intelligent cricketer ever to play for my state or my country, deep into the pages of Nandan Nilekani's recently published book, *Imagining India*.

Dravid had once even read a book of mine, about which I learned in the most curious way. In 2007, India were playing a one-day series in England. Dravid was captain, but not keeping wicket (M S Dhoni was). One would have expected him to stand at slip, but he had placed himself at mid-off, perhaps to advise the bowler and have a clearer picture of the field. After a match in which two or perhaps three catches had been put down in the slips, I wrote to the India captain from my home in Bangalore:

> Dear Rahul,
> You are quite possibly the finest Test batsman in Indian cricket history, and without question the finest slip fielder ever produced by India in ALL forms of the game. You must field there. I understand that with your somewhat erratic bowling you feel the need to be close at hand to guide them. But, all things considered, I think that slip is the place for you, and for the team. No one else in India is remotely as good as you, which is why all these catches go down in the early overs.
>
> With regards
> Ram

Two or three days later a reply came back. This did not refer to my request, but instead noted that he had bought a book I had just published on the history of independent India. 'You are right,' remarked the Indian cricket captain, that 'all our history seemed to stop with Gandhi and there's actually so much that's happened since for us to be where we are 60 years later. I finished

116

about 180 pages so a fair way to go. Would love to talk about it and much more.'

My email to Dravid was unsolicited, unprompted, and impertinent – akin in cricketing terms to a bouncer from a bowler of military-medium pace, it was dispatched to the boundary with a flick of the wrists. The put-down was decisive; and yet so delicately worded. I was told, in the kindest possible manner, to shut up about strategy in cricket and go back to writing history books. (I did.)

VII

One night, early in the second decade of the twenty-first century, I had an asthmatic attack. A heavy dose of pills slowed down the wheezing, and I stumbled into sleep. Next morning, drugged and dopey, I found some profound consolation in the newspaper, whose front page carried a photo of a tall, slim, handsome young man in conversation with a short, plump, middle-aged man of undistinguished appearance. The asymmetry, striking at first glance, was complicated, if not overthrown, by a closer scrutiny of the photograph. For the expression on the younger man's face combined respect with reverence, affection with adoration. In material terms, he was looking down – by a foot, at least. However, in emotional terms, he was looking up, and up, and up.

The two men were Rahul Dravid and G R Viswanath. Vishy was my boyhood hero – because he batted like a dream, because he was a gentle and good man, because he came from my home state of Karnataka, because he was the first Test cricketer I ever shook hands with. I adored him as a fan; but here, apparently, was a man who had scored twice as many Test runs as Vishy who felt the same way about him.

What had brought the two cricketers together was the naming of an underpass after the little fellow, with the honours being done by the taller chap. Later that day – when the steroids had suppressed the asthma altogether – I wrote to Dravid. His reply confirmed in words what that look had conveyed in essence. 'I remember as a young kid,' he wrote, 'rushing [from school] to watch Vishy play in a Ranji game against Hyderabad [towards the end of his career] – there must have been easily 20,000 people at the ground that day. Sadly, those days are long gone.'

A year or two later, Rahul Dravid himself retired from international cricket. His former coach Greg Chappell wrote a fine tribute, which, among other things, recalled the 2006 tour to the West Indies, when, with the Australian as manager, India won its first series outside the subcontinent in twenty years. Chappell singled out the contributions of Dravid and Anil Kumble in particular. As he remarked: 'No team has had two more dogged, resilient and proud competitors; and, for them, the team always came first. There must be something in the water of Bangalore!'

There must be, indeed. Before Dravid there was G R Viswanath; and before Kumble there was B S Chandrasekhar. As a partisan – a notorious partisan – of Karnataka, I have been blessed in having watched and followed the first duo, and in having watched and followed the second. As a young boy, I knew Vishy to be the best Indian batsman who was not from Bombay, and Chandra to be the finest Indian wrist-spinner with the exception only of Subhash Gupte. These were men from my hometown who won Test matches for my country. But it was not for their playing skills alone that I warmed to them. For, as their team-mates and opponents would both have confirmed, G R Viswanath and B S Chandrasekhar were quite simply the *nicest* cricketers of their generation.

As with Vishy and Chandra, it is as much for their character as their cricketing abilities that cricket fans admired Dravid and Kumble. To be sure, our appreciation of character has changed with the times. The words that came to mind with regard to Vishy and Chandra were 'charming', 'decent', and, at a pinch, even 'laid-back'. With Dravid and Kumble, the adjectives one reached for rather were 'courageous' and 'committed', close synonyms of the words preferred by Greg Chappell himself.

These shades of difference reflected the changing sociology of the city. The Bangalore that Vishy and Chandra played for was that of the Mavalli Tiffin Rooms and the unencroached-upon Cubbon Park, a town of tiled bungalows and green barbets calling. M G Road then had more cinema houses than it had cars. The Bangalore that Dravid and Kumble played in was that of Epsilon and Infosys, of glass and concrete and no birds at all, of buses and motorbikes and SUVs all piled up in horrendous traffic jams.

When Vishy and Chandra first made their debuts, Karnataka was called Mysore; and it played its games at Central College, with trees ringing the ground and spectators in makeshift wooden stands. On the other hand, the venue Dravid and Kumble called 'home', the Chinnaswamy Stadium, was built for eternity. With a seating capacity of 60,000, it was floodlit, and ringed by armed security guards.

Playing mostly club and Ranji cricket, with a Test series every other year, Vishy indulged his fondness for beer, and Chandra allowed himself to make more zeroes than any other Test cricketer. On the other hand, playing all day, all year, the naturally unathletic Dravid willed himself to take more catches than any other Test player in history; a record that perhaps got less notice in the flurry of tributes that accompanied his retirement (which understandably focused on his many remarkable innings, at home and, especially, abroad). Despite always being the best bowler for his team, Kumble had also to learn to score runs; he made as many as seven first-class centuries, and once even scored a hundred in a Test match.

Vishy could behave on the cricket field as he did in an idli-and-dosai place in Chamarajpet – that is to say, with an easy, unselfconscious informality. However, in a harder, harsher world, Dravid had to develop skills that Vishy could do without. For, the fans were now more numerous, as well as more demanding. Their attentions were unceasing and at times unforgiving. For its part, the Indian Cricket Board, once run by egotistic and self-important amateurs, was now controlled by professional racketeers. To these demands were added those of the commercial sponsors who the successful modern cricketer had also to please.

These multiple pressures compelled Dravid to craft a public persona that radiated balance and self-control. He had to be decent and honourable; but he could never be spontaneous. There was a gaiety to Vishy's bearing; there is a gravity to Dravid's conduct. That is why we remember the one as 'the best-loved' cricketer of his day; the other as the 'most greatly admired' cricketer of his.

To be sure, Karnataka has produced fine cricketers before and between its two Golden Ages. And it has continued to produce fine cricketers since. As I write the state's openers are K L Rahul and Mayank Agarwal, both of whom have played with distinction for India. The middle order features Karun Nair, who did what even Vishy and Rahul Dravid could never do, score a triple-century in a Test match; as well as Manish Pandey, a superb finisher in one-day cricket and an outfielder in the Azharuddin class.

A quarter-of-a-century after offering my first All-Time Karnataka XI, I would like to offer my second. Placed alongside it is an All-Time Bombay XI:

All-Time Karnataka XI	*All-Time Bombay XI*
1. B K Kunderan	1. S M Gavaskar (captain)
2. Mayank Agarwal	2. V M Merchant
3. G R Viswanath	3. V L Manjrekar
4. Rahul Dravid	4. S R Tendulkar
5. B P Patel	5. D B Vengsarkar

6. R M H Binny

6. P R Umrigar

7. S M H Kirmani
   (wicketkeeper)

7. F M Engineer
   (wicketkeeper)

8. Anil Kumble (captain)

8. R B Desai

9. Javagal Srinath

9. Zaheer Khan

10. E A S Prasanna

10. S P Gupte

11. B S Chandrasekhar

11. P D Shivalkar

12th man: Sunil Joshi

12th man: E D Solkar

Our bowling is better, and even our fielding might have the edge. But we'd still have to win the toss, I think. When Dravid and Vishy have taken us to 350 or 400, Kumble, Sri, Pras and Chandra can set themselves up against those mighty Mumbaikars, with Rajdeep Sardesai and I arguing in the commentary box.

5

Handshakes with Heroes

I

In the 1980s and beyond, as I left cricket for scholarship, I acquired a new set of heroes. One of them was the sociologist André Béteille. He was half Bengali, half French (hence his name), but wholly Indian. When I worked at the Institute of Economic Growth in the late 1980s, he taught next door, at the Delhi School of Economics. On my way to or from the bus stop I would drop into his office to seek his counsel. In later years, I visited him at his apartment in the university campus, and, after he had retired, at his wife's home in the central Delhi locality of Jor Bagh.

André Béteille and I talked of history, politics, society, culture; Nehru, Gandhi, Marx, Weber. He had not the slightest interest in sport, and I was looking for other forms of instruction from him anyway. But one day, early in the first decade of the twenty-first century, when I walked into his ground-floor apartment in Jor Bagh, he smilingly told me that a childhood hero of mine would be phoning soon. I asked for details, but he wouldn't elaborate.

When André was a university teacher I would drop in at his office unannounced. Now I usually fixed to meet him beforehand. On this occasion, I arrived at 4.30, and at the stroke of five, my mentor's phone rang. These were pre-cellphone days, so he walked over to the hallway to answer it. 'Yes, he is here,' I heard him say. 'Please hold on.' André then came back to his study, and said, pointing the way to where the phone lay: 'That's the call I told you would come.'

I walked over, and picked up the instrument. I introduced myself. The caller did so too. He was Mansur Ali Khan Pataudi. He had heard that I was in Delhi, and wished to meet at my convenience. Would I be so kind as to specify a day when I could come over for tea to his home?

I was in Delhi for a three-week-long stint in the archives. The manuscripts section closed at 5 pm anyway, and of course to call on this hero of my youth I was free any time, any day. The following evening I presented myself at Pataudi's house, which (at the time) was the rear part of a Lutyens bungalow on Kamaraj Road, just south of South Block.

The reason Pataudi wanted to meet me was this: the British Broadcasting Corporation wished to interview him for a documentary on the social history of cricket in India. Unlike other Indian cricket captains past and present, he had some idea of the BBC's standing and seriousness of purpose (he had been educated at Winchester and at Oxford). He wanted to be adequately prepared; so he asked his fellow members of the Lutyens elite for the name of a scholar who could brief him. One person led him to another who led him to another who led him to India's greatest sociologist, who suggested my name. (My book *A Corner of a Foreign Field* had just been published.)

I reached Kamaraj Road at the appointed hour. A *darban* directed me to the back of the bungalow, where Pataudi and his wife (the actress Sharmila Tagore) lived. He opened the door himself. He was wearing a crisply creased, off-white, *churidar-kurta*. In the drawing room, an exquisite silver tea set had been laid out, along with some cut sandwiches.

We sat down, and began speaking. I took Pataudi through the main themes of my book: British homesickness, princely patronage, the politics of caste and religion on the cricket field, the growth of cricket since independence and how it became the nation's most popular sport. He listened attentively, asking for an explanation or elaboration from time to time.

Pataudi struck me as an extremely intelligent man. And his manners were immaculate. He addressed me throughout as 'Professor Guha' (although I did not actually hold or earn that title). He handed out the refreshments himself. I had asked for coffee instead of tea. That was a mistake, since this was not a South Indian or Italian home.

The error was trifling compared to what was to come. When our conversation ended, Pataudi escorted me to the gate personally. As we shook hands for the second and last time he said: 'It was a real pleasure meeting you, Professor Guha. I hope we meet again.' I responded by saying: 'Actually we have met before.' Asked, I provided the details. It was some three decades previously, back in December 1974, during the Delhi Test of that year, when I was in search of the complimentary ticket that Syed Kirmani had promised me. One morning, at the Maidens Hotel looking to nab Kiri before he caught the team bus to the Kotla, I arrived at the dining room. My fellow Bangalorean was not there, but two of his team-mates were. One was Pataudi. Now, to his bewilderment, I recounted the story. You were having breakfast with Syed Abid Ali, I said, and I asked where Kiri was, and you told me that he had gone up to his room. 'That was when we had first met,' I said, adding: 'And you were eating a fried egg, sunny side up.'

This was true. I can see that egg on the plate still. True, but spectacularly foolish as well. As I reached the last line of my excessively extended recollection, the look on my host's face turned from confusion to contempt. The visiting scholar and expert, Professor Guha, so highly recommended by the venerable Professor Béteille, had turned out to be a frothing, blabbering fan.

II

A year after meeting Pataudi for the first time, I saw him bat for the first (and last) time. Although he was captain of India for that home series of 1974–5, he missed the Delhi Test because of injury. After the series ended, he announced his retirement from Test cricket. But he would play one more year in the Ranji Trophy, to try and help Hyderabad win the title.

Pataudi's mother came from one of India's richest princely states, Bhopal; his father from the small principality of Pataudi, just outside Delhi. He started his own Ranji career with Delhi, but – like so many good and honest men before him – found the intrigues of the Delhi and District Cricket Association impossible to handle. His sister lived in the city of Hyderabad, in the Deccan; as did his two closest friends in cricket, M L Jaisimha and Abbas Ali Baig. So he shifted allegiance to Hyderabad instead.

In February 1976, I was in Bombay for an inter-college quiz competition. I had a spare day, which I spent at the Wankhede Stadium, watching Bombay play Hyderabad. The visitors were batting when I reached the ground. I saw Baig play some crisp square cuts before mistiming a pull. Pataudi came in, played and missed, played and missed again, before being caught behind off Shivalkar; and Jaisimha scratched around for a bit before being out for a low score as well. They had both been terrific stroke-players in their prime; like so many Indian men in so many different professions, they had stayed on too long at the top.*

---

* This was the first time I had seen Pataudi bat, but in fact the second time I had seen him on the sporting field. In 1967 or 1968, I was with my family in Bombay en route to our annual holiday in Bangalore. My obsession with cricket was well known and widely indulged, on this occasion by my father's elder brother S S Krishna, an engineer with Indian Airlines. My uncle asked someone who asked someone who took me to the Bombay Gymkhana, where Pataudi was that day playing a hockey match. He was the Gymkhana's centre-forward, and a vague memory of his running and waving his stick remains.

As for Jaisimha I never saw him again. But Baig and I met several times in the 1990s. He was living in Delhi, involved in business, in selling sprinkler irrigation sets from Israel as I recall. An uncle and cousin knew him, separately, and in their homes I met him at parties. Baig was a lovely man: gentle, soft-spoken, utterly civilised. I could never get him to talk of his own cricketing achievements: of his hundred on Test debut at Manchester (when he was called up from Oxford to join the touring team, after a campaign led by Keith Miller, who riffing on a famous whisky ad, told the Indian selectors, 'Don't be Vague, ask for Baig'); of the century in each innings he once hit as an undergraduate against a Yorkshire attack containing four Test bowlers, Freddie Trueman among them.

But Baig was willing to speak of cricketers he had played with. Once, at a large party where I had him to myself for about twenty minutes, I got him to talk about the art and craft of wicketkeeping. He thought that the most difficult aspect of this most difficult job in cricket was keeping wicket to wrist-spinners on a pitch of indifferent bounce. Keeping back to fast bowlers, one had time and space to take account of pace and swing; keeping up to finger-spin, one knew that the ball would stay within certain approximate limits. But, with a high-quality wrist-spinner the ball could turn left or right or go straight; the bounce and deviation made more unpredictable by the state of the wicket and the style of the bowler. Reading the hand of a great googly bowler was hard enough; reading him off the pitch, with the batsman often obscuring your vision, even harder.

Baig illustrated his theme with reference to the wrist-spinners and wicketkeepers he had played with. He told me of how Naren Tamhane expertly read and kept to Subhash Gupte; and how Syed Kirmani did likewise to B S Chandrasekhar. Tamhane and Kirmani were both brilliant anyway, but here they also had a special domain expertise, having played for the same state (and zone) with these bowlers before playing with them for the country. 'How I wish I could have seen Naren keep to Chandra,' said Abbas wistfully, 'or Kiri keep to Subhash.'

This conversation was conducted in the early 1990s. Shane Warne may have, just, made his Test debut, so Baig and I did not speak of him. Warne was a great bowler, greater than Gupte or Chandrasekhar. But unlike them he did not have much of a googly. That made his keeper's job slightly easier. I admired how Healy and Gilchrist kept to Warne; but how I wish I could have seen Kirmani keep to Gupte, or Tamhane to Chandrasekhar.

III

A close contemporary of Pataudi and Baig, and from a similarly privileged background, was Hanumant Singh, the second son of the Maharawal of Banswara. Like Baig, Hanumant scored a century on Test debut (against England in New Delhi in 1964) and never scored a hundred for India again. He had however, a long and successful first-class career, and for many years held the record for the most runs in the Ranji Trophy.

Hanumant had played against Durai in inter-college cricket. They were acquaintances, not friends; but the Test player liked my uncle enough to gift him a pair of cream flannels. When I joined St Stephen's Durai gifted them to me in turn. I wore ordinary whites for ordinary games; but for the knockout rounds of the inter-college championship I always wore that special pair of trousers.

I had other connections to Hanumant Singh. Three of my college team-mates were from Jaipur, and hence as besotted about Rajasthan cricket as I was about Karnataka. They had grown up watching Hanumant bat and lead their team. Meanwhile, our captain, Arun (Piggy) Lal, though not Rajasthani by origin, had studied at Mayo College in Ajmer, whose art master was the googly bowler C G (Chandu) Joshi. Piggy told us that Joshi had retired several times from first-class cricket, each time the act reversed by a telegram from Hanumant, asking him to come help Rajasthan in this, their latest, and probably last, chance, to win the Ranji Trophy.

The year I started college, a team other than Bombay at last became Ranji champions. My Karnataka defeated Rajasthan in the final that year, but the captain of the defeated team continued to play on. In 1976 or 1977, I saw Hanumant score a half-century against the Railways in that most desolate of cricket grounds, the Karnail Singh Stadium in Paharganj, hitting some handsome on-drives. Soon afterwards he retired.

Some twenty years later, I met Hanumant Singh in the flesh. He was in Bangalore, on a coaching assignment with the National Cricket Academy. The Chairman of the NCA was Raj Singh Dungarpur, who had played for many years for Rajasthan before becoming manager of the squad that won the 1983 World Cup and, some years later, President of the Board of Control for Cricket in India. One day Hanumant and Raj Singh came to our house for dinner, along with the former Bombay player, Vasu Paranjype, also on assignment with the NCA. Durai, whose idea it was and who had contacted these eminences, came along too.

Some good stories were told that day, mostly by Raj Singh. When Raj *bhai* heard that I was writing a social history of cricket whose heroes were the Dalit brothers Palwankar Baloo and Palwankar Vithal, he said his father (also in his time a princely patron of cricket) had told him that Vithal was as good a batsman as Vijay Hazare. I was delighted to hear this, since Baloo and Vithal had retired before Tests and Ranji Trophy cricket began, and were now totally forgotten. T G Vaidyanthan had insisted to me that Hazare was as good as Sunil Gavaskar, and I was now telling my son Keshava that Gavaskar was as good as Sachin Tendulkar. Hearing that Vithal was as good as Hazare, I could argue that he was, by the testimony of successive generations of credible witnesses, in fact as good as Tendulkar. By the same sort of transitive logic, I could now also say that as a left-arm spinner, Palwankar Baloo was the Vinoo Mankad or Bishan Bedi of his day.

I got Vasu Paranjype to speak a bit too, mostly about one of his early wards, a certain Sunil Manohar Gavaskar. Gavaskar had written somewhere that while supervising his defensive technique, Vasu told him that when Hanif Mohammad played forward at the Brabourne Stadium, the 'thook, thook' of ball hitting the middle of the bat could be heard at Churchgate Railway Station (half-a-mile away). Vasu would not confirm or deny the story, but he did say that when Sunil Gavaskar first toured Australia (as a member of the Rest of the World Team in 1971–2) he sent him a wire carrying these instructions: 'DO NOT COME HOME WITHOUT PAYING YOUR RESPECTS TO SIR DONALD BRADMAN.' (Gavaskar complied.)

My wife, after a hard day at her design studio, had supervised an excellent meal, and then retired upstairs to her bedroom, our five-year-old daughter accompanying her. Keshava stayed back to listen to the stories. Hanumant, who was silent for much of the evening, at length asked my son whether he played cricket, and, receiving the obvious answer, asked to see his bat. This was produced, whereupon the Test centurion and Ranji record-breaker proceeded to vigorously play a series of shadow strokes, including an on-drive as requested by the father of the bat's owner.

IV

The Stephanian cricketers from Jaipur spoke of Salim Durani and Hanumant Singh the way I spoke about G R Viswanath and Erapalli Prasanna. Another college classmate, who did not play cricket himself, venerated Tamil players, S Venkataraghavan above all. His mother, who loved music, had told him of how, at a concert in the Music Academy in Madras, Venkat came early and kept perfect tempo throughout. We were aware of cricket writers who knew their classical music (Madras had its own Neville Cardus in N S Ramaswami); but this was a *cricketer* who did, and a Test captain to boot.

Cardus was a secondary school dropout. This music-loving cricketer, however, had a first-class engineering degree from the MIT (the Madras, not the Massachusetts, Institute of Technology). Another story this friend from Madras told me was of Venkat captaining his company, Southern Petrochemicals Industries Corporation, in a first division match. His side was batting first, and he was down to bat at number four himself. However, shortly after the match began, a messenger arrived from the office, with a message that the boiler had broken down. Now SPIC's cricket captain, who was also its chief engineer, had to help fix it. Venkat obtained a pen and piece of paper from the ground staff, and began sketching the machine, from memory. He then asked the messenger a series of questions, on the precise noises the boiler had made, and the smells it was presently exuding. As he listened, Venkat drew arrows, adding words and sentences indicating what parts seemed to be problematic, and how they might be fixed.

Meanwhile a wicket fell, then another. Venkat pushed himself down the order, to six, seven, eight and nine. By the time the problem with the boiler was properly identified, however, SPIC were eight wickets down. It would be impossible for Venkat to bat at number eleven in a club match. So, when the next wicket fell, he declared. Then his side went into the field, and he took a sharp catch in the first over, and a wicket himself in the second, before stumps were called for the day.

As an off-spinner Prasanna of Karnataka was supreme, but Venkataraghavan of Tamil Nadu was a pretty fine bowler too. In his match reports for the *Times of India*, K N Prabhu had described for me his key wickets in those two Test series we won overseas in 1971. Some years later, I saw Venkat bowl out the Railways on a crumbling pitch, alternating between over and round the wicket. And I would always retain special memories of the fielding display he put on in front of me before the start of play on the second day of the Delhi Test of 1974.

During the Delhi Test of 1993 (against Zimbabwe) Venkat was one of the umpires. I was impressed by how unimpressed he was by Kapil Dev's appeals for balls hitting the pads but evidently going down the leg side. 'Not out!' he barked at the bowler, when a lesser Indian – that is to say, an Indian who had not captained Kapil before becoming a Test umpire – might have been more shamefaced in turning down the greatest new-ball bowler the country had produced, or even given in to the appeal once in a while.

During this Delhi Test, I was invited to a dinner hosted by a cricketing bureaucrat I knew slightly. The Indian team were supposed to show up but didn't. But their manager came. He was Ajit Wadekar, and it was on this occasion that I got him to tell me that it was, in truth, his new shoes which had helped my team win the Ranji Trophy in 1974. I had a longer conversation with Venkat, who had also come along. I told him about the catches I had seen him take in matches, and in practice. He accepted the compliments, and, as Abbas Ali Baig joined us, asked whether he remembered being run out in a Ranji match in 1963 or 1964. He did. Baig and Pataudi had seen fine outfielding in their Oxford days, but rarely in India, and certainly not from a Tamil. So they set off for a single, whereupon a lanky eighteen-year-old debutant at mid-wicket threw down the stumps with Baig a yard out of his crease.

At this dinner I shook Venkat's hands for the first (and as it happens last) time. I commented on their size, adding that now I knew part of the reason why he held so many catches. 'You should have seen Polly Umrigar's hands,' he said. 'They were larger. And he missed even fewer than me.' Baig, who had played

Test cricket with Umrigar (whereas Venkat had merely watched and met him), nodded assent.

Some years later, I met Polly Umrigar myself. It was at a cricket book function in Bengaluru, where he had come along with Raj Singh. I shook hands with Polly, and my then eleven-year-old son did too. It was, in more senses than one, an unequal meeting. As my son's hand went shyly out, the former India captain noticed a plaster on the index finger, and asked, 'How did that happen, Sonny Boy?'

'Playing cricket,' answered the boy, adding, 'it was a return catch.'

'Did you hold it?' enquired Polly.

'No,' said my son, apologetically.

At this point an onlooker butted in. 'You wouldn't have missed the catch,' he remarked, pointing at Umrigar, 'if you had hands like his.'

The onlooker was wrong. It was not the hands, but the genes. My son's father rarely caught a hard-struck cricket ball either.

V

In the first Test I watched, at the Kotla in December 1972, Venkat fielded at leg slip to Chandrasekhar, but at silly point to Bishan Bedi. Throughout that match he and the wicketkeeper, Farokh Engineer, lobbed practice catches at one another. Farokh wore bright red gloves, had his collars up, and walked stylishly between the wickets. Pataudi apart, he was the most glamorous cricketer of his generation.

And he could bat and keep wicket. In that 1972 Test against England, Farokh Engineer scored a fine half-century. In between cuts and drives he played a shot unknown to club and school cricket in Dehradun, the glide down to fine-leg for a single. It was rarely played in the Bombay of Farokh's youth, either, so he must have picked it up in county cricket.

Two years later, Farokh played in a Delhi Test again. On my morning visits to the Maidens Hotel, I saw him several times. I was too shy to go talk to him, but could clearly see how Syed Kirmani venerated him, and was understandably much keener to spend time and take tips from his senior wicketkeeper than to entertain petitions and representations from a junior fellow townsman.

On the fourth day of the match, I saw Farokh bat again. India had a huge first-innings deficit. Engineer opened, and early on ducked an Andy Roberts bouncer, which hit his head a glancing blow (these were pre-helmet days) before going off for four leg-byes. Farokh went off for running repairs, and, after the first wicket fell, came back to give us a courageous display of counter-attacking batsmanship. Roberts was pulled for several fours and a six, and the other fast bowlers driven for boundaries. Engineer got to 75 before being bowled, trying to cut the off-spinner Lance Gibbs.

Three-and-a-half decades after watching Farokh bat in Delhi, I was in his adopted hometown, Manchester. Keshava had just graduated from university, and I had given him a present that was also in effect a present to myself – tickets for five days of an Ashes Test match. We stayed in a hotel near the Manchester United ground and walked every day to that other sports stadium also bearing the name 'Old Trafford'.

It was a drawn match, but well contested, with outstanding centuries from Michael Clarke on one side and Kevin Pietersen on the other. Ryan Harris bowled well for Australia, as did Graeme Swann for England. The cricket was enjoyable, and so was dinner one night, hosted by the hometown boy, Michael Atherton, the guests being this Indian father-and-son and an Australian duo comprising the writer-cricketer Gideon Haigh and the cricketer-writer Ed Cowan.

During the Test we were sitting in an open stand, adjacent to a newly built (and spectacularly ugly) pavilion, meant for members of the Lancashire County Cricket Club. Late on the fourth day, as the match meandered towards a draw, I saw Farokh Engineer on the balcony. He was twice the size of his playing days, but it was recognisably him. He had on a pink striped blazer.

How could we get to meet and speak with this hero of my youth? It seemed impolite to ask Atherton for yet another favour, and perhaps he didn't know him well enough anyway. The person to help must be the son of Farokh's now deceased team-mate for Bombay and India, Dilip Sardesai. So when we returned to the hotel I mailed Rajdeep Sardesai for assistance. The next morning I called him as well. Rajdeep said he was out of touch, but could get the number from a cricket journalist. By the next evening he had. I rang Farokh, introducing myself as a friend of Rajdeep and a fan of his. He asked us to come over for coffee the next morning. We had kept a free day after the Test for visiting bookstores, but this now had to take precedence.

Farokh lived with his English wife in a village ten or twelve miles out of the city. We took a train as instructed, and then a taxi to his home. His wife gave us tea and then left us to speak. We did, in a large airy atrium perfect for a man of Farokh's expansive character. I told our host of when I had seen him play. He was still bitter about being denied the captaincy of India when Pataudi reported injured for the Delhi Test of 1974. However, his mood improved when I reminded him of how he had hooked Roberts. Other stories were exchanged, and the meeting ended with him taking us down to the basement, where the photos, bats and gloves of his playing days were kept.

Farokh was friendly towards me, and exceptionally kind to my son. By now Keshava was twenty-three, and six foot three inches tall. But Farokh only addressed him, 1950s Bombay Parsi style, as 'Sonny Boy'. He so took to him that he insisted on dropping us at the station, in a vehicle gifted by Ferrari. He had advertised for the company, he told us – with the sort of self-deprecating wit that comes naturally to Englishmen but is foreign to Indians (Parsis excepted) – in order to show, or show off, their new car's size.

VI

The cricketers I have thus far spoken about were older than myself. Kapil Dev Nikhanj was born (if Wikipedia is correct) some nine months after I was. I shook hands with him once, long after he retired. This was at the fiftieth anniversary celebrations of the Jolly Rovers Cricket Club in Chennai, where both of us had been invited to speak by the former Hyderabad and South Zone off-spinner, V Ramnarayan.

I spoke before Kapil, and began by recalling the times I had seen him play. I had seen, live, every ball of his first Test hundred, against the West Indies in Delhi in 1978. I told the assembled audience of Chennai cricket lovers about how, through hard drives and delicate late cuts, he got to 94 not out at stumps on the second day. On the third morning, India had to wait until he got his hundred to declare: this he did in the first two balls of the first over, bowled by Norbert Phillip, one going past mid-off for four and the other over square-leg for six.

I then turned to Kapil the bowler, for which I used as my prime exhibit a Test match in Madras itself, played against Pakistan in January 1980. I was there, and so were many members in the audience. On the first day, and on a good wicket, Kapil demolished a high-class batting order with a superb display of swing bowling. Mudassar, Sadiq and Zaheer Abbas were caught behind by Kirmani, diving low to either side. Javed Miandad was taken by Vengsarkar at slip. Checking the scorecard, I find that of the top five only Majid Khan did not fall to Kapil (he was run out). But in my recollection (which the older cricketers of Jolly

Rovers shared) Kapil gave him the most trouble, beating Majid repeatedly, on the inside of the bat and on the outside too.*

To illustrate Kapil's fielding I chose an example from a match everyone in the audience had watched, either live, on television or in one of its many replays. This was the catch he took to dismiss Viv Richards in the final of the 1983 World Cup. I said that as he ran back from deep mid-wicket Kapil had a smile on his face, for he now knew that India were in with a chance. I added that he was the only player in the team who could have taken that catch.

I thought I had given a decent speech, but Kapil's was far better. He began by teasing the audience about his famously poor knowledge of English, which, he said, he was even more embarrassed about after hearing me talk. He knew the residents of Chennai did not like Hindi forced upon them, but could he please, please, speak in that language? Of course, roared the audience, with me joining in the chorus. Having set us up, Kapil then delivered an informative and witty speech in English, whose verve and expressiveness made up for any lack of grammatical orthodoxy. He told many stories, some against himself, one of these aimed directly at me. This chap Guha thought I was smiling when running back to take that catch in the World Cup final, said Kapil, but the real reason is that I had no other choice, for I have buck teeth, which protrude outwards whether I am sad or happy, sleeping or running.

---

* Kapil bowled even better in the second innings, getting seven wickets. I did not see that spell, being on a train to Calcutta that day. In between, he had scored 84 when India batted.

VII

From the time he made his Test debut in 1978 to the time he retired sixteen years later, Kapil Dev was an essential and indispensable part of the Indian team. He was never dropped for lack of form, or because of injury. However, he was once dropped from a Test on disciplinary grounds. This was played against England at Eden Gardens in 1984. I was then still in Calcutta, now getting cured of my Marxism, and coming back to cricket. The father of a friend got me tickets for two days of the Test. On the second of these, I saw the debutant Mohammed Azharuddin score a fine hundred, replete with flicks past mid-wicket and cuts past point. His style was manifestly his own; a fact that distressed his batting partner Ravi Shastri, who after every ball hit against the line would go up to chastise the youngster (fortunately to no avail).

Seven years after watching Azharuddin bat at Calcutta, I was in Oxford, on a research fellowship. I walked past The Parks, saw a match in progress, and stopped to watch. I saw a familiar figure in an unfamiliar role; it was Azhar, who was bowling. I asked around, and found it was a 50-over tie between Derbyshire and the Combined Universities. At lunch, I went to the dressing room and sought my fellow Indian out. We shook hands, and spoke briefly, about cricket, and about the little children we both had at home and missed while away in England.

Through the 1990s and beyond, I saw Azhar play many times, live and on television. I have warm memories of his batsmanship, of course, but even more of his fielding. One of the best catches I have ever seen at the ground was taken by him at second slip during an India–Pakistan World Cup match in Manchester in 1999. It was a bitterly cold day, and as the winds froze us in our open stand, that magnificent left-hander Saeed Anwar was taking the match away from India. Then Venkatesh Prasad got one to move away late, and it caught Anwar's edge. The ball flew fast and low to the left of second slip. Azhar dived to his left and came up with a catch that no one on either side could have taken. It won us the match, but alas could not (*pace* Kapil in 1983) win us the tournament.

I admired Azharuddin as a cricketer, and felt sorry for him as a human being. For it was his singular misfortune to be captain of India in the 1990s, a decade riven with Hindu–Muslim discord and animosity against Pakistan. At this time, the paradigmatic Good Muslim in India was the missile scientist A P J Abdul Kalam, hard at work at building bombs that, if required, could obliterate Pakistan. The paradigmatic Bad Muslim was the mafia don Dawood Ibrahim, born and raised in Bombay, but ever willing to send terrorists to his hometown from his own safe haven in Karachi. Azhar, however, was both a Good and a Bad Muslim, the former when he scored runs and his team won, the latter when he failed and his team lost.*

After that encounter in Oxford in 1991, I watched Azhar play often, and thought of him and his dilemma often too. I saw him at the ground and at the odd cricket function, but did not speak to him again. It seemed that our one meeting would be the last. Then he got entangled in the match-fixing scandal, and that distressed me greatly too.

In 2010, Rajdeep Sardesai and I were shooting a programme on the sixtieth anniversary of the founding of the Indian Republic. Rajdeep got permission to use Parliament House on a Sunday. It was a dull day, made bleaker by the winter haze, and no one was around. After an hour of talking to camera we took a break. As we did we saw a figure familiar to both of us walk over. He was Azharuddin, elected the previous year to the Lok Sabha on a Congress ticket. He rarely attended Parliament and

* For a fuller account of Azhar's tragic situation, see Chapter 16 of *A Corner of a Foreign Field*.

almost never spoke during its debates. What he was doing there on a Sunday I cannot imagine. He knew Rajdeep, of course, and made a good show of pretending to recognise me as well. He was still fine physically; well toned, superbly proportioned, not an ounce of extra flesh anywhere. But he looked distracted and desperately alone. I have never felt so sad at shaking another human being's hand.

VIII

As a boy learning the game in school and college, I was always a mere three handshakes away from a cricketing immortal – from my uncle to V M Muddiah to Hemu Adhikari to Adhikari's own mentor, Vijay Samuel Hazare. As I grew older, I began climbing up this hierarchy of hero worship myself. I met V M Muddiah, and befriended him. Over cups of coffee in his Bangalore home he told me a heap of cricket stories. Most of these, at my prodding, were about the original Holy Trinity of Indian slow bowlers, Mankad, Gupte and Ghulam Ahmed. But there was also one about Hazare.

In the winter of 1958–9, the Services met Baroda in the Ranji Trophy final. Hemu Adhikari knew that the match hinged on how many runs his mentor would make. Hazare was now forty-two, and still batting well, his technique compensating for slowness of eye. Adhikari remembered that ever since the England fast bowler Frank Ridgway had hit him on the head, Hazare was somewhat uncertain against the bumper, at least early in his innings. So Services won the toss, and put Baroda in. The India fast bowler Surendranath knocked over a couple, and Hazare came in at 10 for two. As his captain had instructed him, Surendranath bounced the old man first ball. An intended hook shot flew high into the air, dropping in, and then out, of the hands of fine-leg. 'Now he'll score a hundred!' shouted Adhikari in exasperation. Actually, Hazare made a double-hundred and Baroda won in a canter.

Years after Muddiah told me this story I met Hemu Adhikari himself. He was the chief guest at a cricket party in New Delhi, where one of the accredited invitees, Sujit Mukherjee, had taken me along. As readers of his marvellous *Autobiography of an Unknown Cricketer* will know, Sujit played Ranji Trophy cricket for Bihar and also was on the faculty of the National Defence Academy, where one of his colleagues was the aforementioned Adhikari. There is a passage in the book which tells of how Sujit took the NDA students to the Bombay Test of 1956, where each of them also played, in their mind, every one of the defensive strokes with which Hemu helped save the match for India.

The party was at the home of an old Services cricketer, the other invitees also old Services cricketers. Now my early Dehradun fielding experience – with Durai hammering the fear out of me as he believed Muddiah had said Hemu Adhikari would – had prepared me for a martinet. But the man turned out to be surprisingly gentle, and, for the most part, silent. Unhappily, a TV commentator had also gatecrashed; he spoke continuously. While the loudmouth went to refill his drink I turned the talk around to Adhikari's past, to his memories of Bradman and Lindwall and Miller. I then asked him about his teacher, and asked him, incautiously, about the least known aspect of his hero's game. 'What was Hazare like as a fielder?' was my question. When Adhikari did not answer I put the question once more. 'Why do you ask?' he said. 'All you had to do was put a bat in his hands and glory in the result.'

Some years later I was in Baroda, speaking on an emphatically non-cricketing subject. A local journalist named Vyas kindly set up a meeting with the town's greatest living citizen. Hazare lived in a modest apartment overlooking the Polo Ground in Baroda, the scene of his world record partnership of 577 with Gul Mahommed back in 1946–7. On the door was an exquisite nameplate, the letters lovingly engraved in gold, the work of a craftsman of long ago whose skill must have disappeared with him.

As we climbed the stairs we were greeted by loud barking, from two dogs of indeterminate breed. The dogs were whisked away, and the daughter-in-law of the house took us into the living room. Cups and shields were displayed on shelf and table, these won by the lady's husband and son, both Ranji Trophy cricketers. There was but one memento inscribed to the original sportsman of the family. It was presented to Vijay Hazare on his eightieth birthday, by the Western Railway Workers' Union. Other and more substantial trophies must, I thought, be hidden away in an inner room, safe from an inquisitorial public.

In a minute or two the great man walked in, erect, his eyes alert. He began by saying that he might not be able to talk long or coherently, for the previous day he had been taken to witness (and bless) a schoolboy tournament, walking more than a hundred yards, in the sun, from the road to the pavilion. In the event we spoke for an hour, my questions always answered crisply and directly. Which was his greatest innings, I asked. The triple-hundred in the Pentangular against the Hindus, 309 not out out of a total of 387, in statistical and other terms the finest single-handed show by any batsman in cricket history? The double-hundred in the Ranji Trophy final of 1958–9, a knock which effectively ensured that one of his pupils, the Baroda captain D K Gaekwad, would be appointed captain for the 1959 England tour (instead of his other pupil, the losing Services captain, Hemu Adhikari)? Or the two hundreds in the Adelaide Test of 1948?

The Adelaide knocks, of course, answered Hazare. The Indians had been two days in the field, while Bradman and company scored 674. When they batted in reply, Hazare scored 116 and Phadkar 123. At one point Hazare hooked Keith Miller for three consecutive boundaries early in the over. The fast bowler asked his captain, Don Bradman, for an additional fielder on the on-side, which was refused. Miller then bowled three lollipops, which the batsman politely patted back down the wicket. Bradman did not give the fast bowler another over.

India eventually reached the respectable score of 381. But they still had to follow on. In the first over of their second knock Ray Lindwall had Mankad caught behind and then bowled Amarnath. Hazare went in at 0 for two, and batted for the next six hours, before he was ninth out, for 145. India ended with 277, with the only other serious contribution being Hemu Adhikari's 51. Hazare's second innings was marked by some magnificent cover drives off the spinners Johnson and McCool. Both knocks were chanceless, the hundreds scored against one of the finest bowling and fielding sides in the history of the game.

On the evening of his second hundred, Hazare was taken out for dinner by the great slow bowler Clarrie Grimmett. Years before, in 1937, Grimmett had visited the state of Jath, in western India, on a coaching assignment. Hazare was then employed by the Maharaja of Dewas, the Raja of Jath's brother-in-law. With his boss's permission he joined Grimmett's camp. The Australian bowled Hazare some balls, and came to the sensible conclusion that there was little he could teach him in the batting department. Will you not then teach me the googly, asked the pupil. No, answered the master, for you will not be able to control it. But I will teach you the finger-spun leg-break. This ball then became a key weapon in the armoury of this medium-pacer. I took five hundred and seventy-eight wickets in first-class cricket, said Hazare, a figure remembered with the delight of the batsman who would also be a bowler.

I had been warned that Hazare stayed scrupulously clear of controversy. Unheeding, I asked him to compare men of different generations. Hazare answered politely and indirectly, by praising his contemporary. When I set the names of Merchant and

Gavaskar side by side, he spoke of the other Vijay's exemplary technique, of how he would never loft the ball yet contrive to place it between the fielders. When I asked him to compare Bishan Bedi and Vinoo Mankad, he told the story of the Chepauk Test of February 1952. Vinoo got eight wickets in the first innings, but was bowling ordinary stuff in the second. After the off-spinner Ghulam Ahmed got two wickets in succession, Hazare (who was captain) went over to Vinoo and said in Marathi: 'I have never seen such a strange cricket wicket before. It turns only at one end.' Thus provoked, Mankad began turning them like a top, and with Ghulam bowled India to its first victory in Test cricket.

About the only cricketer Hazare did criticise, albeit very gently, was the senior Nawab of Pataudi. On the 1946 tour of England, Pataudi, much against Hazare's will, commanded him to open the innings against Surrey. I got a *blob*, he recalled to us, the word accompanied by a lovely, low chuckle, the figure carved for good measure with the help of thumb and forefinger. Thereafter his skipper put him down to bat at six or seven, too low for him to make an impact. Then, against the county champions, Yorkshire, India had to bat for half-an-hour late on the first day. Two wickets fell early, so Pataudi sent Hazare in as a nightwatchman, to protect him and the other 'established' batsmen. The next day he scored 244 not out.

As player and captain Hazare was quietly assertive, a gentleman well aware of his own genius. In the late glow of his retirement he retained this distinctive combination of dignity and pride. When we left I asked his daughter-in-law for their postal address. She brought me the master's visiting card, but as I made to put it in my wallet he said, with authority: 'I will sign it.' A pen was fetched, and the paper duly autographed. This was the only autograph I ever possessed; it retained that singular status for many years, until it disappeared when our house was being renovated and belongings had to be packed and unpacked. I live in hope that it may yet turn up again one day.

IX

George Bernard Shaw once said of Frank Harris – a moderately gifted but immoderately ambitious writer of his generation – that 'he has dined at all the great houses in England – once'. So it has mostly been with me and Test cricketers. I met Kapil Dev once, Adhikari once, Hazare once, Venkat once, Umrigar once, Hanumant once. I had only one proper meeting with Pataudi. The only Indian Test cricketers whose hands I have shaken more than once or twice are my two college team-mates and the two generations of cricketers from Karnataka.

There is, however, an exception to the exceptions. This is Bishan Bedi, who is the one great cricketer I count as a friend. The friendship, however, took time to mature. After that first meeting in Durai's house in Bangalore in 1974, I followed Bedi at a distance, via my team-mates who played under him for Delhi. With Bedi's brilliant motivational skills and his own genius with the ball, Delhi won the Ranji Trophy in 1978–9 and 1979–80. The Delhi and Districts Cricket Association responded by stripping him of the captaincy and throwing him out of the playing XI. Some years later he was invited back to his home state, Punjab, to coach and manage its Ranji Trophy team. This time the raw talent was provided by the boys of the Guru Nanak Dev University, the experience by the much-capped Navjot Singh Sidhu and by Gursharan Singh, a capable middle-order batsman who had originally played for Delhi.

In 1992–3, as the Punjab team worked its way through the knockout phase of the Ranji Trophy, I heard, once more, stories of what Bedi would do to young men who strayed out of line. When the opener Sapan Chopra disputed an umpire's decision, his manager made him run ten penitential rounds of the ground after close of play, and also dropped him for the next match. Punjab eventually reached the finals, where they were to play

Maharashtra, in Jalandhar. The visitors had left Pune with the good wishes of the centenarian D B Deodhar, who, like Bedi, knew what it was to captain a Ranji Trophy winning side.

The Punjabis versus the Marathas, a battle of the two most combative peoples of India. It was a close match, won eventually by the home side. When the last Maharashtrian wicket fell, the Punjab captain, Gursharan Singh, grabbed a stump and ran off the field, followed by his men. They made straight for Bedi, at whose feet they laid the spoils of war, the stumps, and prostrated themselves. The Sardar himself then turned and offered the stumps to an old man beside him. This was his coach, Gyan Prakash, who he had brought along that morning from Amritsar. That, so to say, was where it all began, the original inspiration for the 267 Test wickets and the Ranji Trophy victories of Delhi and Punjab.

Meanwhile, in the years since their first meeting on the side-lines of a Ranji match in 1974, my uncle Durai and Bedi had become friends. They visited one another in Delhi and Bangalore, and their wives got along well too. By now I had published my first cricket books, and could legitimately approach him on my own as well. In one of those books I had referred to Bedi's 'whisky-waistline'. Shortly afterwards I bumped into the Sardar of Spin at the Chinnaswamy Stadium in Bangalore during an India–Australia Test match. He contested the accuracy of my description. True, the accumulated kilogrammes showed, but my diagnosis was flawed, for he had been for years on the wagon.

I offered Bishan a conciliatory cup of Mysore coffee, and together we watched Shane Warne trying to bowl out the Indians. When the leg-spinner went round the wicket to Navjot Sidhu, Bedi was deeply upset. 'Why doesn't the lad go back over the wicket,' he said, 'he should bowl in the orthodox fashion, flight the ball and let his art and the wicket do the rest. Why this round-the-wicket nonsense? The Indians will pad him away till the cows come home. I shall talk to him this evening.' Speak to him he did, for when I had dinner with Bedi at his hotel that night Warne had already called, leaving two empty tins of baked beans behind. I was not, alas, privy to their conversation, but I shall not easily forget the pain and worry in Bedi's words that day. The slow bowler was speaking over the Indian, the claims of the craft-guild winning out over the claims of nationality.

In his book *Bishan: Portrait of a Cricketer*, Suresh Menon relates how, in the winter of 1975–6, Bedi played an unofficial Test for India against Sri Lanka in Nagpur, before proceeding to Chandigarh to play a Duleep Trophy match. The Board of Control for Cricket in India had forgotten to book his ticket, so Bedi travelled unreserved in the luggage rack of a third-class compartment. So parsimonious were cricket administrators back then that they paid cricketers 250 rupees per Test match. When Bedi and company won a Test match against New Zealand inside of four days, the Board paid them 50 rupees less!

If Indian players are compensated far better now, it is due to the struggles on their behalf by cricketers like Bishan Bedi. In his book, Menon documents Bedi's role in organising a players' association, that demanded and got fair compensation for cricketers active as well as retired. Bedi was able to do this in part because of the force of his personality, and in part because he was one of the true greats of the game. I did not realise until I read Menon's book that Bedi was the only cricketer who played in India's first Test victories in New Zealand (Dunedin, 1968), the West Indies (Port of Spain, 1971), England (The Oval, 1971), and Australia (Melbourne, 1978).

Bedi is not flawless. Like all men, he is notoriously susceptible to flattery. He does see things always in black and white (the Sri Lankan off-spinner Muttiah Muralitharan's action, for example). He is very bitter about real and imaginary slights. He has a thing or two about Mumbai cricketers in general, and about Sunil Gavaskar in particular, and loses no opportunity to slight them (and him). He is probably (no, certainly) an even worse committee man than I am. On the other hand, he is deeply committed to nurturing young cricketers. And he loves the game far more than he loves himself.

Some years ago, the former British Prime Minister, John Major, made a private visit to Delhi. The British High Commissioner threw a party, choosing the guests with care. In deference to the visitor's political distinction, he invited a senior Union Minister and the serving Chief Election Commissioner. To indulge the visitor's passion for cricket, he had called some former Test players. As a friend of the host, I found my way into the party too. Throughout a long evening John Major ignored the other guests entirely. He focused his attention on Bishan Bedi, with whom he swapped a series of cricketing stories. Several involved the great Yorkshire and England fast bowler Freddie Trueman, who Sir John venerated and Bedi had played against. At evening's end I got in my sole sentence, when I told the chief guest he should write a fan's book with many stories about 'FST' (Frederick Sewards Trueman). 'Why only FST,' acknowledged Sir John. 'I shall tell stories about BSB too.'

I have many stories about BSB. One, which I particularly cherish, relates to a visit I made to Kabul, where our Ambassador (a cricket fan) expressed interest in inviting a famous Indian player to inspire, and coach, young Afghans. I suggested that since cricketers still active would not risk a trip to a land subject to regular terror attacks, they ask a retired player to come instead. Various names were discussed, one of whom was Bedi's. When I returned to India I called my hero-turned-friend. I asked him if the invitation came through at a convenient time, whether he would be willing to go. 'Why not,' answered the Sardar of Spin spontaneously, 'anywhere for cricket.' *Anywhere for cricket* — whereas the unspoken motto of some of his former team-mates is, anywhere (and anything) for money.

X

If, excluding my college contemporaries as well as all Karnataka players, I was to make up a playing XI of Indian cricketers I shook hands with, it would read, in batting order:

1. F M Engineer
2. Abbas Ali Baig
3. V S Hazare
4. H R Adhikari
5. Mohammed Azharuddin
6. M A K Pataudi
7. Hanumant Singh
8. P R Umrigar
9. Kapil Dev
10. S Venkataraghavan
11. B S Bedi

The batting is fantastic, and although the bowling might seem less weighty, one would go to heaven and back to watch Bishan Bedi bowl from one end and Kapil Dev from the other.* Besides, a side with Hemu, Azhar, Kapil, Venkat, Polly, and Pataudi, would field like, well, tigers. There is a preponderance of Test captains, eight in number, nine if one includes Farokh (appointed in public, before the appointment was abruptly withdrawn). I think Bedi would generously propose that Vijay Hazare captain the side, and that Pataudi would – in the same spirit – second the proposal. The manager, of course, would be Raj Singh Dungarpur.

---

* Cf Jim Laker: 'My idea of Paradise is Lord's in the sunshine, with Ray Lindwall bowling from one end and Bishan Bedi from the other.' On reading this book in manuscript form, the historian and cricket writer David Kynaston wrote, as a P.S. to this footnote: 'Pakistan in England in '82 – Imran Khan at one end, Abdul Qadir at the other – I remember fondly.'

6

Sightings of Sachin

I

Every Indian cricket fan claims a special kinship with Sachin Tendulkar. Mine is this: he played his first Test in November 1989, and I published my first book in that same month. For much of his professional career, this historian had his work diverted and his life enriched by the magic of Tendulkar at the crease. I watched him bat many times live, and many more times on the TV. I marvelled at the range of his strokeplay, at his commanding control of both the Test and the one-day game, at his extraordinary ability to master different wickets, grounds, and bowling attacks, and above all, at the cool authority and understated calm with which he bore, for a full quarter-of-a-century, the absurdly inflated and sometimes maniacal expectations of millions of his countrymen.

I was living in Delhi when Sachin Tendulkar made his debut tour of Pakistan, and it was in my old college common room – sitting with students a decade-and-a-half younger than me – that I saw snatches of the sixteen-year-old bat, resolutely keeping out Waqar Younis and Wasim Akram while stroking Abdul Qadir for handsome boundaries. I first saw Sachin in the flesh in a Wills Trophy match at the Feroz Shah Kotla in 1990, shortly after that tour of Pakistan. He did not bat in that match; but I remember, most vividly, his alarm and nervousness as hordes of fans rushed towards him as he went out to field, clutching at his sleeve, his cap, his foot, his arm, as is their wont.

149

Three years later, by which time he was an established Test star, I watched Tendulkar play for India against Zimbabwe at the Kotla. He was involved in a long stand with his childhood friend and schoolmate Vinod Kambli. Zimbabwe had one top-class spinner, John Traicos, who, although now over forty years of age, still had a fine high action, immaculate control, and subtle changes of flight. While Kambli came down the wicket and drove Traicos hard and high, Tendulkar stayed in the crease and deftly worked him past slip and behind square-leg for twos and threes. He looked set for a hundred, but then, when he was about 70, mistimed a drive off an unknown fellow named Ujesh Ranchod. He was caught at extra-cover by Traicos, diving full-length in front of him. This was Ranchod's first (and last) Test wicket – he is probably bragging about it in Bulawayo still. Kambli went on to score a double-century.

The following February, I timed a trip to Bangalore to catch a Test against Sri Lanka. India batted first, and after Navjot Sidhu and Kambli had plundered a rather ordinary attack, Sachin came out to bat just before tea. He started slowly, then accelerated. Muralitharan was then new to Test cricket, and the master took apart the novice, treating him much as he had done the veteran Traicos, milking him through cuts and sweeps. When the second new ball was taken, Tendulkar creamed the seam bowler Pramodya Wickramasinghe for eighteen runs in an over, mostly through the off-side. He had reached 80 not out by stumps. The next morning he proceeded carefully to 96, when he lost his off-stump trying to cut the left-arm spinner, Don Anurasiri.

I had never seen Sunil Gavaskar score a century on the ground, 'live'. When he scored a hundred against Kallicharan's West Indians in 1978–9, it was on the first day, the one day for which I did not have a ticket. The next winter, I watched Gavaskar bat superbly against the Pakistanis at Chepauk. Through a series of dazzling square cuts and straight drives he got to about 75 at tea, but then unaccountably slowed down thereafter. At stumps that day, Gavaskar was 92 not out. Early the next morning, I had to take a train for an interview in Calcutta.

After watching Sachin get a 70 and a 90 the first two times I saw him at the crease, I wondered if the jinx would operate with regard to this Bombay batsman too. In 1995, I moved back to Bangalore; and a couple of years later saw Sachin play in a Test against Mark Taylor's Australians. I had arrived that morning from San Francisco; and by the time I shrugged off customs and jet lag to get to the Chinnaswamy Stadium it was lunch. Four hours of cricket was all I would get, for next morning other business called.

Navjot Sidhu got out soon after the interval, and Sachin came in. He started confidently enough, but I was not sure my jinx would be broken. I remembered Gavaskar at Chepauk, and saw too that Shane Warne was no Ranchod or Anurasiri. However, in three hours of almost chanceless batsmanship Tendulkar had got to his hundred. Of his strokes that day I remember most clearly two rifle-shot straight drives off Michael Kasprowicz, and some lovely late cuts off Warne. He made one error though. The part-time medium-pacer Greg Blewett threw in a bouncer, and Tendulkar was struck momentarily by indecision, for it was the last over before tea. He was a little late on the shot, but the top-edge fell harmlessly between fine-leg and the wicketkeeper. The normally phlegmatic Australian captain, Mark Taylor, fielding at slip, violently stamped on the ground, a gesture that was, in its own way, as sincere a tribute as any other spelt out in this chapter.

So (unlike with Gavaskar) I saw Tendulkar get a Test hundred in the flesh, not merely on TV. A decade later I was to see him exceed this, in another Test against the Australians played in Bangalore. Ricky Ponting won the toss, and chose to bat. With fifties from Shane Watson and Ponting himself, and a hundred from Marcus North, the visitors assembled an impressive total of 478. Surely, we thought, Australia could not lose from here.

When India batted and Sehwag and Dravid got out early, a win for Australia seemed the likely result. Two all-time batting greats had departed; but a third had other ideas. Tendulkar eased the pressure through two fine forcing shots off the back foot, followed by a peach of a straight drive. With young Murali Vijay also playing a steady hand, India had, by close of play, reached 128 for two, with Tendulkar himself on 44 not out.

In the first over of the third day, Tendulkar played two late leg-glances to get to his half-century. Then he hit two lusty pulls off Mitchell Johnson, Australia's fastest bowler, and a man reckless enough to announce before the series began that the Indians were suspect against the short ball. After these four shots, the fielding captain, Ricky Ponting, went immediately on the defensive. The bowlers were instructed to bowl wide outside the off-stump. Tendulkar still found a way to reach the extra-cover fence twice. More fielders were sent out to patrol the boundary. The scoring rate slowed down, with the Indians content with singles and the occasional two.

Australia needed to win the match to square the series. To stem the runs was not enough. Wickets had to be taken. Ponting eventually called upon his sole spinner, Nathan Hauritz, to take advantage of a wearing wicket. That, at any rate, was the theory, to be decisively refuted by three strokes by Tendulkar, an off-drive for four and two sixes over long-on, the last bringing up his 49th Test century.

Shortly after Tendulkar hit Hauritz for his second six, lunch was taken. There was a buzz around the ground and in the press box (where I sat), as we all took stock of this latest landmark. Tendulkar was now ten Test centuries clear of Ricky Ponting, fifteen in front of the next Indian on the list, Sunil Gavaskar, and twenty ahead of the man commonly considered to be the greatest batsman in the history of the game, Donald Bradman.

Through the long afternoon, as Tendulkar further wore down the Australian bowlers, the talk turned to comparing Sachin to his celebrated predecessors. I asked the experienced Mumbai journalist Makarand Waigankar to reflect on Sachin's precise location in the Bombay School of Batsmanship. Waigankar explained how, like Gavaskar, Tendulkar had his talents recognised early, by the scouts sent by the Bombay selectors to study school cricket; how, like Gavaskar, he was fanatically committed to long hours at the nets; and how, like Gavaskar, he was as keen to score runs for Bombay in the Ranji Trophy as for India in Tests. Having situated him historically, Waigankar nonetheless affirmed that in his range of strokeplay and the sheer bulk of his achievement, Tendulkar comfortably surpassed the achievements of Gavaskar, and of other outstanding Bombay batsmen (such as Vijay Manjrekar and Vijay Merchant) who had preceded him.

In between overs, and during the drinks and tea breaks, I spoke also to Peter Roebuck, the former English first-class cricketer who had made his home in Australia, and whose columns appeared in newspapers published in at least four continents. Having watched at least fifteen Test hundreds by Tendulkar as they unfolded, Roebuck wondered how he would write about this particular innings. 'Each made by the same man, but each, of course, constructed so differently,' he reflected. He then spoke of what Tendulkar's innings meant to Murali Vijay, watching from the other end. Was this not the best lesson in batsmanship the young man would receive?

My immediate neighbour in the press box also had plenty of things to say about Tendulkar. This was Suresh Menon, who had covered Tendulkar's first tour, in Pakistan in 1989, where he had watched him being hit on the mouth by Waqar Younis – and battle on regardless. His abiding memory of that tour was of a peculiar complaint of the team manager, the old India cricketer Chandu Borde. Borde had been assigned a hotel room immediately under Tendulkar's, and was woken up at dawn each day by the boy knocking practice balls on the floor of his room.

As we spoke, Tendulkar marched serenely on. At close of play he was just nine runs short of his double-hundred. I learnt from the next day's papers that the last stages of his innings had been watched by, among others, the leader of the Opposition in the Karnataka State Assembly, the Congress politician Siddaramaiah. That morning, Siddaramaiah had gone to work hoping that the BJP Government would be voted out, and that he would stake his claim to become Chief Minister. The plan was foiled when, with the aid of the police, the Speaker chose to disqualify the defecting legislators. While the decision was being challenged in the High Court, the Congress and its allies could not form a new Government. The thwarted leader now chose to leave for the Chinnaswamy Stadium, where, since Tendulkar was still at the crease, he knew he would find pleasure – and consolation.

The next morning, Sachin got to 214 before being bowled. But his work in the match was not done yet. In their second knock, Australia were hustled out for 200-odd, the wickets equally divided between the seamers and the spinners. India knocked off the winning runs fairly comfortably, with Tendulkar getting an unbeaten half-century.

In this Test Tendulkar hit four sixes, two in each innings. All were struck off Hauritz, all between long-on and wide mid-wicket. When he was young Sachin would skip down the wicket and hit the spinner straight over his head. Now, however, he cleared space with his left leg and played absolutely across the line. His first sixes against Abdul Qadir (which I saw on the TV twenty years before this match) had been incomparably more elegant. That said, by these newer, cruder, methods he had won another Test match for India.

II

Tendulkar was superb in Test matches, and magnificent in the one-day game. And yet, the first time I saw him bat live in the shorter format he was unnaturally scratchy and out-of-sorts. This was in the World Cup quarter-final against Pakistan in Bangalore in March 1996. Tendulkar, opening, spent an hour and forty minutes at the crease. I can remember none of it. The scoreboard informs me that he made 31 runs off 59 balls, very slow going by any standards, and not just his. The occasion, so unusually and unexpectedly, had got to him.

Three years later, India played Pakistan in another World Cup match. This time it was in Manchester, and I was there again. It was a bitterly cold day. I sat with Suresh Menon in what was euphemistically called the 'overflow press box'. I suppose the regular press box was enclosed and had some kind of heating. This one was utterly exposed to the elements. But Suresh and I were warmed up somewhat by Tendulkar. While not at his best (perhaps he was freezing too) he was markedly more assured than in Bangalore in 1996. He scored 45, with five fours, one of which, a trademark straight drive off Wasim Akram, I can see still.

Whether in Tests or in one-dayers, Sachin liked to farm the strike. Often, as he played the ball past square-leg or behind point, the stump microphone as well as the straight-field camera would catch him saying: 'Two, two, two.' The problem however was that those who batted with him longest for India could not run as fast as him. Magnificent though they may have been in their strokeplay, Ganguly, Sehwag, Dravid and Laxman were not partial to the sharp single, or to the conversion of slow singles into quick twos either.

In the last week of March 2001, I sat with my son in the BEML Stand as India played Australia in a one-day match. We had just won an enthralling Test series, and our chaps seemed determined to win this lesser contest as well. Certainly Tendulkar did. We batted first, and through strokes of some vehemence he had got to 35 off a mere 26 balls, with four fours and a six. He looked set for plenty more, when one of the four above-mentioned batsmen ran him out. It was the last ball of the over, and so, as he played a ball to deep point, Sachin wanted not two but three. He turned quickly and ran three-quarters of the way down the pitch, but his partner, exhausted by the second run, had stayed firmly put. Sachin went back in desperation and just failed to make his ground. He had completed three-and-a-half runs while his partner (who must, because of his otherwise colossal contributions to Indian cricket, remain unnamed) had been hard put to run two. India went on to lose the match.

Fast forward a couple of years, to another India–Australia one-day match at the Chinnaswamy Stadium, played in November 2003. I was once more sitting in the galleries, where the mood and spirit of the crowd is at its most revealing. The visitors, batting first, scored in excess of three hundred, with both Gilchrist and Ponting scoring hundreds. India lost early wickets, but so long as the little genius was in, we were still in the game. Sachin played a series of magically inventive shots, inside out over cover, paddle sweeps behind the keeper, sublime late cuts, testing the anticipation and athleticism of some of the world's finest fielders. With every four he hit the men (and boys) around me would raise their eyes to the heavens, and intone: 'Sachin! Sachin!' They were privileged to have seen the Divine in the flesh, performing acts of heroism more innovative than our Gods had thought of, and against more devilish enemies too. It was a fabulous innings, made more remarkable by the timid showing of the batsmen at the other end. Sachin got to 89 at a run a ball before he tried one late cut too many, and was bowled.

I last saw Sachin Tendulkar bat live in a one-day match on 27 February 2011. The previous evening, I had attended the opening of an exhibition of cartoons by Abu Abraham, a brooding

Malayali who worked for many years in London and New Delhi before retiring to Kerala. Ranging over fifty years of Abu's work, the show had as its centrepiece his cartoons of the 1970s. These were often prescient, with, for example, a politician saying, before election time, that 'we must consider the relative merits of candidates', and another answering 'yes, especially the merits of relatives'. Another had politician A glumly telling politician B that 'the gains of Pokharan have been cancelled out at Lord's'.

Visitors to the gallery who were much younger than myself would not have caught that reference. I did, immediately, for I was sixteen in 1974, an age when one is just discovering one's love for one's country. Like other patriotic Indians I had saluted the nuclear test in Pokharan that May but been devastated by the humiliation at Lord's in June, when a crack Indian batting side – Gavaskar, Viswanath, Engineer et al. – were bowled out for 42 by the English seamers. Within a single month, I (and other patriots) had passed from exultation to humiliation. Abu, however, had set the matter in perspective. The sardonic, sceptical Malayali had told his readers in 1974 – and was telling me now, decades later – that it was foolish to see either the possession of a nuclear bomb or victory in a cricket match as an index of a nation's worth.

The next day, I was due to be at the Chinnaswamy Stadium, to watch India play England in an early match of the World Cup. Normally, I would have wanted India to win, but Abu's cartoon had confused me. I told a friend at the exhibition that I saw more clearly than ever before the utter worthlessness of sporting nationalism, and would therefore support England on the morrow.

I was a cricketing nationalist as a teenager, but over the years had become less partisan. I greatly admired the West Indian cricketers of the 1970s and 80s – Vivian Richards, Gordon Greenidge and Malcolm Marshall in particular – and the Australian masters of the 1990s, such as Shane Warne, Steve Waugh, and Glenn McGrath. I mostly still wanted India to win, but was not desolated if they lost, especially if this had been to a better or more skilful side. And I particularly deprecated the jingoism that was on display when India played Pakistan. The saddest moment of fifty years of live cricket watching remains the World Cup quarter-final of 1996, also played in Bangalore, when I was the only person in my stand (and possibly in the entire stadium) who applauded Javed Miandad when he walked off the ground for the last time as an international player.

I slept erratically on the night of 26/27 February 2011, juxtaposing, to Abu's cartoon, my own lifelong desire not to see the Indian cricket team humiliated. Juggling my emotions, I recalled that Neville Cardus had once written of how, as a boy, he had reconciled his admiration for the batsmanship of Victor Trumper with the desire to see England win. Before an Ashes Test, he would pray to God that he let his hero make a century – out of an Australian total of 127 all out! I now amended that to fit, and resolve, my own particular dilemma. What I wanted at the Chinnaswamy Stadium, I decided at 3 am, was for Sachin Tendulkar to score a hundred, and I didn't care who won or lost.

I got what I wanted, and in both respects. Tendulkar played a masterful, controlled innings, taking his time while Sehwag blazed away, and accelerating smoothly after his partner got out. I remember this century especially for the demolition of Graeme Swann (who he struck for three sixes) and for two glorious off-drives off James Anderson. His innings was superbly paced; being matched in this respect by Andrew Strauss, who scored an equally accomplished hundred in England's chase. The match ended in a rare tie.

III

Speaking of Sachin Tendulkar's batsmanship, Suresh Menon once wrote: 'Sachin is the one-stop shop of batsmanship. You could watch Sehwag for the straight drive, Dravid for the on-drive, Ganguly for the square cut, Laxman for the square drive, Dhoni for the lofted shots, and so on. Or you could go to Sachin for all of these.'

Sachin Tendulkar played all the shots, true, but he played some more authoritatively than others. The stroke that thrilled this particular *Sachinista* most was the back-foot force, when he would stand up on tiptoe and sublimely stroke Ambrose or Walsh or Akram or McGrath through the off-side for four. The faster they came the quicker they went, to the left or right of cover point. In both Test and one-day cricket, this shot was the one that showed him at his best. The straight drive came a close second, and next perhaps that glorious glide between mid-wicket and square-leg. For delicacy of touch, I also warmed to his late cut; for deftness of placement, to his paddle sweep.

For a full decade following his debut in 1989, Tendulkar was a purely *attacking* batsman. Coming in at, say, 10 for two, he would seek not to stabilise an innings but to wrest the game away from the opposition. This he did frequently, and in dazzling fashion, through slashing square cuts and pulls, and drives past the bowler and wide of mid-on. There was no shot he would not play, no form of bowling that in any way intimidated or even contained him.

Then, in or about 2001, Tendulkar began to slow down. He now ducked the short ball (previously he would have hooked it), and played spin bowlers from the crease. The back-foot force through cover that was his trademark became scarce. He still scored runs regularly, but mostly through the on-side, via dabs, sweeps, drives and the occasional pull.

We now know that this transformation in Tendulkar's game was due to a sore elbow. But while it lasted it appeared to be permanent; I even wrote at the time that 'the genius has become a grafter'. (My embarrassment at recalling this is tempered by the fact that some other writers were even more dismissive.) On the advice of a Bombay doctor, he rested his left hand completely

– he would not even, I am told, lift a coffee mug with it. The treatment worked, for as his elbow healed he recovered his fluency. The hook shot and the lofted drive were used sparingly, but his mastery of the off-side was once more revealed in all its splendour.

Of course, in becoming less of a dasher as he grew older, Tendulkar was merely emulating some great batsmen who had come before him. Jack Hobbs was a different player before and after World War I; Len Hutton a different player before and after World War II. Hobbs stopped playing the cut as his reflexes began to dim; Hutton chose to give up the hook. In their youth, both sought to dominate the bowling from start to finish; in their maturity, to focus rather on building and nurturing an innings.

I know of Hobbs and Hutton only at second hand, but two batsmen I saw decline before my own eyes were Vivian Richards and G R Viswanath. Viv, being a West Indian, simply would not recognise the advance of Anno Domini. So he continued to play as before, unfurling his strokes with a carefree abandon. But whereas he once had the reflexes and power to hit every bad ball and some good balls for four, now he was prone to error. However, he would not adapt. He would still want to score two boundaries an over. When he was in his pomp, he could keep going, and going; but now, with the eyes no longer so sure and the limbs no longer so supple, he would mistime a stroke or misjudge a ball's length and be caught. Between 1975 and 1985, one could count on Richards scoring centuries with a certain regularity. However, in these years of his career, circa 1988 to 1992, what we were more likely to get instead were cameos of thirty or forty.

Gundappa Viswanath adapted his game to age somewhat better than Richards. Once, he danced down the wicket to drive an off-spinner wide of mid-on; or, standing on tiptoe, forced a fast bowler past cover's left hand. But as he grew older, and fatter, and slower, he put away those more exciting (and also more hazardous) strokes. He now got his runs through his trademark square cut (usually played *behind* square) and the leg-side placement. No longer would he leave the crease to the spin bowler; no longer would he meet the fast bowler on the rise. A dashing strokeplayer had become an accumulator. The contrast was most visible in two innings he played in Tests in Madras: the 97 not out he stroked against the West Indies in January 1975; and the double-hundred he grafted against England seven years later. The first knock is still remembered by those who saw it; the second was forgotten within weeks.

The exception to this general rule was Viswanath's brother-in-law and fellow batting genius, Sunil Gavaskar. As he grew older, Gavaskar's range of strokes actually expanded. In the first part of his career he only drove along the ground; now, he was to be seen lifting spinners and even medium-pacers over mid-on. Like Hutton, Gavaskar had put away the hook shot; but when confronted with the West Indian pacemen of the 1980s, he brought it back, to good effect. One reason that Gavaskar could innovate as he did was that he had a superbly organised batting technique. His footwork and balance were immaculate. Since he was already perfectly in position, it was easy for him to go from stroking the ball between fielders to elevating it above them. Besides, unlike Vishy and Viv, Gavaskar took good care of his constitution. His reflexes did not decline as quickly; with his technique being what it was, he could go on playing his shots until the end of his career.

Like Vishy, Sachin had a tendency to put on weight; and he had a back problem to boot. As he grew stiffer and slower he changed his game. Now, he almost never came down the wicket to slow bowlers; instead, he chose to work them for ones and twos behind the wicket. Once a ferocious hooker and puller, he now preferred to get under every short ball sent down by bowlers fast, fast-medium, or even merely medium. In his heyday, his most thrilling – and effective – shots were hit on the rise, straight back along the ground, or either side of cover point. Now, however, Sachin could no longer trust himself to meet the ball on the rise; so he went back or forward and played the ball down in front of him.

In this, the second phase of his international career, Sachin remained a most highly valued member of the Indian team. For one thing, he still got runs, if not in quite the authoritative manner that he once made them. For another, his unparalleled experience and sharp cricketing brain were at hand to proffer advice to the Indian captain in Tests as well as one-day matches. Still, to those of us who followed his career from his first Test, the longer he played the more ambivalent we became. For a decade, and more, we were favoured with the fabulous treats of a genius; now we had to make do with the humdrum offerings of an (undoubtedly accomplished) craftsman.

I saw Tendulkar bat many times for India. But I never ever saw him bat for Mumbai. Other people were sorry about this, too. Once, shortly after Javagal Srinath retired from first-class cricket, I asked him whether he had any regrets. Only one, answered Sri – that while he had often bowled to Sachin in the nets, he had never done so in a Ranji match. The crazy, packed, schedule of international matches all through Tendulkar's career meant that he almost never got to play in the last stages of the Ranji Trophy. That was a shame. I saw Gavaskar bat against Prasanna and Chandrasekhar for Bombay against Karnataka; I would have given anything to have seen Sachin bat against Srinath and Kumble for Mumbai against Karnataka. I think that this did not – could not – happen might be one of Tendulkar's few cricketing regrets as well.

IV

Sachin Tendulkar made his international debut in 1989. His first years in Test cricket were played against a background of rising social conflict in India. The Mandal Commission Report, advocating affirmative action for intermediate castes, had sparked a series of clashes between different castes. The opening out of the Indian economy had provoked fears of rising inequality and joblessness. There was an insurgency in Kashmir, and continuing tension along the border in Pakistan. A right-wing Hindu revival was threatening the country's secular fabric. During the decade of the 1990s, thousands of people lost their lives in bloody riots between rival religious groups.

The social tension was accompanied by political instability – between 1989 and 1998, India was governed by no fewer than seven different prime ministers. It was in this atmosphere of hate, suspicion, fear and violence that Sachin Tendulkar scored his first hundreds in international cricket. The skill and versatility of his batsmanship made millions of Indians temporarily forget their everyday insecurities and come together to cheer their new hero.

There had been fine Indian batsmen before Tendulkar. Merchant and Hazare in the 1940s, and Gavaskar and Viswanath in the 1970s, were world-class players. Yet their game was based on technique and artistry, whereas Tendulkar exuded power and domination. He was a magnificent attacking batsman, who took the game to the bowlers. Although he was a little man, he stood up to the best fast bowlers of the day – South Africa's Allan Donald, Pakistan's Waqar Younis, West Indies' Curtly Ambrose, Australia's Glenn McGrath – hooking, cutting, and driving them with authority. Because he was a small man, his conquest of these fearsome foreigners made Indians marvel even more at his achievements.

163

Tendulkar would have been great in any age, yet he was lucky that his cricketing career coincided with the rise of satellite television, as well as with the growing importance of one-day cricket. The achievements of Gavaskar and Viswanath could only be admired by those in the cities. On the other hand, Tendulkar could be appreciated in small towns and villages too. Meanwhile, his style of batsmanship was extremely well suited to limited-overs cricket, which was rapidly replacing Test matches as the main form of the game in India (and beyond). There was also far more international cricket played nowadays. These factors all helped Tendulkar become more recognisable than any other cricketer of the past.

In the early years of his career, Tendulkar brought solace and consolation to a divided nation by the quality of his batsmanship. There were few credible role models elsewhere – the politicians were manipulative and corrupt, the film stars voyeuristic and exhibitionist, the entrepreneurs self-serving. By the end of the 1990s, however, he commanded attention by the sheer weight of his cricketing achievements. He was well on the way to becoming the most prolific batsman in the history of world cricket, scoring more runs and more centuries in both Test and one-day cricket than any other player. Indians love records; in this case, the fact that we are so miserable in other sports, and perform so pathetically at the Olympics, made us cling to Tendulkar all the more.

In living memory only Vivian Richards and Graeme Pollock had so dominated the best bowlers in the world. While they batted, Richards answered to the few million black people of the Caribbean, Pollock to the few million white people of South Africa. But Tendulkar now had placed on him the burdens of one-sixth of humanity; what's more, he had often to carry them alone. Richards and Pollock each embellished batting sides of staggering depth and consistency. One had Gordon Greenidge to bat before him and the likes of Clive Lloyd and Alvin

Kallicharan to follow. If the other got a duck, he returned to the pavilion in the assurance that Barry Richards or Eddie Barlow would get the runs needed by his side. However, while Indian batsmen excelled at home they were notoriously fragile abroad; given a bouncy wicket, they fell quicker than you could spell 'coalition government'. In the first seven or eight years of his career, Tendulkar batted in an overseas Test knowing that if he failed his side would fail too. (Later, Dravid, Sehwag and Laxman came to take some of the burden off him.)

In these years, Tendulkar knew not where he would play his next innings. He knew not whether his team-mates would bat more than a few balls each with him. He knew only that his bat had, willy-nilly, to make up for the fact that the United Nations authoritatively asserted that India was the 146th most developed nation in the world. That he was so marvellously cool about this was perhaps the most remarkable thing about him. Look into yourself, dear reader, and examine afresh how you react to a child who wails at night, to a computer that crashes when you are finishing a book, to an examination paper that is to be answered at eight o'clock the next morning. We routinely respond with anger or disbelief to the most trivial tests of character. Yet this man met with complete equanimity the intensely magnified and completely unfair expectations of a billion of his countrymen.

His adversaries knew not of these burdens. They saw only the cricketing genius, and rose to honour it. The compliment he might cherish most, it having come from a great contemporary, was offered at the end of a tournament in Sharjah in 1998. Here, Tendulkar hit centuries against the Australians in successive matches; the first hundred got India into the final, the second hundred helped them win it. At the end, Shane Warne walked around to the Indian dressing room to ask his tormentor to sign (left-handed) on his T shirt.

Even Englishmen, who are otherwise so parsimonious in praise of their opponents, unbent in the case of Tendulkar. After the

Princess Diana charity match in July 1998, Mike Atherton suggested that the authorities at Lord's be prepared to rename the W G Grace Gates. Eight years earlier, a greater England opener had borne testimony to the genius of Tendulkar. When Sachin batted at Headingley in the Test match of 1990, Sir Leonard Hutton told Freddie Trueman that he could not remember when he had last seen such quick and assured footwork. Trueman repeated the remark on the BBC, adding his own endorsement of Tendulkar's genius. This was the only known occasion on which either of those Yorkshiremen is known to have paid a compliment to an Indian. The next year the Bombay cricketer became the first overseas professional to be contracted to Yorkshire. A little brown boy had found his way into the hearts and chequebooks of the most insular and tight-fisted community in the universe.

V

In cricketing terms, Sachin Tendulkar defined the Age; indeed, he *was* the Age. In the history of the game there have been only three other cricketers who, in terms of skill and social impact, can be compared with him.

There was, to begin with, the bearded doctor William Gilbert Grace. Grace was the first batsman to play all round the wicket: as his friend and contemporary K S Ranjitsinhji pointed out, before WG batting was like a one-stringed lute, after him it became a many-chorded lyre. Grace could bat and he could bowl: he took more than two thousand first-class wickets. And he could field: usually at short point, looking down hard and meaningfully at the batsman. He was mammoth in size and personality, a vigorous, extroverted and often domineering character who was the best known Englishman of his time.

Once, when Grace's county was playing away from home, the ground's management put up a sign outside the gates: 'Admittance sixpence; a shilling if the Doctor is playing.' The next player for whom one could comfortably double the admittance fee was Donald George Bradman. He brought to the art of batsmanship a clinical and almost frightening efficiency. 'The glorious uncertainty of cricket,' claimed Neville Cardus, 'is not threatened by Bradman.' The Don remains the only cricketer to have an entire strategy worked out against him. The strategy was called Bodyline, and it was reckoned to have worked, since it brought down his batting average to a mere fifty-six.

On Bradman's tours of England, one Australian official was exclusively deputed to answer his letters. The Don never played cricket in India, but was adored here nevertheless. He retired in 1948, and five years later decided to make another visit to England, as a journalist. As it happens, his aircraft made an unscheduled stopover at Calcutta's Dum Dum airport. Word got around, somehow, and within minutes there were five thousand cricket-crazy Indians on the tarmac, screaming for him. Bradman hastily got into an Army jeep and took refuge in a barricaded building.

After Grace and Bradman came Garfield Sobers. He started out as a slow left-arm spinner, took to batting, and then also to swing bowling. All along he fielded superbly, in the slips or at short-leg. His great Pakistani contemporary, Hanif Mohammad, once claimed that 'God has sent Garry Sobers down to earth to play cricket'. He was, without doubt, the most accomplished and variously gifted man ever to grace this most graceful of games.

Sobers won matches with the bat, with the ball, and often-times with both bat and ball together. He broke a sheaf of records as well. Yet his impact would never be reckoned in quantitative terms alone. When, in the summer of 1966, he scored 722 runs in a Test series against England, and took twenty wickets and ten catches to boot, the novelist J B Priestley wrote that 'it was not only his feats with bat and ball that compelled my applause; it was his style and manner; the way he carried himself, the way he moved'.

Where Grace and Bradman were single-minded in their pursuit of success, Sobers did not appear to play to win; though his side often won nevertheless. His cricket and his personality were marked by charm and sparkle. The enjoyment was visible, and the sportsmanship self-evident. He was a creature of the 1960s, the cricketing counterpart of that other combination of fun and genius, the Beatles.

Sachin Tendulkar, however, was more like the Don, utterly focused on the job at hand. One would never see him, as one often saw Sobers, practise a golfing stroke in the field. Or, as one also often saw Sobers, in a nightclub at play's end. But we must not be judgemental; greatness has many avatars, and we must learn to cherish and equally respect all of them. Certainly no one since Bradman had quite such a range of strokes, quite such an ability to dominate attacks quick and subtle, on wickets dusty or green. Moreover, in social terms Tendulkar had to bear a burden the others could not even remotely contemplate having to carry. Grace was loved by fifteen million Englishmen. Bradman was idolised by ten million Australians, Sobers worshipped by a similar number of West Indians. But Sachin was answerable to a billion hyper-expectant and too-easily-dissatisfied Indians.

Future cricket historians will speak of the Age of Tendulkar, as we speak of the Age of Grace and the Age of Bradman and the Age of Sobers. What is particularly endearing is that these cricketers represented four different countries, in four separate continents. Yet, and this is what marks them out from everybody else, one never had to share the colour of their passport to revel in their greatness. J B Priestley naturally wanted the West Indies to lose, but, watching Sobers, 'admiration came seeping through the mud walls of partisanship'. Australians and South Africans, and even Pakistanis, have felt exactly the same way about Tendulkar.

VI

It is useful to remind ourselves that Sachin Tendulkar's cricketing achievements were not restricted to his batsmanship alone.

It is striking how effective, as bowlers, have been some of the game's greatest batsmen. Consider, for instance, Vivian Richards and Allan Border, who would be on anyone's shortlist of the finest batsmen in modern cricket history. Their bowling skills, by contrast, were meagre. Both pretended to be finger-spinners, but neither could (on a decent wicket) turn the ball more than an inch. Neither had a puzzling flight, or a well-concealed change of pace, or zip off the wicket. In sum, they each lacked all the attributes of a wicket-taking slow bowler. Yet the number of wickets both took (in Tests as well as one-day cricket) was quite out of proportion to the talents given them by the God of Bowlers. The explanation lies not in science but in psychology. For when they came on to bowl they brought with them their awesome reputations as batsmen, captains, and cricketers. The novice Test player, especially, would have his resolve tested by the sight of Richards or Border with the ball.

Something of this kind also explains Sachin Tendulkar's curious successes at the bowling crease. True, he could bowl the lot: inswing, outswing, off-break, leg-break, the googly. But he bowled them so slowly and with such lack of control that even a decent schoolboy batsman would back himself to safely milk him for four runs an over. That he got as many as two hundred wickets in international cricket was to be explained, I think, largely by his name and his iconic status.

In 1998, all the major cricketing countries came together to play a 'mini World Cup' in Bangladesh. When Brian Lara came up against Tendulkar in that tournament, he batted with paranoid care against a part-time bowler. That night Lara displayed a fear not of his opponent's innocuous off-breaks but of his own declining reputation. How would it look if Lara the batsman got out to Tendulkar the *bowler*?

In fact, unlike with his batting, Sachin's bowling actually improved with age. When he started out, he bowled dibbly-dobbly swingers with the new ball and off-spin with the old ball. However, around the turn of the millennium he turned to bowling wrist-spin instead. He had prodigious powers of turn, and bowled a decent googly too. In one-day matches, he would come on around the thirty-fifth over, when the batsman, seeking to accelerate, would find it hard to score boundaries against balls bowled from round the wicket and spinning around the stumps.

Sachin's wrist-spin also played a part in two famous Test victories. On the last day of the epic Calcutta Test of 2001, he got three wickets, all lbw. The left-handers Adam Gilchrist and Matthew Hayden were both done by leg-breaks. These were two fantastic strokeplayers, and Tendulkar must have relished getting them out, while surely cherishing even more his dismissal of Shane Warne, out to a googly he could not read. Three years later, when India won at Adelaide, Sachin dismissed Damien Martyn and Steve Waugh, two top-class batsmen caught at slip pushing forward to a leg-break that turned more than they thought it would (or could).

In his youth, Tendulkar fielded capably at slip. As he grew older he was normally placed at mid-on, where he was never fleet of foot but always had safe hands. Which fan who saw it will easily forget the remarkable, match-and-series winning catch he took, high over his head at long-on, to dismiss Inzamam-ul-Haq under the lights of the Gaddafi Stadium in Lahore?

Tendulkar was venerated by his fans, and much admired by his opponents as well. And he could always count on the frank adoration of his team-mates. Indian cricket was long marked by personal rivalries and parochial jealousies; if that seems now to be behind us, this was the handiwork of a generation of gifted and selfless cricketers, among them Kumble, Dravid, Laxman

and Ganguly – and Tendulkar. One image captures it all. A cake
was being cut to mark victory in a hard-fought one-day series in
Pakistan some years ago. The first slice was offered to the man of
the tournament, Yuvraj Singh, who immediately turned the plate
towards his hero and said, 'Pehlé Sachin bhai ko.' *The first one is
for our elder brother, Sachin.*

VII

Chapter Thirteen of C L R James' *Beyond a Boundary* begins like
this:

> A famous Liberal historian [G M Trevelyan] can write the
> social history of England in the nineteenth century, and two
> famous Socialists [Raymond Postgate and G D H Cole] can
> write what they declared to be the history of the common
> people of England, and between them never once mention
> the man who was the best-known Englishman of his time. I
> can no longer accept the system of values which could not
> find in these books a place for W G Grace.

I knew these words well – as well as many others in that book. I
was reminded of them when, shortly before the 1996 World
Cup, I was sent two bulky volumes, then recently published, on
the history of Bombay/Mumbai. Edited by two senior sociologists, and appearing under the imprimatur of the Oxford
University Press, they contained some thirty essays by leading
scholars of the city and the region, covering its politics, economics, social and cultural life, community and religious features,
and more. Cricket went entirely unmentioned, as did the most
famous Indian cricketer, who was also the most famous
Mumbaikar, of our time. But, unlike C L R James, I was neither
surprised nor outraged. I knew that Indian academics as well as

academics of India were prone to miss the social and cultural importance of cricket and cricketers.

Shortly after these books were published, something of altogether greater significance happened in Mumbai; the Wankhede Stadium was furbished with floodlights. The first match played under these lights was between India and Australia in the early stage of the World Cup. Australia batted first, and powered by a silky century by Mark Waugh reached an (at the time) impressive total of 258. Sachin was normally more comfortable batting first than chasing; but, as so often, the Australians brought out the best in him. Opening the innings he played a series of searing shots all around the ground. It was thrilling to watch, on television; and must have been an absolute feast for those fortunate to be at the stadium. When Tendulkar had got to 90 off 84 he went down the wicket to Mark Waugh, who was bowling his off-breaks. Waugh, seeing him come, bowled it wide, to have him easily stumped.

India went on to lose that match by 16 runs. They qualified for the knockout rounds, however, where they beat Pakistan in Bangalore before being humiliated by Sri Lanka in Calcutta. All through the tournament the screaming crowds and the shrieking newspaper headlines had told us that Sachin would surely bring the Cup home, playing at home.

This was Tendulkar's second World Cup. He played a third, a fourth, and a fifth, scoring reasonably each time. However, the trophy still eluded him, and his team. Finally, on his sixth attempt in 2011, India won its second World Cup. Sachin had a couple of decent outings, although he failed in the final, played at the Wankhede. When the match and championship were won, Virat Kohli and Yusuf Pathan carried their (our) hero on their shoulders for a victory lap, for (as they said) having carried Indian cricket on his shoulders for twenty-one years prior to that.

I myself thought Tendulkar should have quit the game after that World Cup victory. His two great predecessors in the Bombay School of Batsmanship had retired when at the top of their form: Vijay Merchant after scoring a Test century, Sunil Gavaskar after an excellent World Cup tournament in 1987. Once he was done with cricket, Merchant turned to running his textile business and to working for the rights of the disabled. Once he had hung up his bat, Gavaskar went from the playing arena to the commentary box. I knew that Tendulkar did not have a family firm to fall back upon, nor the command over language to comment publicly on the game. But I still thought the right thing for him, and us, was for him to get out at the top.

Instead he stayed on, and on. He still occasionally scored fifties and more, but was manifestly not the batsman he once was. In September 2012, I saw him play at Bangalore against New Zealand, where he was bowled for a low score in the first innings. As he got out, I heard a man in the row behind me say: 'Time to think of retirement.' This was a heartlessly cruel remark, especially in Bangalore, where India's greatest batsman had played some magical innings over the years.

There was worse to come. In the second innings, when Sachin scratched around for an hour before being bowled again, the murmurings became louder. More people in the pavilion began voicing thoughts unthinkable a year previously, when, after India's World Cup victory, there was a widespread demand for Sachin to be immediately conferred with the country's highest civilian honour, the Bharat Ratna.

Later that year, India played England. During the Mumbai Test, Sachin got out for 8 in each innings, both times to Monty Panesar, a slow left-armer who would scarcely have troubled him at all even two or three years previously. When he was dismissed for the second time he was booed – and this was his Mumbai. Surely he should retire now? He would not. He stayed around for another year, until he had played his 200th Test match, a record he (and his admirers) hoped would stand for all time.

It must be said at once that Indians, and Indian males especially, are not very good at retirement. Perhaps the example of

Bhishma Pitamah, the great greybeard in the epic *Mahabharata*, is too compelling. Bhishma went into battle at a very advanced age, thus to provide a mythical justification for warriors and rulers down the ages to keep going for ever too. In staying on far too long, Sachin Tendulkar was in the company of, among other famous and powerful Indians, the dairying genius Verghese Kurien, the corporate head Ratan Tata, and the Prime Ministers Jawaharlal Nehru and Manmohan Singh.

But one still wishes that Tendulkar had taken his cues from Merchant and Gavaskar instead. It was not just that he kept going beyond his prime, but that in his (as it were) cricketing dotage he took the cricketing public for granted.

I have spoken of the century that I saw Sachin score in Bangalore against England in March 2011. This was his 98th hundred in international cricket. Later in the same World Cup he scored his 99th, against South Africa at Nagpur. Now he, and a billion others, hoped that the century of centuries would come in the World Cup final. It did not, although India won the championship anyway.

Later in 2011, India were due to tour the West Indies and then England. Tendulkar skipped the first tour. I cannot now remember what the official excuse or reason was, but we all suspected it was because, having failed to score his 100th hundred in a World Cup final, he wanted to score it at the Home of Cricket. The first Test of the England series was to be played at Lord's. In the event Tendulkar failed in the Lord's Test, and did not get to the three-figure mark in the rest of the series either. He then toured Australia, where in the four Tests of the series he got a couple of fifties, but no hundreds.

A person less crazy for records would have retired. Not Tendulkar. Finally, in March 2012, he scored his 100th hundred, a full year after his 99th. It came in a one-day match against Bangladesh, and arrived so slowly that despite Tendulkar scoring a century, his team lost.

Surely now he would retire? No, for there was yet another record to be broken. In early December, with the series against England and New Zealand having concluded, Tendulkar had played a small matter of 198 Tests. Our next set of scheduled Tests was against South Africa, in South Africa. But the man known as India's greatest ever batsman did not now want to face Dale Steyn and Morne Morkel on the fast and seaming wickets of their country. So hastily, greedily, the desperately broke West Indies Cricket Board was bribed with two Tests in India, the second of which, played naturally in Mumbai, was to be Tendulkar's 200th in all. It was altogether a disgrace, whose one saving grace was that even on a slow wicket against a mediocre attack, the hometown hero could not, would not, score a century in his last international innings.

VIII

It would not do to end this tribute on a sour note. So let me in conclusion recall two proposals I made which involved Sachin Tendulkar. In February 2005, the Indian Hockey Federation organised its first Premier Hockey League championship. The Hyderabad Sultans defeated Sher-e-Jullundar to win the final, played at the Gachibowli Stadium in Hyderabad. The home side's heroes included two Pakistanis: the defender (and drag-flick specialist) Sohail Abbas and the goalkeeper Ahmed Alam. After the match, the players and their supporters were on top of the world; and in Ahmed Alam's case, on top of the goalposts, which he climbed as soon as the final whistle blew.

After the tournament had ended I wrote these paragraphs in the *Telegraph* of Calcutta:

I think that the success in this respect of the Premier Hockey League calls for emulation by other sports, especially that South Asian sport *par excellence*, cricket. Some years ago the novelist Mukul Kesavan suggested that Test and one-day matches between nations, the staple of international cricket, be supplemented by an inter-city tournament. The time has come to revive that suggestion. Kesavan had a global tournament in mind, but we might begin with South Asia alone. And begin on a modest scale, with a week of Twenty-Twenty matches played alternately in India, Pakistan, Bangladesh and Sri Lanka, between teams representing the cities of those countries. Each side would be composed, as are football teams in Europe, of a mix of locals and outsiders.

The possibilities are intriguing. Think of Sachin Tendulkar playing (under contract) for Karachi, a port city not dissimilar in character and culture to his native Mumbai. Or of Virender Sehwag turning out for Multan, with that city's most famous batsman, Inzamam-ul-Haq, appearing for Delhi. Sourav Ganguly will of course captain Dhaka, and Muttiah Muralitharan might play for (and even captain) Jaffna.

I wonder if either Subhas Chandra or Lalit Modi (or both) read these words. At any rate, not long afterwards Chandra started his Indian Cricket League, shortly superseded by Modi's Indian Premier League. This was unfortunately restricted to teams and cities in India alone. Tendulkar played for the Mumbai Indians, not the Karachi Kavaliers as I had once fondly hoped. Some Pakistani cricketers did play in the inaugural IPL; but then, after the terror attack in Mumbai in November 2008, Pakistanis were barred from the tournament altogether.

After the Mumbai attack, bilateral series between India and Pakistan were put on hold. However, in the winter of 2012–13 the two sides played three one-day matches in India. They were well-attended as well as incident-free, whereupon the chairman of the Pakistan Cricket Board, Zaka Ashraf, suggested that the two countries play each other regularly, for what might be called the 'Jinnah–Gandhi' Trophy.

Reading of this proposal, I wrote another column in the *Telegraph*. If peace prevailed, I said, then 'we may indeed push for regular tours between the two sides'. However, I added: 'To the idea of naming it for the Fathers of their Nations there are two serious objections. One is cricketing – neither Gandhi nor Jinnah really had much interest in the sport. The other is political – namely, whose name should come first?'

So I considered other names such a trophy could carry. Perhaps the Lata Mangeshkar–Noor Jehan Trophy, to take account of the other great popular passion of the two nations, films and more particularly film music? Or the Iqbal–Tagore Trophy, to honour two great writers?

On reflection, I concluded that it seemed best to name a cricketing trophy after a cricketer. Since there existed the Border–Gavaskar Trophy (for Australia–India series) and the Warne–Muralitharan Trophy (for Australia–Sri Lanka series), one could perhaps think of an 'Imran Khan–Kapil Dev Trophy', named after two great all-rounders. But, since Imran was now a controversial political figure in Pakistan, I rejected this idea too, urging that we think instead of naming this trophy after a single cricketer alone. There were precedents – such as the Frank Worrell Trophy for Australia–West Indies contests, and the Basil D'Oliveira Trophy for England–South Africa series.

Following this model, I argued that Test series between India and Pakistan should henceforth be played for the 'Sachin Tendulkar Trophy'. For no man had quite defined Indo–Pak cricket in the way that he did. Or for so long – he first played Pakistan in a Test match in 1989, while he last played against Pakistan in the World Cup semi-final of March 2011. For twenty-two years, in all forms of the game and in all venues, how much Sachin scored and when he got out often decided which way the match would go. Some of his greatest innings were played against Pakistan – several in a losing cause, as in that epic hundred in Madras, when, after winning by a mere 13 runs, Wasim Akram and his team had the Chepauk crowd rise to them.

The fans and (even more) the cricketers of Pakistan venerated Sachin Tendulkar. I remember the late Raj Singh Dungarpur telling me of how, at a reception at Buckingham Palace during the 1999 World Cup, the young Pakistani players merely wanted to be in the presence of Sachin, to touch his blazer and be photographed with him. To name this trophy after Tendulkar would be a proper tribute to a truly great player, whose appeal so effortlessly transcended the barriers of nation and generation.

Having made this suggestion, I acknowledged however that

> Some jingoistic Pakistanis might cavil at the trophy being named after an Indian player alone. To them I offer this answer – after Mumbai 2008, it took great magnanimity and far-sightedness for India to resume cricket ties with Pakistan at all. If you want to separate cricket from politics, and if you want regular ties between the two countries, then a Tendulkar Trophy may be the most pragmatic and most workable solution. Besides, Sachin is a great sportsman, who … has always conducted himself with dignity and self-effacement, as did Worrell and D'Oliveira in their time. If Australians and South Africans can put cricket above partisanship I trust the Pakistanis can, too.

In sporting terms the proposal was, I think, unexceptionable. However, with a right-wing Hindutva regime now in power in India, and Pakistan in political turmoil, there is at present little prospect of cricketing ties between the two countries being resumed any time soon. My own hope is that we can have a Tendulkar Trophy played for, if not in my lifetime, at least in Sachin's.

7

A Hindu's Pantheon

I

The late Verrier Elwin, a son of a British Bishop who became one of India's great pioneering anthropologists, was once asked to sum up the difference between Hinduism and Christianity. He said that whereas the Christian believed more in God, the Hindu believed in more Gods.

Theologians shall dispute this, but it always seemed to me that Elwin's witticism nicely captured the key difference between the Indian cricket lover and the foreign one. For, while the Englishman of my age had eyes mostly for Ian Botham, the Australian for Allan Border and the Pakistani for Imran Khan, the Indian, inclusive in his sympathies and generous to a fault, would worship those three great *firangis* alongside his own Sunil Gavaskar and Kapil Dev.

Growing up, I followed, and supported, FUCC, Karnataka, and India, but as a good Hindu my pantheon was capacious enough to include people who played for clubs and states and countries other than my own. As a boy, long before I had been to a Test match, which was also long before live television entered Indian homes, I learnt to admire – or worship – foreign cricketers by reading or hearing about them.

My first *firangi* hero was the Australian Keith Miller, whose *Cricket Crossfire*, bought for me by my father from a shop on Dehradun's Rajpur Road, was probably the first book (of any

179

kind) that I ever read from cover to cover. Miller's affection for India and Indians shone through. He had first come here in 1945 with an Australian Services side, made up of cricketers who had fought in the war. In England, this Aussie side had spread joy and cheer, their matches at Lord's and elsewhere signalling the end of death and deprivation. In India, too, they received a rapturous welcome, for these men were warm and approachable, not stand-offish like the British Tommies.

T G Vaidyanathan, who saw the Australian Servicemen play in Madras, always insisted that Keith Miller was the 'best looking cricketer, *ever*'. Before the war, Miller had been marked out as a rising young man of Australian cricket, a batsman who had scored a hundred against the great leg-spinner Clarrie Grimmett before he had turned twenty. In this Services side he also doubled up as new-ball bowler, taking to the role only after A G Cheetham, the speedster originally selected, went home. But on Indian wickets he wisely went back to his first love. Like the great Victor Trumper he did not always carry his own kit, and was prone to picking up the first bat he saw lying around. Before he went to the crease in the Calcutta 'Test', Miller picked up a new bat belonging to his mate Dick Whittington, saying, 'I promise I'll be careful.' Three of the first four balls he faced, bowled by the miserly Vinoo Mankad, were deposited into a lily pond that lay just beyond the stand at long-on. It was the longest over ever bowled in Eden Gardens. Miller finished with 82, but so strained his back with the effort that he did not bowl fast again on tour.

Miller's achievements were considerable, but again, it was *how* he played the game that made an impression on Indians. He was not obsessed with records, one reason he did not always get along with Don Bradman. During the 1948 Australian tour of England, the first county side to claim all ten wickets against the visitors were Essex. They dismissed Bradman's side for 721, the runs scored in a single day. The captain himself made 187, but Miller deliberately played over his first ball, and was bowled. To bully second-raters on a flat track was not his way.

In *Cricket Crossfire* Miller wrote with admiration of Mankad, Mushtaq Ali, C S Nayudu and the other Indians he played against. He wrote also of how, in 1948, when the ship carrying the Australian touring side to England docked at Bombay, Vijay Merchant invited Don Bradman for dinner at his home. The Australian captain declined the invitation, which his compatriot thought churlish. These were the words from Miller's book as I remember them: 'The great Indian opening batsman swallowed his pride and came to see Bradman aboard our ship.'

Miller played again in India in 1956, this time as part of an official Test side. He had to sit out the Madras Test due to injury. Watching Vijay Manjrekar square cut Ray Lindwall for two successive fours, Miller told the journalist sitting next to him: 'Those were beautiful shots. I wish I was bowling to him.' Until the end he retained a deep affection for the people and cricketers of the subcontinent. In 1976, Miller accepted an invitation to play in a series of matches in Pakistan organised as part of the birth centenary celebrations of Mohammed Ali Jinnah. His friends thought he was daft, for it was twenty years since he had retired from the game. Miller's answer showed the kind of man he was. He told his friends that four current Australian cricketers had been invited, but all refused, apparently because the terms were not attractive enough. Miller felt that he had to go, for otherwise his country would be unrepresented. He went to Pakistan and played for free, but with a borrowed bat.

The first Australian team I have aural memories of is Bill Lawry's side of 1969–70. Like their predecessors they brought plenty of beer with them; Lawry's men were, it seems, so suspicious of Indian water that they even used the booze to brush their teeth. The captain was described by Rajan Bala, in the Calcutta *Statesman*, as 'tough, tenacious and taciturn'. (That is how I remember him, too, although my son knows him only as a loquacious character on Channel Nine, yelling 'he's got him' or 'it's out of here'.) This was a side with batsmen who hit hard and bowlers who bowled fast, as Australians are expected to.

The first Australian side I actually saw play came ten years later. It was a team depleted by the chequebook of Kerry Packer, and was to lose the series, 2–0, to an Indian side led by Sunil Gavaskar. I witnessed snatches of the Bangalore Test, a match ruined by rain. Players of world class were Kim Hughes, a batsman with a lovely flowing style, particularly off the front foot, and the fast bowler Rodney Hogg. Hogg had serious no-ball problems in Bangalore, being called fifteen times in one session. Hughes switched him around afterwards, but then the other umpire no-balled Hogg three times in one over. The fast bowler sent the stumps flying with a kick and departed the field in anticipation of being ordered off it.*

Also in the side that toured India in 1979 was Allan Border, a man so certain of his abilities that he registered as a 'professional' with the Australian Cricket Board before he became a Test cricketer. In Bangalore, Border scored a fluent forty-odd. When he hit Kapil Dev past cover point for four, I heard a man behind me say, in Tamil, 'Harvey maadri adchaa.' *He played that stroke just as Neil Harvey once did.* Certainly he had Harvey's footwork and his cracking shot through the off-side, half-cut, half-drive, lighting up the arc between backward point and extra-cover. He might even have been the better all-round batsman. And unlike Harvey, who had to play a devoted second

---

* Instead of agreeing to bowl from the other end, Hogg should have followed the example of his compatriot Ernie McCormick. On the first morning of the first match of the 1938 Australian tour of England, played at Worcester, McCormick was no-balled eighteen times. After lunch his captain, Don Bradman, asked if he would like to be switched around. 'No. I"ll bowl from the same end,' answered Ernie, 'the umpire's hoarse.'

fiddle to Richie Benaud, Border was to lead his country in a staggering number of 93 Test matches. Indeed, the subcontinent was the making of him as captain, when in 1987 he led a team of untried youngsters to victory in the World Cup, thus beginning Australia's march back to the top of world cricket. The previous year his bold declaration in Madras had set up the second tied Test. The hero of Chepauk, Dean Jones, had been motivated to play his eight-hour innings by a chat before the match with his captain, when over a bottle of lemonade (!) they discussed how Jones should take over the pivotal number three position.

I watched a lot of Australian cricket and cricketers in the 1990s, both live and on television. I admired the batsmanship of the Waugh brothers and, even more, of Ricky Ponting. No man has strode so purposefully to the crease, and no batsman – not even Lara or Tendulkar – so quickly established his presence there. He liked to begin with boundaries – cuts and hooks for choice. The faster the bowler, the quicker the ball went to the boundary. He was lightning quick on his feet while batting, between the wickets, and in the field. He was fantastic in the slips, and brilliant at cover and mid-wicket too.

However, Miller apart, my favourite Australian cricketers were googly bowlers. In school and college, I devoured books by and about Arthur Mailey, Bill O'Reilly, and Clarrie Grimmett, and in middle age had the good fortune of watching a great deal of their most famous successor, a man whom the *Oxford Companion to Australian Cricket* claimed had 'captured the imagination of the Australian public and had a greater impact on Australian cricket' than any player since Don Bradman. But even Bradman was not the subject of a study by two Cambridge scientists. These researchers, with the unlikely names of Loof Lirpa and Heinz Bohnen, concluded that Shane Warne's success was a consequence of the ball 'spinning backwards around its own axis a certain number of times faster than it is travelling forward'. The 'ratio of spin to forward velocity' for Warne's deliveries averaged 56.86, well above the mean.*

How, one wonders, would the late Bill O'Reilly have responded to this exegesis of the wrist-spinner's art? Stuff the science, he would have said, and return to the basics. What mattered about Warne was not his forward or backward velocity, but the curving arc to his flight, his immaculate control, his sharp-turning leg-break, his whizzing flipper, and, to cap it all, his big-match temperament. This was a leg-spinner whose captain would bring on to bowl in the last over of a match with two wickets to get and four runs to play with.

Warne had an outstanding record against all countries except India. When he came to the subcontinent in 1996, for the World Cup, it was to prove, to himself as much as to others, that he was in all conditions the best bowler in contemporary cricket. Certainly there were some Indians who greatly looked forward to seeing him bowl. One morning at Jaipur, when Warne warmed up before the match against the West Indies, a short, stocky, middle-aged man walked across the Sawai Man Singh Stadium to shake his hand and say, 'Son, you have a great talent. I hope you keep bowling for years to come.' Warne was foxed until Ian Chappell, who was standing alongside, introduced the new fan. 'Shane, you are speaking to Erapalli Prasanna,' said Chappell, 'the greatest slow bowler of *my* generation.'

In March 1998, Australia came to play a three-Test series in India. The papers billed it as a *mano a mano*, Tendulkar versus Warne, and as it happened in the first match the tourists played, against Mumbai, Tendulkar scored a double-hundred and Warne took none for eighty-odd. Then in the first innings of the first Test, at Chepauk, Tendulkar hit Warne for one four but was caught at slip off the next ball. Was the bowler hiding something in the warm-up game? When the home side batted again, seventy

---

* As reported in the *Asian Age*, 5 April 1998.

runs behind, Tendulkar played what may be the finest attacking innings by an Indian in the annals of Test cricket. (I say this on the basis of what I read, for I was ten thousand miles away at the time, spending a term at a university in California.) He scored 155 in four-and-a-half hours, with twenty fours and four sixes, two of these off Warne, one a cross-batted swat over mid-wicket, the other orthodox enough, over extra-cover. In the second Test, played at Eden Gardens, the Bombay Blaster hit 79 off 86 balls, and his mates Azharuddin (163) and Nayjot Sidhu (97) also hit powerfully in an Indian score of 633 for five declared. Warne's final figures were 47–4–147–0, by some distance his worst ever.*

The batsmen of the subcontinent, one might say, put the Indian sign on Shane Warne. They could read the bowler from the hand, where sundry Englishmen, West Indians, South Africans and New Zealanders apparently could not. Where *firangi* batsmen played Warne with painful and generally fatal care from the crease, Indians would dance down the wicket and drive him through the covers or wide of mid-on. Because of their superior understanding of the wrist-spinner's art, they also made good (but to the bowler deeply frustrating) use of the pads. To a Warne ball flighted just outside off-stump, Michael Atherton or Daryll Cullinan would play tentatively forward, for they could not be certain that it was not the straighter one or zooter. The same delivery would be kicked away by Tendulkar or Laxman, knowing well enough that it was a leg-break. Where one kind of batsman would edge this ball to slip and depart, the other kind would prepare for the next one, and perhaps hit it for four.

For all his lack of success in India, and against Indians, I had plenty of time for Warne. He was a fabulous bowler, and so was that other Aussie wrist-spinner, Stuart MacGill. Sadly, whereas O'Reilly and Grimmett won Test matches and Test series

---

* Almost as bad were his figures in his first ever Test, at Sydney, also against India: 45–7–150–1.

playing together, the selectors of Warne's time picked MacGill only when playing on rank turners. In 2005, for instance, MacGill toured England without playing a single Test. As it happened, I was in London at the time of the last Test, which was played at The Oval. I did not try to get a ticket or press pass – and would probably have got nowhere if I had. But the night before the Test, I had dinner with Australia's leading cricket writer, Gideon Haigh. I asked him why MacGill had been so comprehensively sidelined. Surely now, with his side 2–1 down in the series, and the Ashes at stake, he would be picked for tomorrow's Test? Haigh shook his head. The Australians, he said, would stick to their old policy of picking three seamers and one spinner.

But the third seamer had been found seriously wanting, I answered. In any case, with Warne and Brett Lee batting so well down the order, they could drop a batsman. Playing three seamers and two spinners made sense, especially as this Test simply had to be won. Haigh shook his head once more. The Aussie brains trust, he said, believed in choosing MacGill only on his home ground, Sydney, or when Warne was unfit or banned.

Stuart MacGill was not in the playing XI for any of the five Tests of the 2005 Ashes series. The profound unwisdom of that policy was made manifest later in 2005, when a 'Super Test' was played between Australia and a World XI. For it was MacGill who dismissed, in both innings of this Super Test, England's most destructive batsman in the Ashes series, Andrew Flintoff, who holed out in the deep, beaten in the flight each time. English batsmen are notoriously fallible against high-quality leg-break bowling. How many wickets might MacGill have got if he had played in England in 2005, instead of the palpably off-colour Gillespie or the manifestly ageing Kasprowicz?

Shane Warne was a genius, Stuart MacGill an artist. No wrist-spinner in the history of the game had a cooler temperament than Warne, or better control either. His variations were many and subtle. MacGill was more typical of the orthodox leg-break bowler – he bowled many wicket-taking balls, but also his fair share of full-tosses and long-hops. And he was fallible; while he could run through a side, if a batsman with quick feet and sure hands got after him he could rather quickly go to pieces as well.

At one stage in this Super Test of 2005, MacGill and Warne were bowling in tandem. It was a sight that demanded that all else be put on hold. I stayed stuck to my sofa, until I heard Michael Holding say to me (and to a million others): 'Notice that where Warne's line is leg-stump, MacGill bowls on off-stump and outside. This is because he turns the ball much less than Warne.' Holding is a commentator I otherwise admire; this, however, was a serious lapse, emanating from the fact that he was a fast bowler himself, who played for a side that only had other fast bowlers.

Actually, when Holding began his Test career the peerless Lance Gibbs was still playing for the Windies. But Gibbs was a finger-spinner. Perhaps Holding's only playing experience of leg-spinners was a few Tests against Pakistan, which at the time had both Mushtaq Mohammed and Abdul Qadir. But since he retired, and took to television commentary, he had seen much of this art at close quarters – as purveyed by Warne, Anil Kumble, Paul Strang, Mushtaq Ahmed, and others.

There were three reasons why MacGill's line was more off-stump than Warne's. First, because of his higher action Warne got more in-drift, directing his delivery towards leg-stump, there to land and abruptly spin away in the other direction. Second, MacGill flighted the ball more, seeking to draw the batsman out of the crease to drive, thus to edge to slip, or mistime to cover, or miss altogether and be stumped. Third, unlike Warne, MacGill had a fabulous googly, which made an off-stump line so much more appealing. After being served a succession of leg-breaks, the batsman deceived by a wrong-un was then more likely to be bowled or leg-before-wicket than if the regular 'line' was, as in Warne's case, towards leg-stump.

When I heard Holding say what he did, I was tempted to get up and chuck the sofa at the screen. Then I checked myself; fast bowlers will think like fast bowlers, I told myself, let me simply shut my ears and watch. If this is how I felt, imagine the feelings of the man sitting next to Holding in the commentator's box. This was none other than Richie Benaud, Mr Cricket himself, and in his own playing days a not inconsiderable exponent of the once international art of leg-break bowling.

It took Richie Benaud forty-eight hours to respond. In the second innings Warne and MacGill were bowling together again. This time, the dominant voice over the box was that of an Indian commentator, who chatted on, and on. When he allowed Benaud to get in a word edgeways, Richie simply said: 'MacGill is a HUGE spinner of the ball.'

In a long interview the day this Super Test ended, Anil Kumble expressed his surprise at MacGill sitting out the Ashes summer in England. 'He is a very fine bowler,' said Anil. 'And very different from Warne. If he had played the Tests in England, the Ashes would still have been with Australia.' This was not mere trade union chummery, but the honest appreciation of a fellow artist.

II

The first West Indian cricketer to be greatly admired in India was Frank Worrell, even though he never played a Test match in this country. He was not part of the West Indies touring side of 1948–9 because of a dispute over terms (the authorities wanted him to stop spending his summers playing League cricket in England.) Ten years later, when the West Indies came back, he was not there either. The reason given this time was that Worrell was busy finishing a degree at Manchester University, but it is more likely that he opted out after Gerry Alexander was appointed captain. (Not that he had anything against Alexander personally, but the point had to be made – the best and most experienced cricketer in the side should lead it, regardless of the shade of his skin.)

While Worrell never represented his country in a Test match in India, he came with the three Commonwealth sides that toured the subcontinent between 1949 and 1954, taking catches, claiming wickets, scoring runs, runs, runs. He himself counted as one of the best innings of his life the unbeaten 223 he hit in Kanpur, in the fourth unofficial 'Test' of the 1949–50 series. The runs were made on a surface he was not used to, coir matting, and against Hiralal Gaekwad and Ghulam Ahmed, two real devils on the mat. In the next 'Test' in Madras, the West Indian scored 161 in another exhibition of classical batsmanship. The Indian captain, Vijay Hazare, wrote later that 'watching Worrell perform always gives one mixed feelings. On the one hand with every minute he becomes a thorn in the flesh of the fielding side. But even when smarting under the blows one cannot but admire his artistry.' In 1950–1, Worrell again scored a century at Kanpur. On this visit he was also captain for three of the Tests, standing in for the forty-five-year-old Englishman, Les Ames. His side won the series, and Worrell had demonstrated that white men could play under a black leader with no detriment to performance or ability. Indians were already convinced of this, but it took another ten years for the message to finally reach the West Indies.

'And off the field, what a man!' wrote Vijay Hazare of Frank Worrell. 'Affable, suave and courteous, Worrell was always good company. Always immaculately turned out, he was ready to enjoy a chat and a drink with anyone (even those like me who drank nothing stronger than a cup of tea). Though he possessed strong views on many subjects he talked without giving offence.'

Countless Indians who did not have the good fortune to play against him or speak to him likewise worshipped Frank Worrell, both for his cricket and for his character. I knew that from many people, my uncle Durai onwards; and this was recently confirmed afresh during a visit to Madurai, when a veteran Gandhian, knowing of my non-Gandhian interests, presented me with what must surely be the only cricket book ever promoted by a Gandhian organisation. This was R Perumal's *Cricketing Reminscences*, published by Sarvodaya Ilakkiya Pannai, Madurai, in 1992. The author of this book was a university cricketer in his youth. In the mid-1960s, when he was Registrar of Madurai Kamaraj University, he hosted another lapsed cricketer, the visiting Rector of the University of the West Indies, Sir Frank Worrell. He met Worrell at Madurai airport and took him for a tour of the University. As he recalled, 'Sir Frank was an engaging conversationalist. He was well read and he held his own with the professors of the university. He conversed on a wide range of topics and had a happy knack of putting everyone at ease.'

Following these meetings, Registrar Perumal took Rector Worrell to the famous Meenakshi temple. Afterwards they had dinner at a local eatery, the otherwise carnivorous host tucking in with relish to the dosai and sambar. A room had been booked for Worrell at the well-appointed guest house run by the uncrowned Kings of Madurai, the TVS family; but the cricketer had made his own plans for the night. He had chosen to stay at the modest home of his sporting mate N Kannayiram, a fast bowler who had toured the West Indies with the Indian team in the early 1950s. As Perumal wrote, 'in spite of my earnest entreaties Sir Frank insisted on going to Kannayiram's house after dinner and I had no alternative but to agree. That was Sir Frank all over. Friendship to him was all that mattered.'

In Worrell's own mind the subcontinent would always have a special place. When he died in March 1967, aged only forty-two, he was buried on the campus of the University of the West Indies. The chosen site overlooked the cricket ground on one side, the sea on the other. I have seen, somewhere, a picture of the tombstone. Here lies buried, it says, 'Sir Frank Mortimer Maglinne Worrell, West Indies Cricketer.' Look closer, and between the name and the profession one can read, in smaller print, 'BA (Manchester); LLD (Punjab).' One degree acquired through diligent study, the other bestowed upon him in recognition of his contributions to sport and to humanity. Lancashire, North India, the Caribbean: of which other cricketer shall it be said that he was revered in places so widely separated by culture and geography?*

The greatest West Indian cricketer was Garfield Sobers. I am too young to have watched Sobers in the flesh, a continuing regret. In 1966 I was eight, not old enough to be sent to watch his team play in Delhi, a city one hundred and fifty miles from where I then lived. But I saw him now and again in the *Sport and Pastime*, photos of him cutting and sweeping and hooking and driving. Also one of him in Hyderabad, in mufti, a forkful of biryani in his left hand, saying – so the caption ran – '*Maan*, this is great stuff.' Next to Sobers stood the dimunitive Anjou Mahendru, a Bollywood starlet he was briefly engaged to. Some thirty years later I saw them together again, in the stands at Sharjah. Anjou was at first sitting with Pammi Gavaskar, a row behind Sir Garfield, as he now was. Possibly at Mrs Gavaskar's urgings, Anjou moved over to the row ahead. The Indian cameraman focused on them but the results were not encouraging. Sir Garfield looked determinedly at the field of play, never at the lady sitting beside him.

---

* In February 2019 I was in Calcutta, where I saw several posters put up for 'Sir Frank Worrell Blood Donation Day'. I made some enquiries. Back in 1962, on a tour of the West Indies, the captain of the Indian team, Nari Contractor, had his skull cracked open by a bouncer. His life was saved by Caribbean doctors, aided by donations of blood from, among others, Frank Worrell. For many years now, the Foundation Day of the Cricket Association of Bengal (which falls in February) has seen blood donation camps organised in memory of Worrell, in a moving tribute from the citizens of Calcutta to this best-loved of foreign cricketers.

On his first tour of India, in 1958–9, Sobers hit three hundreds in the Tests, at Bombay, Calcutta and Kanpur respectively. Eight years later he scored none, resting content with five half-centuries in five innings. In Bombay the tourists were 90 for four chasing 191, the wickets all falling to B S Chandrasekhar. After lunch Sobers came in to join Clive Lloyd, playing in his first Test. If one of them went the tail would be exposed. Sobers now told Lloyd to attack Chandra, by playing him as a googly bowler and driving him through the off-side on the rise. With the captain showing the way the pair added a hundred runs in an hour-and-a-quarter, and the match was won. As they walked off, Lloyd thanked Sobers for his advice. I was doing it for myself, came the reply, for I had to get to the Mahalaxmi race course – I have good tips for the four o'clock and the four-thirty.

Sadly, none of Sobers' Indian innings have been captured on film. My own best views of Sobers the batsman lie in two films shot Down Under, sent to the Australian High Commission in New Delhi, and shown by me to the students of St Stephen's College every year between 1974 and 1979. The first film, somewhat indistinct, is of the Brisbane tied Test, and has shots of Sobers in his innings of 132. The second film, of altogether superior quality, highlights his 254 for the Rest of the World against Australia at Melbourne in January 1972, an innings that Sir Donald Bradman insisted was the finest knock ever played in Australia. Sobers had missed the previous Test through injury, being absent while Dennis Lillee, in his first season in international cricket, claimed eight for 29. In this match the young lion was subject to a battering, chiefly through the off-side, with a few soaring hooks thrown in. There was a time when Lillee was bowling to Sobers with a deep point and a deep cover, these bisected time and again by drives played on tiptoe. When Kerry O'Keefe came on to bowl his leg-spinners, Sobers hit him for two successive sixes, from the crease each time, the first over long-on, the second over long-off, each with a gloriously extended backlift and follow-through.

My last sight of Garry Sobers on the television was at the Recreation Oval at Antigua, the home ground of Viv Richards. In chronology and cricketing greatness, Richards comes roughly between Sobers and Brian Lara. The match of which I speak was the one in which Lara made 375. After his 366th run, play was interrupted, as the previous record-holder walked into the field to officially pass on the baton. The shoulders drooped slightly, the knees were a little more 'knocked' than before, but all who saw him that day knew they were, once more and fleetingly, in the presence of a greatness the like of which no cricket field will ever see again.

III

The first English cricketer to make an impression on my consciousness was Ken Barrington. When he came with Ted Dexter's side of 1961–2, Barrington made a deep impact on Indian crowds. He endeared himself by doing imitations of cricketers they had recently seen, such as Garry Sobers and the gum-chewing Australian Ken Mackay. When he was thrown a pair of sunglasses by a spectator, he put them on and even bowled in them.

The man Barrington most resembled, on the other side, was Vijay Manjrekar, who like the Englishman died of a heart attack much before his time. Both were batsmen who kept their strokes under wraps for hours after they came in, waiting until they got to 60 or 70 before unfolding the lofted drive or the hook. Both fancied themselves as slow bowlers, although their captains generally thought otherwise. In this series they matched one another stroke for stroke, almost exactly, for one scored 594 runs in the five Tests, the other 586. In the Indian dressing room Manjrekar was also known as a prankster and mimic.

Manjrekar, however, was for us 'gar ki murgi dal barabar', a known product, whereas Barrington had the charm and appeal of the exotic outsider. Throughout the land, boys as well as men were to imitate the way he played forward, the way he sent down his leg-breaks, the way he took up his position in the slips. The first team I followed, Friends Union Cricket Club in Bangalore, had within its ranks a fine all-rounder who bowled high tossed leg-breaks, batted with care and orthodoxy, and did his hair up in a puff like the England player. I believe his mother named him Rajanna, but we knew him only as 'Ken'. (That, fifty-five years later, is what I still call him.) When I played college cricket in Delhi, there was a chap who played for Salwan Club, which is a team of Punjabis. He was known, simply, as 'Bringtin'. I have no doubt that in Calcutta there is a former club cricketer, now in his late seventies, who likes to answer to the name of 'Bearing-tone'.

Years later, an English journalist asked Barrington the secret of his success in India. 'Eggs and toast, old chap,' replied Ken, 'that is all I ordered wherever I went in the subcontinent.' I retold this tale to an older colleague of mine in the Nehru Memorial Museum and Library. 'Nonsense,' he replied. 'During the Test match at Eden Gardens I myself threw him an orange, which he caught, peeled, and ate fully.'

I never saw Barringon bat (or eat), alas. The first English cricketer I admired on the field was Alan Knott, as I narrated in the opening chapter. In that Delhi Test of 1972, Geoff Arnold started with some sighters, way outside off-stump and leg, and Knott collected them, *horizontally*. It was my first sight of a wicket-keeper diving, for schoolboy stumpers were taught to move with their feet, and in any case in India they then kept mostly to slow bowlers.

Four years later, in the Delhi Test of 1976, Knott impressed me more with the bat. The first hour was packed with action. Mike Brearley was run out by Brijesh Patel, a brilliant underhand flick from short cover. Graham Barlow came in for his first Test innings; mesmerised by Bedi, he put a ball tamely into the hands of short-leg. Bob Woolmer was lbw to Chandrasekhar, and then Keith Fletcher was bowled, the off and middle stumps hurtling out of the ground. England were 70 for four at lunch. I walked over to where my friend Shivy was sitting. 'That was a decisive session,' I crowed. 'Didn't I tell you, they can't play Indian spinners, on Indian wickets at least. We will now win the match, and the series.'

After lunch Amiss and the England captain put on fifty, but then Greig was lbw to Venkatraghavan. Alan Knott came in, and in an hour-and-a-half of inspired batsmanship transformed the match. Venkat was cut past slip, Chandra pulled and lofted. The wicketkeeper seemed always to play against the break, successfully, for his footwork and eye were exceptional. Before one knew, Knott was fifty not out. Bedi came on, belatedly, and held him in check, but there were still runs to be had from the other bowlers. Knott was finally out to a classic left-armer's dismissal, stranded down the wicket as he made to drive over cover. By then he had scored 75, out of a stand of 101. He had put heart into Amiss, and the men to follow. With the opener going on to score 179, England finished with 381, a total from which they could not lose. In the event, although it was Amiss who scored a hundred and John Lever who took ten wickets, Knott's was the knock that defined and won the match.

Alan Knott was perhaps the first authentically great English cricketer to play for England in India. In the 1950s and 1960s, many top English players ducked tours of the subcontinent. During the war, Denis Compton played a season of Ranji Trophy cricket, but he never played a Test in India. Nor did Len Hutton, Peter May, Jim Laker, or Freddie Trueman. They thought the competition beneath them, and were turned away by tales of heat, dust, dirt and disease. Even Geoffrey Boycott only came because he wanted to break a world record; no sooner had he done that than he ran away mid-series to join a rebel tour in apartheid South Africa.

The greatest English cricketer to play in India was the incomparable Ian Botham. Botham played his cricket much as Keith Miller did – with not a thought for the morrow (or the record books). He drove on the up like Miller, he fielded in the slips like Miller – hands on hips, most of the time – he got wickets with bad balls like Miller. He also made friends easily with cricketers from other countries. When asked why he did not join a rebel tour to South Africa in the days of apartheid, he answered, 'Because I would not be able to look Viv Richards again in the face.'

Botham toured India in 1981–2, when by his own standards he had a moderate series: four fifties (with a top score of 66), and sixteen wickets in the five Tests. The way the series was played one could hardly expect him to shine, for the rival captains, Gavaskar and Fletcher, outdid one another in the matter of safety-first tactics and time wasting. But there was one day in Indore, playing for MCC against Central Zone, when Botham decided to remind us of who he really was. In the city of C K Nayudu he hit 118 in little over an hour, his scoring strokes being nine singles, two twos, sixteen fours and seven sixes. He was in such cracking form that when he walked off the ground and an orange peel was thrown in his direction, he drove it with his bat back into the stands.*

Two winters prior to this, Botham had stopped over in Bombay for a week. The occasion was the one-off 'Jubilee Test' (marking fifty years of the Indian Cricket Board), and the captains for the match were G R Viswanath and Mike Brearley. Both believed in brighter cricket, and Brearley knew always how to make his best man perform. In what must rank as the finest

---

* This innings is lovingly described in Scyld Berry's *Cricket Wallah*, one of the best books on cricket in India.

all-round performance witnessed in a match in India, Botham scored a brisk hundred and took thirteen wickets as England won by ten wickets.

Those days my mind was preoccupied with scholarly rather than sporting matters, so I did not often get to watch the cricket on television. Botham's innings I completely missed, but I did see some of the seven wickets he claimed in the second innings. With any ball, and without Vaseline, this fellow could move it late both ways and at a brisk pace. It was a quite outstanding display of the swing bowler's art, and also the last time Botham would win a Test with the ball. The beef and the beer soon got to his waist, and by the time he was in India next he was but a handy bowler, not a great one. The additional pounds had destroyed his balance, the body no longer able to swivel at delivery time, the arm no longer quite so high. Of course as a batsman and slip fielder he was still of world class.

IV

When I was growing up, we looked kindly on cricketers from New Zealand. These were the men who allowed us our first series victory in Test cricket, when they came over here in 1955–6, as well as our first successful series overseas, when we went over there in 1967–8. We practised on them the affectionate condescension we had ourselves received from the English and the Australians. We wrote about them the way the correspondent of the *Melbourne Age* or the editor of the *Wisden Cricketers' Almanack* used to write about us. 'England went on to win by an innings, but only after Vijay Hazare had batted *bravely* for India.' 'Australia won the match, and hence the rubber four-nil, but in a spell of *artful* slow-bowling Vinoo Mankad showed that the *best* of the visitors are not *noticeably* inferior to the [*worst* of the?] hosts.' Substitute John Reid and Bert Sutcliffe for Hazare and

Mankad, and you have the *Times of India* or *The Hindu* writing about New Zealanders in the 1950s and 1960s.

The first time I myself recognised that New Zealand were a proper cricket side was in the summer of 1973, when I listened to *Test Match Special* as these minnows, led by Bevan Congdon, almost chased down a target of 450 plus to win a Test in England. One of the younger members of that side was Richard Hadlee, who did more to make New Zealand a power in world cricket than anyone else. Hadlee was the son of a Test player and the younger brother of another. Though he could wield a bat, he is known more for what he could do with the ball. In February 1976, playing at the Basin Reserve in Wellington, one of the coldest and most inhospitable cricket grounds in the world, he destroyed Bishan Bedi's side with seven for 23, the wickets taken in eight overs. All this with no help from the umpires too, for three Indians were bowled and four caught. Exactly two years later, and on the same ground, he took six for 26 to see his country to their first win over England. For another decade and more he would destroy batting sides all over the world with his pace and his fabulous control of swing and cut.

In 1988, aged thirty-seven, Richard Hadlee came to India to get the few wickets he needed to go past Ian Botham's record of 373 Test wickets. I saw him on and off on the telly, struck by the lovely rhythmic run-up, the high action and the late movement this way or that, exactly which decided by a last-minute flick of the wrist. It was evident the Indian batsman could not 'read' him. It was in Bangalore on 12 November 1988 that Hadlee had my old college mate Arun Lal caught at second slip to go past Botham's record. I saw that on the box, for I had just moved to take up a job in Delhi. If I'd had the sense to join work a month later, I would have seen it at the ground.

Hadlee's own record of 431 Test wickets was broken, of course, by Kapil Dev. When Kapil went past him, the New Zealander told an interviewer that the Indian had played many more Test matches than he had. Especially in this country that was regarded as bad form. But Hadlee might not have had to make the point if Kapil himself had been wise to it. When Sunil Gavaskar scored his thirtieth Test hundred, for example, almost the first thing he told the assembled reporters was that Donald Bradman had scored his twenty-nine Test centuries in far fewer innings. I myself do not consider Hadlee's remark to be ungenerous. Fast bowling is awfully hard work – would one not remember the wickets and how quickly they came? After Kapil Dev had retired as well, there was this lovely conversation on television between Hadlee and that fine English fast bowler Bob Willis. They were commentating on a World Cup match played in Ahmedabad, and the talk went like this:

Hadlee: 'This is the ground where the great Kapil Dev broke
    the world record for the most number of Test wickets.'
Willis: 'And whose record was that?'
Hadlee (mischievously): 'It wasn't yours.'
Willis (wistfully): 'No – my legs gave out after 325.'

If Hadlee was by some distance the best New Zealand bowler ever, the finest batsman produced in that country was Martin Crowe. He too was a brother of a Test cricketer. Crowe was chosen to succeed Viv Richards as the overseas professional at Somerset, and made a decent fist of it. At his best he was as good as any in the world. Like Bradman he liked to drop the ball at his feet first up and call 'one'. He batted as if piloting a sleek limousine, moving smoothly from first gear to top. He had a preference for the on-side, but could cut and cover drive too. He could also bat for a very long time.

I saw Martin Crowe bat on two occasions, and on both occasions he was done by the umpire. In 1987, he played in a World Cup match in Bangalore. India scored 250 in their fifty overs, and the fate of the match now depended on how long Crowe would bat. He started slowly, as was his style, but then played a glorious on-drive for four off Kapil Dev. Kapil quickly took himself off and brought on the spinners. Crowe now had to play himself back in. The first time he tried to attack the slow left-armer Maninder Singh he was beaten in the air. He tried hard to regain his ground, but was given out stumped. The television replays showed that the ball had dropped out of the wicketkeeper's hands before he had broken the wicket. If there had been a third umpire in those days, Crowe might have gone on to win the match for his side.

In 1994, Martin Crowe came again with a New Zealand side to play in India. A leg injury had kept him out of international cricket for the better part of the previous two years. He had an indifferent series, not all of it his fault. I saw him in the Bangalore Test, where he was caught at slip off Anil Kumble in the first innings. In his second knock he began with two rasping drives, promising much. Then he was beaten by a Kumble googly and given out lbw. It was both high and going down the leg-side, the decision of an incompetent umpire named S K Bansal. Crowe walked off towards the pavilion, where I was sitting. His face displayed no emotion, but he had his bat held astride like a guitar, which he pretended to strum. Soon afterwards he announced his retirement.

V

Indian cricket fans of the 1950s and 1960s patronised the New Zealanders, and they patronised the Sri Lankans even more. They were considered merely as good as a Ranji Trophy side; in fact, for many years the proudly independent country of Ceylon played the Indian state of Madras annually for the Gopalan Trophy. But the Sri Lankans, undeterred, kept on producing top-class cricketers regardless.

Readers of this book will have gathered that it is biased towards the 1970s, the decade when I myself played and talked cricket almost non-stop, before being claimed by the pressures of the workaday world. In November 1975, in between the visits to India of Clive Lloyd's West Indians and Tony Greig's Englishmen, a Sri Lankan side arrived to play three unofficial Tests. It is a sign of how slightly they were still regarded by the hosts that the 'Tests' were assigned to unconventional venues: not Bombay, Calcutta or Madras but (if memory serves) Hyderabad, Nagpur and Ahmedabad. Delhi was allotted the match against the North Zone. In those days, when satellite TV had not yet entered India, the chance to witness a match like this was, for the college cricketer learning the trade, simply priceless.

As it happened I could go only for one day of the match, for the St Stephen's cricket XI was otherwise engaged on the other two. But I was lucky enough to see what I still regard as the most blistering attacking innings of my life, Vivian Richards' undefeated 192 only excepted. It was played by Louis Rohan Duleep Mendis. An adoring father had, by choice or by accident, bestowed on his son the names of two great batsmen. The boy was to take after Kanhai rather than Duleepsinhji, after the sometimes savage West Indian rather than the delicately wristy Indian.

This day at the Kotla, a warm winter sun beating down on all of us, Duleep Mendis hit 112 at a run a ball. First he took on Madan Lal and Mohinder Amarnath, two Test opening bowlers. Madan was hooked and pulled, Mohinder hit with the swing high over mid-wicket for four, and then for six. Bishan Bedi brought on Rajinder Goel, a slow left-armer who would have played Test cricket with distinction had he not been born in the same country at roughly the same time as his skipper. Goel was pummelled through the off-side, time and again. For a ball just a little short of a length Mendis made to square cut, but as his bat was still coming down he realised it was the arm ball, coming in fast rather than spinning away slow. Somehow he arched his bulky frame further to the leg and still hit it past slip for four. Bedi now put himself on to bowl, reluctantly. He was hit for one towering six, the ball soaring high into the blue sky before landing just short of the sightscreen. A last shot that sticks in the memory was played against the break, off the stumps, for four or maybe for six.

In all this Mendis spared one of the North Zone bowlers. This was the young leg-spinner Ashwin Minna, who had come to wider attention after taking masses of wickets in university cricket. Though Minna bowled more loose balls in an over than Bedi and Rajinder Goel did all day, Mendis was gentle on him. Why swallow the second-class stuff when the thoroughbreds were available for the taking? It was as if Mendis was saying, through his bat, that his side was already worthy of a higher status than the International Cricket Council was then willing to grant it.

In 1982, when Sri Lanka travelled to Madras to play their first proper Test match versus India, Duleep Mendis scored a hundred in each innings. Two years later he almost did the same thing at Lord's. With a conspicuous lack of grace the English authorities had allowed the Sri Lankans a solitary Test match. At the Home of Cricket the Sri Lankan batsmen taught their former rulers a thing or two about the game they professed to have invented. The first day-and-a-half was dominated by an innings of classical elegance played by Sidath Wettimuny. At every interval he was spoken to by the Pakistan opening batsman Mohsin Khan, phoning in from Manchester. Mohsin had scored a double-hundred at Lord's on his first Test appearance there. Wettimuny himself just failed to get there, being dismissed for 187, but his exit brought in the rampaging Mendis. He scored a furious hundred, reaching his century with a four and a six hit off Ian Botham. The next time around Mendis scored only 94, being caught on the boundary. A few yards to right or left, and he would have joined George Headley as one who had scored two centuries in a Lord's Test match.

Despite the likes of Mendis and Wettimuny, nothing in the history of Sri Lankan cricket quite prepared the world of cricket for the events of 1996. Cricketers and cricket watchers from all countries still saw them as charming fellows, spirited chaps really, who would play a dazzling innings or two before graciously shaking hands, as sporting losers will, with their opponents. How then did a team of part-timers and no-hopers become World Champions?

I am not about to provide a full answer or explanation here. Let me just unfold the roll, once more, to take in the names, richly resonant as Sri Lankan ones always are: Jayasuriya and Kaluwitharana, Tilekaratne and Mahanama, Gurusinha and Wickremesinghe, Vaas, Dharmasena, and Muralitharan. And let us stay a while longer with the two thus far unmentioned, the captain and vice-captain of that 1996 World Cup winning side.

With the possible exception of Erapalli Prasanna, no man has looked less like a Test cricketer than Arjuna Ranatunga. Consider the consequence of a shot played by him down to third man. He rolled up the wicket for a single, side to side, bat held horizontally between the two hands, reminding this viewer of a fat bandmaster who for years used to conduct the passing-out parade at the Indian Military Academy in Dehradun. One thought that this fellow should be somewhere else, if not at the head of a steel band, in a corporate boardroom at least.

The impression of laziness was reinforced by the way Ranatunga batted. No batsman was more economical in effort. The ball had been bowled, but for four-fifths of its flight there was no movement of hands or feet from the batsman. Ah, you will say, but the best play the ball late. They do, but when they get to it, it shows. Not with Ranatunga. The backlift was minimal, the feet shuffled slowly, wrist and eye doing the work. He evolved a style all his own, albeit a hugely effective one. That style was stamped most sharply on the shot he played to the first ball he received in the World Cup final of 1996, a deft, last-minute, and breathtakingly chancy dab down to fine third man for four.

Aravinda de Silva was shorter than Ranatunga, but almost as round at the waist. This man, you would say when you first see him come out to bat, should also be sent for a fortnight's incarceration to the Jindal Health Clinic in Bangalore. But wait, let him make his way to the crease. His bat comes down from on high, his feet reach out decisively for the ball. Willow strikes leather with a smack. He runs busily up and down the wicket. Ranatunga was *sui generis*: but De Silva could justly be regarded as an updated, postmodern version of Duleep Mendis. There was the same power, the same range of strokes, the same kind of controlled violence of batsmanship, saying – *Give us a bat, and a match, and we Sri Lankans are as good as anyone else in the world.*

In the month of March 1996 they were, too. It fell to Aravinda de Silva to play match-winning innings in both semi-final and final. In the first of these matches, at Calcutta, India had made their plans for the deadly duo of Jayasuriya and Kaluwitharana. But they had forgotten about De Silva. He came in to bat five minutes into the match, his face shining with determination. His side were 1 for two, but his first three shots were all crisply struck boundaries: a cover drive off Javagal Srinath, a late cut and a whipped on-drive off Anil Kumble. Venkatesh Prasad came on, and was hit for two fours; both pull shots, the second landing inches inside the fence. In Prasad's next over he went for two fours on the off-side, hit gloriously on the up. Azharuddin took out mid-wicket and sent him to strengthen the covers. De Silva now played his first proper one-day shot, a slog through the spot just vacated, opportunistic and arrogant. This was his ninth four, taking him to 43, out of his side's 48 for three. The tenth was a flick off Srinath, the eleventh an off-drive, the twelfth a lofted stroke between cover and extra. A dozen boundaries had been met by silence, and Geoffrey Boycott remarked meaningfully on television, 'I don't think this crowd is here to watch the cricket. They just want to see India win.' The crowd's desires were openly stated when De Silva departed, dragging a leg-break from Kumble onto his stumps. He had scored 66 in forty-seven balls, and the balance of the match had shifted for ever.

When, three days later, De Silva came to the wicket against Australia at Lahore, his side were batting second. They were, at the time, 23 for two, a moderate improvement on 1 for two. Their target was 242. The situation called for modulated aggression, not the Mendis-inspired mayhem of Calcutta. The seam bowler Damien Fleming was leg-glanced for four and then on-driven, the batsman picking the slower ball early. Shane Warne came on, and was struck for two crunching cover drives. De Silva now cooled it for a while, then took Paul Reiffel also for two boundaries in an over, an off-drive and a slash past point. The fifteen overs were up, the fielders were out, and a more dreary phase of the game began, with the runs now milked in ones and twos. Asanka Gurusinha, face twitching, beat Aravinda to the fifty, by one ball only (and he had something of a head start too). After the Guru left, Ranatunga carried on his work. De Silva continued in even keel, but stirred himself with eight overs to go, and with forty-one still wanted. He now off-drove Reiffel, his first boundary for some fourteen overs, and next ball flicked him through mid-wicket. Glenn McGrath came back, and was sent in the same direction. De Silva's century came up with his twelfth boundary, which was a leg-glance off Fleming.

The final at Lahore was depicted as a 'grudge' match, the little fellows having revenge on the bullies who had victimised them the previous winter – when Sri Lanka played in Australia, and Muralitharan was called, unfairly, for 'throwing' – and who had displayed a racist arrogance in not coming to Colombo for a preliminary match on the grounds that the city was not 'safe'. The representation was not inaccurate, but no one seemed to have commented at the time on an odd irony. In about 1991 or

1992, De Silva had almost made up his mind to emigrate to Australia. A colleague, Ravi Ratnayake, had already done so, fed up with the one Test in three years and the three one-day internationals in a year that his team were allowed by the International Cricket Council. De Silva's cricketing future looked bleak, and with Sinhalas and Tamils butchering one another at home, might he not mark out a life as a businessman in Australia? It took the visit to his home of the Sri Lankan Board President and Secretary, and the printed appeal of thousands of his admirers, to make Aravinda change his mind. Soon more Tests were being played, many more one-dayers too. An Australian of Sri Lankan origin came on assignment to Colombo – this man, Dave Whatmore, then worked with Ranatunga and Duleep Mendis to shape the side that would win the World Cup. But had things turned out otherwise, the man who had batted so beautifully in Calcutta and Lahore might so easily have been selling carpets in Perth.

Muttiah Muralitharan excepted, the best Sri Lankan cricketers have tended to be batsmen. In the days before they became a Test-playing nation they had F C De Saram and M Sathasivam, both attacking strokeplayers. Then came Mendis, Wettimuny, Ranatunga, De Silva and Sanath Jayasuriya, followed by Mahela Jayawardene and Kumar Sangakkara. Both were world-class batsmen: Mahela, silky and elegant, cutting and cover driving; Kumar, brisk and efficient, working the ball off his legs and slashing it past point. For the first decade-and-a-half of this century they held Sri Lanka's batting together. Mahela was also an excellent slip fielder; Sanga, a high-quality wicketkeeper.

Jayawardene appears to be an immensely likeable man. His mate is nice enough, but really stands out for his intellect. Sangakkara is – and not just for a cricketer – unusually thoughtful, well-read and wise. These attributes are all present in the 2011 MCC 'Spirit of Cricket' lecture he gave at Lord's, where he ranged widely over history, sport, and politics. Halfway through his Lord's lecture, Sangakkara referred to the pogrom against

Tamils in Colombo in 1983, noting that his own, proudly non-sectarian, family gave refuge to thirty-five Tamil friends on the run. Towards the end of the lecture, he returned to the theme of inter-faith and inter-community harmony. When he played cricket for Sri Lanka, said Sanga, '[W]ith me are all my people. I am Tamil, Sinhalese, Muslim and Burgher. I am a Buddhist, a Hindu, a follower of Islam and Christianity.'

Sangakkara gave his Lord's lecture on 4 July 2011. On the last day of the same month, I was in Colombo, speaking in memory of Neelan Tiruchelvam, a remarkable lawyer-scholar who lived (and died) for the cause of racial and religious harmony. In the course of my talk I mentioned Sangakkara's MCC lecture, adding that no Indian cricketer, dead or alive, could have spoken with such intelligence or empathy. I was being absolutely sincere – but perhaps I should have added that no English, Australian, West Indian, Pakistani or South African cricketer could have spoken like that either.

The next day I was at a dinner where Sangakkara was also present. We hardly got to speak, but when we did, he said that among the things he most enjoyed on tours of my country was the opportunity to drink Old Monk. This further endeared him to me. A great batsman, a superb wicketkeeper, a passionate and truthful public speaker, and a lover of good, strong, rum too. What a cricketer – what a man.

VI

On a flight from Berlin to Copenhagen in February 1995, I picked up a copy of the *International Herald Tribune*. I turned, of course, to the sports page, to find listed these two astonishing scores:

Davis Cup tennis, Copenhagen: End of first day: Denmark
  2 Sweden 0.
Test match cricket, Harare: End of second day: Zimbabwe
  544 for four declared; Pakistan 79 for three.

At Copenhagen airport I asked the cab driver what had happened
in the tennis doubles. They won, he said, shrugging his shoulders. I was at the tennis the next day, sitting between a Swedish
lady and her Danish husband, watching Stefan Edberg and Jonas
Bjorkman win the reverse singles and restore some sense to the
form book. But in distant Harare the underdogs would not be
pipped at the post. As I found out later, the Zimbabweans won
by an innings against a side that liked then to think of itself as
world champions. True, that title was awarded for honours won
in the shorter and lesser game, but in 1995 Pakistan was a high-
class side at Test level too. As for the Zimbabwean cricketers,
their formal credentials were indicated by a list of current occu-
pations helpfully provided (by a British newspaper) after their
win. The side included chicken farmers, cattle ranchers, company
executives, lawyers, even a big game hunter. Only one of the
eleven was officially listed as a 'professional cricketer'.

In that epic match against Pakistan Andy Flower scored 156,
his kid brother Grant 201. The cricketing history of all countries
is marked by the deeds of brothers. Think of the Bannermans and
the Chappells and the Waughs of Australia; the Graces of England;
the Pollocks of South Africa; the Amarnaths of India; the Grants
of the West Indies; the Hadlees and the Crowes of New Zealand;
and most emphatically, the Mohammeds of Pakistan. Had Robert
Mugabe not destroyed his country's economy while also damaging its cricket, the Flower brothers might also have come to be
spoken of in the same breath as the Waughs and the Chappells.
In an earlier chapter, I have written of how the Flower brothers
bravely resisted Kumble and company at the Feroz Shah Kotla in
1993. Five years later, I saw them, on TV this time, almost bring

off an amazing win over Australia at the same ground. Zimbabwe were set 295 to win in 50 overs, against a side which bowled tight and fielded maniacally. Andy Flower joined Grant after the fall of the second wicket at 98, and they added 121 at better than a run a ball. The target was within reach when a Warne flipper rolled along the pitch and disturbed the younger Flower's leg-stump. In the next over, Andy was run out after a stunning piece of fielding in the covers by Mark Waugh. Although it was not quite clear that he had not regained his ground, the third umpire gave him out. In the opinion of Ian Chappell (an Australian) the batsman was 'hung on insufficient evidence'.

One Flower was two years old and the other in his mother's womb when their team-mate John Traicos appeared in his first Test. This was for South Africa against Australia, in the winter of 1969–70. Traicos was by profession a lawyer, born in Egypt of Greek extraction. His mother chose a wonderful middle name for her boy, Athanasios, as well as a town with a lovely name, Zagazig, to give birth to him. In his prime, Traicos was an off-spinner right out of the top drawer. Starting behind the bowler's back, the right arm came over in a sweeping curve: this enabled him to bowl a beautiful floater. Tall and slender, he had superb control, and was a magnificent fielder off his own bowling to boot.

Traicos first came to India for the World Cup held here in 1987. As a sometime off-spinner myself I loved to watch him bowl on television. There was a legal precision to all that he did – the brisk licking of the fingers, the balls delivered in rapid succession, the no-nonsense collection of the returns. The records show he was never collared in the six matches he played in the tournament.*

---

* Here are the figures: 10–2–28–1 against New Zealand; 10–0–36–0 versus Australia; 8–0–27–2 versus India; 10–0–43–1 versus New Zealand; 10–0–9–0 versus India; and finally, 10–0–45–2 against Australia. Six wickets in as many matches, and an economy rate well below four runs an over – a record a Kumble or a Warne could be proud of.

By the time Zimbabwe achieved Test status, Traicos was forty-three. The control remained, though not the zip off the wicket. In the Delhi Test of 1993, he bowled steadily, without ever looking like taking wickets. As a bowler, at least, although as a fielder he took a stunning catch in the covers, diving forward, to get rid of Sachin Tendulkar. Two years earlier, in his country's first ever Test match, he had sent Tendulkar on his way with the ball. Remarkably, Sachin had not even been born when Traicos first played Test cricket. As someone said at the time, it took a Greek to do it.

VII

I have a vivid boyhood recollection of listening to radio commentary on a Test played in Dacca between Pakistan and England. The home side were batting, and when a tailender came to the wicket the cheers from the crowd were louder than they had been for the top batsmen in the side. This was because he was, remarkably, an East Pakistani, the first person from this, the larger of the two wings of the country that Jinnah created, to play Test cricket.

My memory says that this fellow was an off-spinner called Nazir. But the internet (more reliable in this case) informs me that his name was Niaz Ahmed, and that he was a medium-pace bowler. The Test was played in what was not yet Dhaka in March 1969. Niaz batted at number ten in this, his second and last Test match (the first was in England in 1967), scoring 16 not out, each run met with more applause than the many others scored by his (West Pakistani) team-mates.

In his book on Pakistan cricket, *Cricket Cauldron*, Shahryar Khan writes, 'There was a club-level cricketer from Dhaka called Niaz Ahmed who was Pakistan's perennial 12th man for quite some time, the Pakistan Cricket Board attempting to give the entirely unconvincing impression that East Pakistan was on the verge of national representation. The fact was that no effort was made by the governments of Pakistan or by the cricket boards to promote cricket in East Pakistan.'

The cheering for Niaz in that Dacca Test of 1969 was in part cricketing, in larger part political. The East Pakistanis were discriminated against even more substantially in economic and political than in sporting matters. By the late 1960s, the movement for an independent state of Bangladesh had begun gathering momentum. It finally achieved success in December 1971.

It took a long time for Bangladesh to achieve full cricketing status. They first qualified for a World Cup in 1999. In that tournament they upset Pakistan, a result described by the Prime Minister, Sheikh Hasina, as 'the greatest day since Liberation'. Some years later I was watching on TV when they nearly beat Pakistan in a Test match in Multan. Pakistan had been set 261 to win in the fourth innings. While wickets fell steadily at one end, the hometown boy, the great Inzamam-ul-Haq, kept going at the other. When the eighth wicket fell there were still more than fifty runs to get, and Bangladesh were odds on favourites. They did not get home in part because Inzy kept majestically calm, in part because the Bangladesh captain trusted only himself, bowling on from one end when he was visibly tired and ineffective.

In 2005, Bangladesh played their first Test at Lord's. I was in London, and watched the first day in the company of the Karl Marx biographer and cricket nut Francis Wheen. The visitors batted first, and were clearly overawed by the place and occasion, being bowled out before tea. Both Francis and I were however impressed by one batsman, Mushfiqur Rahim, who had then just turned seventeen. He batted assuredly for an hour-and-a-half before falling lbw to one that kept low.

That match Mushfiqur played as a batsman, but soon he was keeping for Bangladesh as well. I saw, on television, every ball and every run of his match-winning knock against India in the 2007 World Cup. Early in his innings he came down the wicket to Harbhajan Singh – then the best off-spinner in the world

– and hit him over his head for six. He ended with 56 not out. Through that shot and that knock, Mushfiqur secured his place in this Hindu's pantheon. I remain a great admirer of his glove-work, his footwork, the crisp cleanliness of his strokeplay and the manifest maturity of his cricketing brain. By helping his side win Tests and one-day matches against more fancied teams, Mushfiq has been the architect of many great days since Liberation.

VIII

Some might find it odd that I deal last with a country which was, in Test match terms, one of the first. South Africa played its inaugural Test in 1889, whereas West Indies joined the ranks only in 1928, India in 1932, Pakistan in 1952. But then these countries played with anyone at all, while the South Africans would break bread only with their fellow whites, playing against England, Australia, and New Zealand alone. Nor, of course, would they contemplate the admission into their own teams of a black or coloured South African player, however gifted.

For an Indian of my generation, it was the South African side of 1969–70 that one knew, or knew of, best. This team had hammered the Australian team that had just hammered us. It was all-white, true, but it was also the best in the world. When, in 1971, Ajit Wadekar expressed regret that his side, that had just beaten England and the West Indies, could not play the South Africans for the title of 'world champions', we knew this to be bravado, a challenge thrown in the safe knowledge that it could not, in the prevailing political climate, ever be accepted. For how would our bowlers bowl to Barry Richards or Eddie Barlow or Graeme Pollock? Or our batsmen face up to the pace and bounce of Mike Procter and Peter Pollock?

Some answers were provided twenty years later, when India finally did play South Africa. Apartheid was in the process of being dismantled, Nelson Mandela had been released from jail, and his country had been readmitted to the International Cricket Council. The South Africans came here in 1991 to contest three one-dayers, and made a tremendous impression with their fielding. In the first match in Bombay, Jonty Rhodes effected two run outs and took three catches, one of which was taken at full stretch, body at least four feet off the ground. We had read of Colin Bland, the South African who once ran out an English batsman by throwing a ball between his pads to hit the stumps. But Rhodes appeared akin to one of those characters out of Hindu mythology, taking off in the air to do battle with someone a million miles away. As for the other members of the team, we noticed that a few could bat, and one could bowl very fast indeed.

The next winter, India went to South Africa for a full tour. Ajit Wadekar was the manager of the Indian side, and I wonder whether he ever recalled the challenge he had once offered. India were beaten easily in both varieties of the game, yet this team of South African cricketers could not hold a candle to the side of 1970. Possibly the only Springbok playing in 1992 who would have commanded a place in that team was the fast bowler Allan Donald. To watch Donald bowl, even on TV, was a thrilling sight. Never was he less than in complete control of his body and his craft. He had a very long run-up, but not one foot appeared to be in excess. The words that came to mind when watching Donald bowl were *symmetry, poetry, beauty, grace*. With another kind of fast bowler these might be *terror, power, fear*. This is not to say that Donald was, either in the cricketing or the physical sense, not 'dangerous'. However, he made sparing use of the bouncer, obtaining his wickets as much from movement as from pace, through skill as well as strength.

Allan Donald would comfortably walk into an all-time South African XI; and so, perhaps even more easily, would his younger contemporary Jacques Kallis. If my son was with me watching television when Kallis walked out to bat, one of us would say to the other, 'Here comes the MVP.' This term, borrowed from baseball, fitted Kallis better than any cricketer since the peerless Garry Sobers. Kallis was one of the three or four best batsmen of his generation. He scored more than 13,000 runs in Test cricket, with 45 centuries. But he also had the small matter of 292 Test wickets and 200 Test catches to his credit. Through the first decade of the twenty-first century, Jacques Henry Kallis was, without question, world cricket's Most Valuable Player.

When Kallis made his international debut he was principally an off-side player. I remember one of his first one-dayers, when he came in with four or five wickets down, and South Africa needing about 40 runs off eight overs. He played a series of dazzling back-foot drives behind and past point and got his side home.

A few years later I saw Kallis strike an even more brutal note, as he powered his team to a win in a match against Sri Lanka being played in Bangladesh. He hit the great Muralitharan for a series of sixes (five in all, as I recall) over mid-wicket. Those elegant drives past point, and those muscular hoicks to leg, were less in evidence in later years. Assigned the role of innings-builder, Kallis relied more on leg glides and off-drives to make his runs. He remained a very accomplished batsman, and a very prolific one.

When he began his career, Kallis swung the ball prodigiously, both in and out. I recall a series in England where he was given the new ball, with Donald coming on first change. Later, as he became older and his body filled in, Kallis slowed down and lost the ability to move the ball late and dangerously. But he remained a very effective bowler, able to contain batsmen on the go, and to break partnerships.

Kallis was also a cracking good fielder. He was normally placed at second slip, where the edges come fast in any case, and faster than normal if the bowler is named Donald, Ntini, or Steyn.

Countless times on the telly I saw an edge fly rapidly towards Kallis, the pace and pressure of the ball pushing him backwards, from where he rose, smiling, the ball in his hands, the white floppy hat still in place.

One of my few regrets as a cricket fan is that I have never watched the South African Test team play live, at the ground. I have seen almost all the great moderns in the flesh – Wasim, Waqar, Imran, Miandad, Inzamam; Lloyd, Kallicharran, Richards, Greenidge, Roberts, Holding, Marshall, Lara, Walsh, Ambrose; Botham, Knott, Underwood, Gooch, Anderson; Ponting, Warne, Steve Waugh, Border, McGrath, Gilchrist; Martin Crowe; Andy Flower. Two I have never seen bowl or bat before me are Allan Donald and Jacques Kallis. Of course, thanks to the magnificent work of generations of (anonymous) cameramen, I was able to watch plenty of them on the box. But it would have been even nicer to have seen them in the flesh.

IX

In middle age, I have got to know three former English cricketers; all Cambridge educated. They are Mike Brearley, Mike Atherton, and Ed Smith. I have met them perhaps half-a-dozen times each, the conversations often beginning with cricket but always ranging far beyond the boundary.

The meeting with a *firangi* cricketer that made the most profound impact on me, however, took place when I was a college student. A friend in St Stephen's was attracted to the Moral Re-Armanent movement, and an itinerant preacher took him to a summer camp where he met Conrad Hunte, the great West Indies opening batsman who had joined MRA after his career ended. This led to an invitation to Hunte to speak at the college's 'Informal Discussion Group'. As the most cricket-mad of my friend's friends, I was asked to chair.

The meetings of the IDG were held after dinner in the college staff room. Hunte had agreed to come only on condition that he speak about moral rather than sporting questions. Fortunately, seeing what the crowd wanted he changed his mind, and after a few homilies on the importance of being polite to your mother and faithful to your wife (he had been neither, until he joined the 'Movement' and forsook rudeness and adultery) he told some cricket stories. One story related to the Brisbane tied Test; the last over of which he lovingly rehearsed, ball by ball, mentioning but not spending excessive time on the spectacular run out he had himself effected.

The second, and even better, tale was about a hundred Hunte scored in the Bombay Test of 1966–7. The tourists had identified the wrist-spinner B S Chandrasekhar as their main threat, so Hunte, as the batsman with the best technique, was asked by his captain Sobers to take as much of Chandra as possible. As he described it to us, he played the bowler with a loose top hand, so that an edge would not carry to slip, if it was the leg-break, or to short-leg, if it was the googly.

By these methods, Hunte kept out Chandra all day, allowing the strokemakers to make merry against the lesser bowlers. With Kanhai, Lloyd and Sobers blazing away opposite him, the West Indies scored in excess of 400 and quite easily won the match. As he concluded a story meant to reflect well on his own cricketing technique and the tactical skills of his team, I could not help interject mischievously, by saying, 'Mr Hunte, perhaps it was Chandra who won in the end. You, a West Indian, took a full six hours to make a mere 101.' Hunte, laughing delightedly, agreed.

The questions from the audience kept coming. All were cricketing, and all were answered at length. Word of this meeting in St Stephen's got around the sporting fraternity in Delhi, and a few days later Hunte was invited to play at the Feroz Shah Kotla in a benefit match for, if memory serves, Abbas Ali Baig. He agreed, putting on his whites for the first time in a decade.

That night at my college helped bring Conrad Hunte back to the sport he grew up with. After Nelson Mandela was released from prison, Hunte moved to South Africa, where, in a shanty town outside Johannesburg, he set up a coaching clinic for black kids. In December 1997, I opened the newspaper to find the West Indian was visiting my city, and in a cricketing capacity. A women's World Cup was on, the South Africans were playing in Bangalore, and the great former opening batsman was their coach. I walked over to the Chinnaswamy Stadium, located Hunte and reminded him of when and where we had first met. We had a fairly long and entirely pleasurable conversation, which featured, among other things, the commemoration back in the 1960s of the independence of his country from British rule. As part of the festivities, a cricket match was arranged between Barbados and the Rest of the World. That little island of two hundred thousand people was taking on the globe, emboldened by having produced Weekes, Worrell and Walcott in the past and Hunte, Sobers, Nurse, Hall and Griffith in the present. I thought this a lovely conceit. It was rather cheeky, he admitted, adding, 'if only we had borrowed just four Guyanese, Rohan [Kanhai], Clive [Lloyd], Basil [Butcher] and Lance [Gibbs] we would have beaten them, too!'*

---

* In fact, Kanhai and Gibbs played for the visitors, alongside (among others) Bill Lawry from Australia, Chandu Borde from India, Tom Graveney from England, and Mushtaq Mohammed from Pakistan. Rest of the World won by 262 runs. The match was played in March 1967; Barbados had achieved its independence the previous November.

8

Some Favourite Pakistanis

I

A mere sixteen families are said to control Pakistan's economy, a textbook case of exploitative oligopoly. But that might seem like egalitarian socialism when compared with the state of Pakistan cricket, which for many years appeared to be run by two households only. One of these families was plebeian, as befitting their base, the trading port of Karachi. The other was feudal, and lived in the town of kings, soldiers, and poets – Lahore. In fact, a lyrical sociologist (were there such an animal) could use the story of these two cricketing families to write a larger social history of the nation. Punjab versus Sindh, land versus commerce, indigenous Pakistani versus imported Mohajir. This divergence in class and cultural origin was deeply marked in the men from the two homes: in their dress, in their deportment, in how they played the game, in how they viewed the enemy.

The First Family of Pakistan cricket were the Mohammads of Karachi, but before that of the princely state of Junagadh. As a business house they were a closely held partnership, five brothers who worked and schemed together. Economic historians tell us that capital does not always follow the law of primogeniture. Certainly not in this case, where the two elder and the two younger brothers deferred to the one who lay between. He was the unquestioned Master, albeit a 'little' one.

Hanif Mohammad was born in 1935, moving to Pakistan when he was twelve. By then his game had already been elaborated in his native Junagadh. The story is told of how Hanif would bat on after sundown, the unwilling bowlers shifting the game from a side street to the main one, to play on under one of the three lighted lampposts that the Nawab allowed his subjects. After they shifted to Karachi the boy came under the tutelage of Jaoomal Naoomal, a skilled all-rounder who had once bowled Don Bradman (while playing for the Indian Gymkhana against the 1930 Australian side), and also appeared in the first Indian Test XI, at Lord's in 1932. Naoomal (incidentally, a Hindu who had stayed on in Pakistan) spied in the lad a future Test player. So as to keep up his confidence, and prepare him for Test matches played over thirty hours, he instructed the umpires of Karachi (most of them his pupils, too) never to adjudge Hanif out leg-before-wicket.

Hanif was not long out of short pants before he returned to India, with Abdul Kardar's team of 1951–2. Also in the side was his eldest brother, Wazir, an able middle-order batsman and the maker of two Test hundreds. (The brother next in age to Wazir, Raees, narrowly missed selection, but the two younger to Hanif, Mushtaq and Sadiq, each played many Test matches for Pakistan.) From then until he retired in 1970 it was a case of 'if you get Hanif out, you win'. The uncertain abilities of those who followed him placed a dreadful burden, and like Sunil Gavaskar, Hanif had to put his strokes in the bank locker for days on end. He became, only partly out of choice, the best defensive batsman in world cricket.

My all-time favourite cricket story stars Hanif. It relates to a Test played in Bridgetown in the third week of January 1958. The West Indies, batting first, scored 579, Conrad Hunte and Everton Weekes scoring hundreds. They then dismissed Pakistan for 106, Roy Gilchrist taking four for 32. Following on almost five hundred behind, Hanif had to carry his team-mates through the last three days of the Test. That gifted wicketkeeper-batsman, Imtiaz Ahmed, helped, scoring 91 in an opening partnership of 152. Two days still remained. Alimuddin, with 37, Saeed Ahmed, with 65, and brother Wazir, with 35, each stayed with Hanif for an hour or two.

Watching the play on the fourth day, and from a palm tree high above square-leg, were a group of Bajan boys. As the afternoon sun rose higher one of them could no longer stand it. Delirious from the heat, from Hanif's relentless *thook thook* and doubtless from a steady intake of palm wine, the boy fell off the tree and landed on his head some forty feet below. He was taken to hospital, recovering consciousness twenty-four hours later. Inevitably his first words were: 'Is Hanif still batting?' He was.

In this match-saving marathon Hanif scored 337 runs in 970 minutes. It remains the longest innings in first-class cricket, and we may reckon it one of the bravest. I am not a statistical man, but some of the bowling figures must be quoted: Gilchrist, 41–5–121–1; E Atkinson, 49–5–136–2; Smith, 61–30–93–1; Valentine, 39–8–109–2; D. Atkinson, 62–35–61–1; Sobers, 57–25–94–1. In their desperation the West Indians even called upon Clyde Walcott to bowl ten overs.

I was born too late to watch Hanif bat, but we once sat in the same row of the Chinnaswamy Stadium's Diamond Jubilee Box. When Pakistan played India in Bangalore in 2005, I got a message saying that the Chairman of the Pakistan Cricket Board (then Shahryar Khan) wished to see me. I walked over from the Members Stand to where the VVIPs sat. Mr Khan was as courteous and well mannered as his cousin Tiger Pataudi, but with just a trace of pomposity. He had read my book *A Corner of a Foreign Field*, and was thinking of writing something similar on Pakistani cricket. As we spoke, Younis Khan and Inzamam-ul-Haq were in the middle of a very long partnership. Three seats to my right, and watching the cricket intently, was a little old man with hair dyed henna, eating peanuts out of a blue plastic bag. It was Hanif. Seeing him in the flesh brought to mind a story from a tour of Australia in the 1960s. When Pakistan played South Australia at Adelaide, Sir Donald Bradman walked into their dressing room and asked to meet the batsman who had broken his record score of 452. Hanif got up, and apologetically said, 'Sir, you will always be the greatest.' The Don looked him up and down and replied, shaking his head, 'So you are the fellow. I always thought that the batsman who took the record away from me would be six feet two inches tall. But you are shorter than me!'

A near contemporary of Hanif is the poet-policeman Keki N Daruwalla. In 1946, Keki moved to Junagadh with his father, who had been appointed tutor to the Nawab's children. When he went looking for cricketing playmates, Keki was directed to the home of the Mohammads. Sizing him up as not up to their 'level', Wazir and Hanif left him to face, without hope, the fizzing top-spinners and googlies of the four-year-old Mushtaq.

Mushtaq Mohammad was the youngest player to play Test cricket, and also the youngest to score a Test hundred. He was a strokemaker with a fine record against all except the quickest bowling. He captained Pakistan in the 1978 series against India, when cricketing relations between the two countries were resumed after seventeen years. The series was played in Pakistan, but telecast live in India. Although Mushtaq was very much a batting all-rounder, I remember him, from those matches, as a bowler with a wonderful side-on action, curving flight and sharp turn, a classical 'leggie' who never bowled quite enough in international cricket.

Mushtaq led Pakistan to victory in what, in its combination of warmth and sharp rivalry, can only be called the 'Friendship–Grudge series', competed as it was beween postcolonial cousins who had fought two wars since they last met on the cricket field.

The runs were scored and the wickets taken mostly by other Pakistanis. For his part, Mushtaq contributed shrewd captaincy and a blinder of a catch that swung a match. This was the second Test at Karachi, when Syed Kirmani and that always underrated tailender Erapalli Prasanna were taking India to safety. In what would have been the last over of Imran Khan's last spell Prasanna edged an outswinger, which flew fast and low to the left of second slip. The ball was travelling, and Mushtaq was built like a tub. Cricketing genes rather than physical ability lay behind a late lunge that came up with the catch, and India were done for.

In the 1950s, three Mohammads played together for Pakistan. Three appeared in the same team again in the 1970s, when Sadiq came in for the retired Wazir. Sadiq was brought up, forcibly, as a left-hander, the strain showing in his style, or lack of it. But he was a dogged opening batsman, whose best innings for his team was, as then was invariably the case for cricketers from the subcontinent, in a losing cause. This was in Headingley in 1971, when he scored a battling 91 in four hours, with sixteen fours, taking his side to within 25 runs of what would have been their first series win in England. I followed every run of his effort, on a then state-of-the-art Grundig radio in my aunt's house in New Delhi.

I don't know if Mushtaq and Sadiq have any children, but Hanif's son, Shoaib, played often for Pakistan and should have played even more. He was as solid as his father and as stolid as his uncle, an opening bat who could bowl a useful off-break. He was also, by far, the best fielder ever produced by the House of Mohammad. But he had the misfortune to achieve cricketing adulthood when a man from the rival *biradari* in Lahore was captain of Pakistan. Shoaib was at times not taken on tours, at other times not included in the playing XI, always on account of old animosities of which he had no part. On one tour of England, in 1987 as I recall, he did not play the first two Tests, and was brought in, belatedly, for the third. He scored an immaculate fifty, and as the clapping died down Trevor Bailey spoke out on the BBC: 'And the lad did not play in the previous Tests. The Mohammad family back in Pakistan will be asking a few questions about this. Especially old Mrs Mohammad, I think.' The reference was to Shoaib's grandmother, the lady who had brought up all her boys as cricketers.

II

For many years, the only woman listed in *Wisden's* Births and Deaths was Mrs Henry Grace, the mother of WG and two other England players. *The Pakistan Cricket Annual,* if one exists, should likewise memorialise Amir Bee, the mother of the Mohammads of Karachi, and also, at a pinch, three proud Pathan women of Lahore. These were the sisters who each produced a Test player who became a Test captain.

Javed Burki, the son of the eldest of these sisters, was an Oxford Blue who made a couple of Test hundreds, led his team on an unsuccessful tour of England in 1962 and then disappeared into the working world, into politics or administration or business. (I have forgotten which, though some would say that in Pakistan they are all more or less the same thing.) The second of the cousins had a longer and more distinguished cricketing career. Majid Khan made his debut in 1965 as a seventeen-year-old fast bowler, then called Majid Jehangir. Jehangir was the name of his father, a new-ball bowler for Cambridge University and (undivided) India who is best remembered for having killed a sparrow at Lord's: killed with the ball, that is, not a catapult or .303 rifle. The son soon decided that it was a batsman's game, although the reason given for his giving up bowling was a bad shoulder.

I once heard Bishan Bedi say of Majid Khan that he was the best bad wicket player of his experience. Bedi came up against

Majid often, for India against Pakistan in 1978–9, and before that, for Northamptonshire against Glamorgan in the English County Championship. Those were the days of uncovered wickets, when all county sides had a slow left-arm spinner to hand, for the rain-affected wickets that came into play every other week. And Bishan Bedi, as we know, was the finest of the tribe. One day at Swansea a crowd of approximately four hundred fans was treated to Majid against Bedi, footwork against flight, the loveliest and now scarcest of cricketing sights. Bedi spun it like a top, the ball occasionally taking a divot out of the wet mud that passed for a wicket. Majid rushed out to take it on the full, to drive. Every now and then he would feint to come forward but then lie back and cut through point. Bedi did him in the end, stumped. Since Majid had by then made 70, one might say that the result was approximately the same as that of the India–Pakistan war of 1965; that is to say, a draw, dead even.

Majid was a cold warrior, a man who rarely displayed emotion and never talked to opponents on the field. But I do remember a show he put on at the Gaddafi Stadium on 1 November 1978. Pakistan needed 120-odd to win the Test, in an hour and a half. Sent in first, the innovative Majid was frustrated by Kapil Dev bowling wide of the wicket. At length the Pathan uprooted the off-stump, and made to place it several feet further to the off. It was altogether atypical, but then it was his home ground, and he was batting against the old enemy. In the event, Pakistan got to their target easily, the winning runs being hit by Majid's younger cousin, Imran Khan.

Those who watched that catalysmic (if one was an Indian) series of 1978 would have thought that the bond between Majid and Imran was the bond between brothers. So it was, then. When Pakistan were in the field, every alternate over one saw the older Khan, at slip, wait for the little kid to come up from fine-leg to bowl. Majid would take his cap, conveying it to the umpire, all the while talking to Imran of what variations he might now try (at least that is my fancy – for all I know, they could have been discussing the rents paid by their tenants in Sargodha or the cuisine of a Chelsea restaurant). Imran and Majid have since fought, bitterly: at the time of writing they have not spoken to each other for twenty-five years. Their behaviour has been moderate in the extreme, when one considers what a Pathan generally does to a brother with whom he disagrees.

In 1978, Imran was a tearaway fast bowler who sometimes seemed to want more to scare batsmen than to actually get them out. At the other end his partner Sarfraz Nawaz bowled a classically full length, but then he didn't have Imran's pace. Sarfraz could make the cricket ball do all except talk. His enemies alleged that he was the acknowledged Master of Tampering, who knew how to change the shape of a ball, its weight and texture and colour too. But this MT was an honest double MS as well, a master of swing and of swerve. Sarfraz was known sometimes as 'Sufi', an egregious nickname when one compares the mystics' softly romantic feelings with the bowler's fearsome look and fiery temperament. It was in his nature to fight with captains, umpires, team-mates, managers, mentors, and pupils. For a while he and Imran were very intimate: he called him 'Boy', answering to 'Big' in return. They later had the mother of all quarrels, after which Big called Boy a KGB agent, a CIA agent, a drug runner and a spokesman for imperalism and for finance capital.

When India toured Pakistan in 1982–3, Imran was both captain and main bowler. But it was quickly evident that Sarfraz had passed on to Imran some of the more legitimate tricks of the trade. He now bowled fast and full, and much has been written of the dipping late inswingers with which Imran destroyed the Indians that year. But one cannot forget the variety, the bumper sparingly but cleverly used, the late outswinger served up after a series of four balls that went the other way.

As a bowler Imran had an action all his own, not to be recommended to the young. But his batting was straight out of the coaching manual, left elbow held up and bat close to pad. He had a succession of English coaches, and the pedigree showed: Aitchison College, Lahore; Royal Grammar School, Worcester; Worcester College, Oxford. He was very much a front-foot player, a slow starter who warmed up with drives either side of the wicket. He was certainly good enough to hold his place in any international side as a batsman. His last significant contribution to Pakistan cricket was with the bat, the studied, slow, careful but ultimately critical 72 he made in the 1992 World Cup final in Melbourne.

Imram is now a full-time politician, at the time of writing the Prime Minister of Pakistan. He is now into his third marriage, to a woman mystic (the first was to a British heiress). In his second career in the spotlight he remains a charismatic and controversial man. However, among the many photos I have seen of Imran in his various roles, the one that stays in the mind is of him playing a flashing square cut, with Kris Srikkanth leaping for cover at silly point. In this photograph Imran is, as always, immaculately attired, sleeves rolled down to the wrist, a green cap with the star of Pakistan placed firmly and proudly on his head.

III

Pakistan's greatest batsman after Hanif Mohammad was also from Karachi. But whereas Hanif was a gentle man, always polite to team-mate and opponent alike, Javed Miandad was a street fighter who took his rights and some of the rights of others too. I first saw him bat on the telly, during that Indo–Pak series of 1978, and can still recall the shock I received when he hit Chandrasekhar – the destroyer from my native Bangalore – out of the ground at Lahore. Four years later he caused a great deal of anguish to another outstanding slow bowler, Dilip Doshi. In one match the Indians were staying in a hotel which looked over the ground. When it was Javed's turn at the wicket, he kept asking Doshi the number of his room. The bowler wouldn't answer, but an eavesdropping Gavaskar asked Javed why he wanted to know. 'So that I can hit my next six into it,' came the answer.

It is a joy to remember that this Pakistani took his toll of English spinners too. David Gower tells a wonderful story of an early encounter Javed had with Ray Illingworth. Now 'Illy', a canny Yorkshireman, liked in county matches to come on to bowl the last over before lunch, when, with English batsmen at any rate, one could safely go into the pavilion with the splendid figures of 1–1–0–0. The first time he played against Miandad, for Leicestershire against Sussex, Illy came on, ritually, to bowl just before one o'clock. Javed hit him for three boundaries and a two; Illingworth's figures were 1–0–14–0 at lunch.

In December 1979, I saw Javed play in Bangalore. On the first day of this first match of a six-Test series, Mudassar Nazar batted dourly from morning until dusk, scoring a hundred. The man sitting next to me had his ear cocked to All India Radio, where the great Lala Amarnath referred to the opener, time and again, as 'Nazar Mohammed'. That was his father, against whom the Lala had played back in 1951–2. The confusion was understandable, for Mudassar's father was also caution personified, scoring 124 in 515 minutes in the Lucknow Test of that season. The senior Nazar took his risks off the field, retiring prematurely after a jump out of a third-floor window, a leap necessitated by the imminent entry into the room of the husband of the lady he was currently courting. (One might question Nazar Mohammed's timing, but not his taste, for the lady in question was the beautiful singer and actor, Nur Jehan.)

Anyhow, on this day in Bangalore, while Mudassar Nazar blocked at one end, at the other end the more adventurous Pakistanis unfolded their wares. First came Zaheer Abbas, who played some gorgeous leg glides off Kapil Dev, almost Ranji-like in their perfection. When Dilip Doshi came on to bowl he cracked the spinner past cover and mid-wicket before being stumped for 40. That brought in Javed, who for a long session between lunch and tea toyed with the spinners, cutting Doshi and driving the off-spinner Shivlal Yadav through the on-side, himself yards down the wicket. After Miandad was dismissed, for 76, we were allowed a brief glimpse of Wasim Raja, a left-hander with dreamy eyes and a rollicking off-drive.

Almost twenty years later I saw Javed Miandad on the TV, playing his last innings on the ground where he had learnt his trade, the National Stadium in Karachi. The occasion, England versus Pakistan in the 1996 World Cup: the background, the hero's return to the national side after three years in enforced exile. When he came in to bat the stadium erupted. The cheering was so wild and prolonged that even the unsentimental Javed smiled and shook his head in happy disbelief. Commentating at the time were two Englishmen. One, the spiteful kind, remarked that the reception was calculated to ensure that no umpire would dare give their man out lbw. He was at once put in his place by his colleague, Geoffrey Boycott, a man who knew well what respect and honour from a cricketing community signifies. 'Nothing of the kind, Charles,' scolded the man who had scored his hundredth first-class hundred in a Test played in front of his own home crowd. 'It is a deeply felt tribute to a great player.'

Many years later still, a package arrived for me in the mail. It weighed in excess of a kilogramme; but the return address assured me that it was not a bomb but a book. It had been sent by the Karachi branch of the Oxford University Press, who I knew to have published a series of fine works on the history and politics of Pakistan. This one, however, was something else: an autobiography of the great Sindh, Sussex and Glamorgan cricketer, Javed Miandad. Javed, or more likely his publisher, had titled this book *Cutting Edge*. In years of watching him at the ground and on television, I cannot remember many edges. But there were plenty of cuts, slashed hard through point. In addition he drove capably, was adept at playing off his legs, and could pull and hook too. He was not a particularly elegant player, but a greatly effective one.

I have written of Javed's mastery of spin. Unlike so many of his countrymen, Miandad was a fine player of fast bowling as well. He got solidly into line, and knew where his off-stump was. He had a marvellous record against Australia and the West Indies, the sides that had the best new-ball bowlers. Beyond his technical abilities, he paced his innings very well, and was a superb runner between the wickets.

This cameo assessment of his batsmanship is mine, not Javed's. His autobiography itemises his main achievements, but naturally cannot analyse them. What it does do, however, is to provide an extended and absolutely frank assessment of his relationship with Imran Khan. In character and background, they were a study in contrast. One was an aristocrat who went to Oxford via a Lahore public school, the other a plebeian, educated (for the most part) on the streets of Karachi. One cavorted with artists and millionaires in London, the other kept strictly to his native social milieu. They were different, but they were also contemporary. Thus it was Pakistan's good fortune that its best ever bowler came to cricketing maturity at the same time as its best ever batsman.

In his book, Javed was generous in his praise of Imran the cricketer. As a bowler he was 'irreplaceable'. The 'combination of pace, guile and reverse-swing made Imran absolutely lethal'. Then, 'having mastered fast bowling, he turned his attention to batting ... with great method and application'. Indeed, 'Imran's capacity for hard work is an example to all aspiring cricketers'.

Miandad also handsomely praised Imran's leadership skills. When the Pathan became captain of Pakistan, 'he led from the front and created an atmosphere in which there was no room for mediocrity. He made selection strictly performance-based.

Everyone feared for their place in the side, and it motivated them to give of their best.' It helped that unlike some other Pakistani cricket captains, this one was squeaky clean. For, as Miandad pointed out, 'Imran's is a famous name in cricket, but the great thing is that it also remains an unvarnished name. There have been no scandals, no allegations of him being anything less than impeccably honest.'

At the same time, Miandad was critical of Imran the team-man. For the better part of a decade the two men alternated as captain. 'As I did for other Pakistan captains, so I gave my best for Imran as well,' wrote Javed, adding, 'I was hurt when Imran did not return the gesture.' He wrote of a series against Sri Lanka when 'Imran didn't give me his full cooperation'. At other times, the Pathan would opt out of the side when he was not named skipper. Thus Imran played in only 13 of the 34 Tests when Javed was captain, whereas Javed played in as many as 46 of the 48 Tests when Imran led the side. Yet, says Miandad meaningfully, 'both of us won the same number of Tests for Pakistan – fourteen. I was present in each one of Imran's Test victories, but he was present in only five of mine. All of his wins came from a full-strength team, while more than half of mine came from a team with a second-string bowling attack from which our best bowler was missing.'

Cutting Edge also dwelt at length on the major team rivalry of Miandad's career, India versus Pakistan. There were analyses of Tests and series between the two sides, and a not excessively self-congratulatory recounting of the famous last-ball six in Sharjah. Miandad advised the Indian Cricket Board to prepare fast pitches if they wanted to produce their own equivalents of Imran, Waqar and Wasim. And he meditated reflectively on the linking of sport with patriotism. 'A nation's self-esteem cannot be held hostage to its sporting fortunes,' he remarked. 'One has to stop seeing cricket as a proxy war and a cricket loss as a political failure.'

The words in this book might have been polished by the ghostwriter (Saad Shafqat), but the sentiments appear to be Miandad's. Indeed, the book has a directness notably absent in south Asian autobiographies, whether sporting or otherwise. There are some sharp cricketing judgements. Gavaskar, says Miandad, was a better batsman than Tendulkar, Abdul Qadir a better wrist-spinner than Shane Warne, and Muralitharan without doubt the best off-spinner in the history of the game. There are some perceptive bits of psychology as well. Consider this, which applies equally to India as it does to Pakistan: 'Many of our star players, after they have become successful on the field and have received some public recognition, develop an inordinate sense of their own importance. They cease to be team players and expect special treatment. This divisive attitude disturbs team unity and keeps us from rising to our true potential.'

This frankness should not surprise us; what might are the bouts of empathy, so unexpected in a man reckoned to be one of the toughest competitors in the history of the game. When Pakistan dramatically beat the Kiwis on their home turf in the semi-finals of the 1992 World Cup, Miandad recalled his side's own loss in the same stage of the tournament five years before. 'Having been in the Pakistan side that lost that greatly hyped-up World Cup semi-final against Australia in 1987, I identified with the New Zealand team. I was sad for them and for the New Zealand public.'

Even more striking, perhaps, are Miandad's comments on the aftermath of the 1992 World Cup final. After Pakistan won, Javed held his captain in a long embrace, and then wrapped the national flag around him. Later, Imran, speaking as the victorious captain, did not so much as mention his players, dwelling instead on the cancer hospital he was building in his mother's memory. To the independent observer, that victory speech was a disgraceful exhibition of egotism. How must it have felt to the slighted Pakistan team?

Listen to Miandad. It appears he was not angry or hurt; rather, he could 'sympathise with Imran on this count. His public-speaking skills were modest to begin with, and now he was asked to deliver such a high-profile speech when he had just crowned his cricketing career with the achievement of a lifetime.' Imran meant well, says Miandad. That he said all the wrong things was only because he was emotionally overwrought. 'I should know,' comments Imran's great team-mate and rival, 'because it was an intense emotional moment for me as well. I had a huge lump in my throat – but at least I had the option of *not having to speak.*'

IV

The summer following the 1992 World Cup, Pakistan were touring England. Miandad was captain, Imran having finally retired. Pakistan won the Test series, but sections of the British press complained about the alleged doctoring of the ball by Wasim Akram and Waqar Younis, prompting Akram to respond that his critics were 'racist' and 'bad losers'.* When I arrived in London in mid-August to work in the British Library, the one-day internationals were being played. I landed the evening of the Lord's match which, as the next morning's newspapers informed me, was incomplete. Pakistan had scored 204 in their 50 overs, and England were 15 for one in reply when the rain came down, forcing play into a second day. The game was finely balanced, and Ian Botham was 12 not out, three cracking boundaries hit off Wasim Akram.

I was staying in the Indian YMCA along with my old college friend Shivy, now living in New Haven in Connecticut, and on his first visit to England. We would have given much to watch

---

* https://www.independent.co.uk/news/wasim-swings-ball-tampering-row-to-racism-1548561.html.

the match, but the newspaper was categorical – all tickets had been sold out. 'Let's go to Lord's anyway,' I told Shivy, 'I can show you the precincts, and we can go later in the week to see a county match.'

We had reckoned without that great universal institution, the black market. Taking the subway to St John's Wood, we emerged into the light to join a line of people walking towards the ground, carrying hampers and valid tickets. When we reached Lord's our companions waved their tickets and walked briskly through the turnstiles. We watched for a while, and then made to go. As we did, Shivy's eyes lighted upon a fellow in a blue blazer lounging under a tree. 'That fellow is a tout,' he said with the conviction of a long-time watcher of Hindi films. So he was. Thirty pounds changed hands for two tickets – in view of what followed, it was a steal.

Play had just begun when we arrived at our seats on the upper tier of the Compton Stand. Years ago, in the 1970s, Shivy and I had watched our Indian side lose Test matches to England, the West Indies, and Pakistan. Then our enjoyment of Vivian Richards and company had been toned down by despair, but this day at Lord's we were strictly non-aligned, free only to glory in the game.

Almost immediately Robin Smith was out, setting the pattern for an innings in which England lost a wicket every time they appeared to have the match under control. Botham was joined by Fairbrother, a cheeky left-hander with the remarkable Christian names of Neil Harvey. His first six scoring shots were all off-side boundaries. 'Another half-hour of Fairbrother and the match is over,' I told Shivy. It was a remark calculated to get him out, and sure enough next over Aqib Javed bowled him through the gate.

In came Allan Lamb, arguably England's best one-day batsman but, at thirty-eight, less than a certainty for that winter's tour of India. Lamb was quickly into his stride, working the ball away for ones and twos and smacking the half-volleys for four. Meanwhile Botham was in a torment. Shivy and I were a hundred yards away, but through his white helmet we could still feel the indecision in his mind. Like Lamb, he had been dropped halfway through the Test series, and wanted desperately to go to India. With his partner batting the way he was, all Botham had to do was push for singles, rotate the strike, and his side would be home and dry.

He did play thus for a while, but like his great adversary Kapil Dev the nudge and deflection were always foreign to his style. The seam bowlers and the leg-spinner Mushtaq Ahmed gave him nothing to hit, but when the slow left-armer Aamir Sohail came on to bowl, impulse got the better of self-preservation. Marking out a fresh guard, Botham hit Sohail powerfully off the back foot for four. He then watched, chomping at the bit, as Lamb took strike for the first five balls of the spinner's next over. Sohail knew as well as we did what Botham wished to do with the one ball he got to face. He artfully flighted it just that bit wider of off-stump, and the batsman, committed to the charge, missed and was stumped.

Botham walked disconsolately off the ground, for the last time it seemed as an England player. In came Graeme Hick, also to have an early slog off Sohail and be bowled off the inside edge. At 139 for five, the match was nicely poised. Lamb was joined by Richard Blakey, a Yorshireman making his international debut. He showed little sign of nerves, the score mounted, and Pakistan appeared to be out of it. Then with only thirty to get Lamb went to sweep Mushtaq, and was caught off bat and pad for 55. Now the excitement mounted. As wickets fell the asking rate climbed; crucially, Pakistan had in reserve three overs each of Waqar Younis and Wasim Akram. When England were fourteen short of the target Blakey was bowled by Waqar for a brave 25. Two runs later, Akram disposed of Chris Lewis and Phillip DeFreitas in a single over.

Now, we thought, Pakistan would surely win. But ten and jack, Dermot Reeve and Richard Illingworth, took no risks, and pushing the singles, brought down the deficit. When the last over began England needed four to win with one wicket standing, the kind of script that might have been written by the promoter of the first one-day international. Reeve took a single off the first ball, leaving Illingworth on strike. All of us expected Waqar's inswinging yorker, the most feared ball in cricket, best played while watching from the other end. The batsman, who thought likewise, brought his bat firmly alongside his front pad, but in a clever piece of double bluff Waqar bowled a fast outswinger. The off-stump went cartwheeling down towards the pavilion, and Pakistan had won by two runs.

Shivy and I made slowly towards the exit. We were followed by the voice of the adjudicator, Clive Lloyd, describing the match over the public address system as one of the finest he had seen. Too tired to talk, we walked down St John's Wood Road to the tube station, at the end of a day that had made us twenty years younger.

Later that week the team to tour India was announced, and both Ian Bothan and Allan Lamb were not in it. His career over, Lamb now went to the press with a story of how the Pakistani bowlers had been tampering with the cricket ball almost since the birth of their nation. The accusations were given wide and sympathetic coverage. I particularly remember a tabloid story which carried Lamb's claims alongside a photograph of the cricketer outside his suburban home, surrounded by wife, children, and sheep dog – a picture that spoke louder than a thousand words.

The ball-tampering controversy of 1992 helped reinforce stereotypical English images of the Pakistani, a man singled out by his colour (brown), his religion (Islam), his language (incomprehensible), and most of all, by his coming dangerously close, through mass migration, to the very citadel of British civilisation. That same autumn, indeed, I was travelling on the upper deck of a country bus in Oxfordshire, sitting in the front seat while being taunted by some skinheads from behind, who mixed invective with the throwing onto me of empty beer cans. In years of travelling and living in the West this was the only (and admittedly mild) instance of racial abuse I have encountered. It is noteworthy, though, that the louts called me a 'bloody f***** Paki'.

The last word on the cricketing summer of 1992 must be that of Geoffrey Boycott. Asked to comment on the allegations of ball-tampering against the Pakistanis, he answered that 'on present form Waqar and Wasim would bowl out the England team with an orange'.

V

Four years after the Lord's thriller, I watched Pakistan play India in my hometown, Bangalore. I took my seat early, for it was the quarter-final of cricket's World Cup. When I arrived Imran Khan and Sunil Gavaskar were walking around the ground, the Pathan in *salwar khameez*, the Maharashtrian in regulation shirt and pants. The last time they had met at this spot was during a Test match ten years previously, when Sunil scored 96 and Imran led his team to a 16-run victory. On the far side the present Pakistan captain, Wasim Akram, was bowling to his wicketkeeper, closely watched by the coach, Intikhab Alam. There had been much speculation as to whether Wasim would play, for he had a strained thigh. After five or six balls he came off towards the pavilion, shaking his head.

Apparently, when the news that Wasim had dropped out of the match reached the Pakistan dressing room there was *gadar*, a commotion. Javed Miandad thought he should be made captain for the match, on account of his long experience and the dread

236

the Indians held him in. Salim Malik also advanced his claims. In the event it was the official vice-captain, Aamir Sohail, who walked out for the toss. He lost it, and came out again leading his team. In the first over Miandad could be seen moving fielders without the consent of the captain. This went on for about half-an-hour until Sohail took the bull by the horns, and sent the veteran away to third man, where no one could hear him.

The Indian openers began cautiously. The occasion had got to Sachin Tendulkar, while Navjyot Sidhu at the other end was expected to drop anchor anyway. The innings proceeded at a steady clip, like a mail train, *rat-tat-tat*, too fast to be a passenger and too slow to be an express. Sachin scored a subdued thirty-odd, before being bowled by Ata-ur-Rahman. The Indian captain, Mohammed Azharuddin, flicked here and there, until he was caught brilliantly by the wicketkeeper Rashid Latif, jumping away to his right. Vinod Kambli got a few, I cannot remember how or how many. All this while Sidhu was playing solidly along the ground. He remembered himself only once, pulling Mushtaq Ahmed violently over mid-wicket. When he was finally out, cutting at Mushtaq, for 93, India were 190 for five, with only ten overs remaining. They could get 240 at best, we thought, not really a winning score.

Ajay Jadeja thought otherwise. Almost the first attacking stroke he played off Waqar Younis flew high in the air, way behind point, not close enough for sweeper cover, and too wide for third man. It earned him three runs, but it was the kind of shot that drives bowlers mad. Never had I seen a mishit land so perfectly in no-man's land. Now Jadeja proceeded to hand Waqar the thrashing of his life. He drove him for six over his head and then cross-batted his slower ball into the crowd. In between Anil Kumble hit Waqar over mid-wicket, a tailender's shot, and next ball drove him through cover, an all-rounder's shot. The great fast bowler went for forty in his last two overs, and India ended with 287.

Pakistan began brilliantly. Aamir Sohail and Saeed Anwar reached fifty in five overs, all authentic cricket shots. Aamir's square cuts and Anwar's cover drives were simply out of this world. Yet the silence that greeted their strokes was eerie – not a soul clapped. (Behind the sullenness lay two kinds of chauvinism, for India's new-ball bowlers were both from Bangalore.) Kumble came on, and was lofted first ball by Anwar for six, way over long-on, the batsman easing himself into the stroke. At the other end Sohail was laying into Venkatesh Prasad. Words were exchanged. Sohail played two breathtaking square drives on the up, off successive balls, and walked towards the bowler. Next ball he charged down the wicket and missed. The middle and off stumps were askew, and Prasad showed him the way to the pavilion. The crowd erupted. Soon afterwards Javagal Srinath had Anwar caught off a mishit, with another local boy, Anil Kumble, running backwards at mid-on to take the catch.

After 15 overs Pakistan were 115 for two, well above the required run rate. I can recall little of the middle phases of the innings, of how numbers three and four, Ijaz Ahmed and Inzamam-ul-Haq, came in and were out. But I can see Miandad walking in at number six. On his way to the crease he had to pass the non-striker, Salim Malik. Malik did not speak to his new partner, merely extending his left fist. Javed tapped it with his own, jauntily. The confidence seemed breathtaking.

Miandad and Malik were both acknowledged masters of the one-day game. Their records against India were exceptional. Four or five years ago that meeting of fists would have signalled the end, for the home side that is. But it was quickly evident that Javed was past his best. The body was ageing. Once he would be away in the first overs, working the ball in the gaps and running hard. Now he felt obliged to play himself in. The legs would not follow the brain either. His first fifteen runs all came in singles. The overs ticked away, and the run rate approached seven. Malik had to do something. He tried to loft Kumble, missed, and was given out lbw. He was a yard or two down the wicket, but then the umpire was not one of ours, so it must have been out.

Rashid Latif came in, without a helmet, as no contemporary batsman had dared to do since Vivian Richards and Sunil Gavaskar retired. He was at the wicket for about a quarter of an hour, long enough to play three shots of uncommon beauty. He began with an on-drive for six off Kumble. Srinath came on for his second spell, and to a bowler of genuine speed Latif casually strolled down the track and hit him over the sightscreen and into the stands. The next one was short, expectedly. A flashing square cut sent the ball skimming in the air, low and parallel to the ground, to land just inside the fence. This was high-voltage stuff, and it could not last. Azhar cleverly brought on his slowest bowler, Venkatapathy Raju. Latif went after a lollipop which drifted away in the flight, beating him, for the easiest of stumpings.

When Latif went I knew the contest was over. Not so my uncle, in the next seat to mine. He, like countless others, would not forget Miandad's last-ball six against India at Sharjah, which won his side the match. When that shot was played, back in 1986, I was living in Connecticut. Everyone around me had seen the shot on television or heard it on the radio; I had only read about it when the Indian papers arrived at my university two weeks later. And where I now saw the man, ageing, they saw the myth, who would hit the last ball of this match also for six. But I could see that Miandad was playing from memory, without the power to even reach the boundary along the ground. Nine an over were required when he was run out by a direct hit. When he walked off the ground I stood up to applaud him. 'Why are you clapping?' asked an obnoxious fellow from a row behind. 'You should clap him too,' I answered, recklessly. 'This is the last time any of us will see him bat.' 'Thank God I shall never see the bastard again,' came the reply. How did I ever think that an uncertain internationalism would be equal to a single-minded patriotism?

<h1 style="text-align:center">VI</h1>

Before Waqar and Wasim there was Imran Khan, and after them have come Shoaib Akhtar and Mohammed Amir. Because of cricketers like these, Pakistan has been identified as a land of fast bowlers, whereas in fact they have produced some quality spin bowlers too. From youth to late middle age, my own life as a cricket fan has been greatly enriched by watching – albeit mostly on TV – four googly bowlers from across the border.

The first of this quartet was Abdul Qadir, who made wrist-spin glamourous long before the name of Shane Warne was known to the cricketing world. Qadir had a thrilling run-up and action; beginning with a lick of the fingers, he stood poised on his toes, ran four brisk steps sideways before releasing the ball with a quick final jump. He had them all: the leg-break, the googly, the top-spinner and the flipper too. Like Warne, he bowled extremely well in one-day cricket, being perhaps the first spinner to bowl regularly in the death overs. Had he the benefit of DRS he would have taken many more wickets in all forms of the game. I remember listening to the radio while he bowled for days in an England tour (of 1982), with the home batsmen putting their left leg down the wicket, bat tucked behind pad, in the knowledge that conservative umpires always gave batsmen the benefit of doubt on the front foot. Today even the English umpires would be compelled to give those out lbw.

Unlike the English and the West Indians, we Indians generally played Qadir well. I remember a Test on our 1982–3 tour when, after Imran and Sarfraz had run through the top order, Kapil came in and hit Qadir all over the place: inside out over cover, past square-leg, straight down the ground. But here too there were exceptions. In that same Test, Arun Lal had bravely and successfully seen off the new ball, and was inching towards his fifty. Then Qadir came on to bowl. Remembering Piggy's second-ball duck against Bhagwat Chandrasekhar on his first-class debut, I told my cousin, with whom I was watching, that I now feared for my old college captain, who was always vulnerable against quality wrist-spin. Sure enough, Qadir gave him two high-tossed leg-breaks which he left alone, followed by a fizzing top-spinner which Piggy played back to, and missed. He was struck low on the back pad, right in front of middle stump; and given out lbw, in perhaps the easiest decision ever awarded by a Pakistani umpire in favour of a Pakistani bowler.

I was then twenty-four, and my own (and always undistinguished) cricket career was already long over. But a Pakistani youngster then aged twelve, watching Abdul Qadir bowl as I was, chose to emulate him. This was Mushtaq Ahmed. Although he was short and pudgy whereas Qadir was supple and slim, he modelled his action on his hero's: from the lick of the fingers to the swift sideways run, though his build precluded that dramatic final jump. Like his mentor, Mushy bowled beautifully in both Test and in one-day cricket. He played a critical role in Pakistan's 1992 World Cup win, but I remember equally well his winning a Lord's Test by dismissing the three best English batsmen – Graeme Hick, Robin Smith, and Allan Lamb, all white South Africans by origin. If memory serves, one was caught behind off a leg-break, a second bowled by a googly, and the third leg-before to a top-spinner.

After Mushtaq came Danish Kaneria, only the second (or perhaps third) Hindu to play Test cricket for Pakistan. His action and delivery were more orthodox, as were his methods. He flighted the ball more than Qadir or Mushtaq, and turned it more too. However, he had less variety, the googly serving as the main or sole foil to his stock leg-break. But he was a superb bowler nonetheless. I can recall as I write two magical dismissals I saw on TV, in different continents and against different teams. One was of the right-handed Englishman Alec Stewart, done in the air as he came down the wicket, beaten by a sharp-turning leg-break to be stumped. The other was of the left-handed Australian Mitchell Johnson, a firm-footed hitter, seeking to strike a full ball over the bowler, only to find that it was a googly and not a leg-break, which missed the flailing bat and took the off-bail.

The most recent exponent of the Pakistani art of googly bowling I have seen is Yasir Shah. More open-chested in his delivery than his predecessors, he shares with them fine control, prodigious powers of spin, and the ability to take on the best. I saw, on television, a great deal of the 2016 Test series in England, a gripping contest which ended with both sides winning two matches apiece. The best bowler for the home team was Jimmy Anderson, a master of seam and swing and a real joy to watch when on song. For the visitors it was Yasir who asked the most searching questions. Since the Tests in England started when it was late afternoon in Bangalore, I could get a full morning's work on Mahatma Gandhi (and other such solemn subjects) before turning to the cricket with a clean conscience. It was a happy and fulfilling summer of binge watching, which I enjoyed all the more being from (as it were) a neutral country. May there be others to come.

VII

It has always seemed to be that the relationship of Inzamam-ul-Haq to Sachin Tendulkar was similar to that of Wally Hammond to Don Bradman. In 1928–9, Hammond toured Australia with the England team and scored 905 runs in the series. He was the world's best batsman, the world's best slip fielder, and a handy medium-pace bowler besides. He was set to be the world's greatest cricketer for the foreseeable future; except that, in the same Australian summer, a certain D G Bradman made his Test debut. He failed in his first Test, was dropped, but came back later in the series to score a hundred. A year-and-a-half later, Bradman toured England, scoring 974 runs in the Ashes series of that year to beat Hammond's record. And he fielded (in the covers) as well as his rival did in the slips. He did not bowl; but then he did not need to. Because Bradman batted so supremely well, Hammond spent the rest of his career somewhat in the Australian's shadow.

By the 1990s, in terms of intensity of interest and fanaticism of fan following, the India–Pakistan rivalry had replaced England–Australia as the most important contest in world cricket. When the 1992 World Cup came around, Tendulkar had already been three years in the game, scoring dazzling Test hundreds in England and in Australia. At this stage, Inzamam was relatively unknown. Although he was older than Sachin, he had come to international cricket later. However, in this World Cup India were knocked out early, whereas Inzamam played the innings of the tournament, a rapid-fire half-century in the semi-final against New Zealand. After the victorious Pakistanis returned home their captain talked up his protégé. Inzamam, said Imran, was as good or even better than Tendulkar.

That did not quite turn out to be the case. Tendulkar remained the greatest cricketer of his age. Inzy had to be content with being the Walter Hammond of his day. Like the Englishman, he suffered from being an almost exact contemporary of a batsman playing for the country which his own country most wished to defeat. And whereas the England–Australia rivalry was merely sporting, the India–Pakistan rivalry was political, religious and military as well.

For these reasons, cricketing history has somewhat condescended to Inzamam-ul-Haq. That is a pity, for he was a magnificent player. He had a languid grace, playing all around the wicket, always with time to spare. Like his great rival he played all the shots in the book. And he was much better while batting with the tail than Tendulkar, as well as more reliable in the fourth innings of a Test match.

The Inzamam innings I remember best was played in Bangalore in March 2005. Pakistan won the toss, chose to bat, and lost two quick wickets. Now numbers three and four, vice-captain and captain respectively, got together in a long act of retrieval. While Younis Khan played himself in carefully, Inzy chose to attack, driving the fast bowlers through the off-side and pulling and sweeping the spinners. Both got big hundreds, taking their side to an impressive first-innings total of 570.

When India replied, Sehwag scored a brilliant double-century, but the home side still conceded a lead of over a hundred. However, the wicket was still playing well, and it did not seem that there was time enough to force a result. Inzamam thought otherwise. Younis and he both scored at a fast clip before Pakistan declared at 261 for two. A day's play remained, but India failed to bat it out, crumbling in the face of astute bowling changes made by the visiting captain.

I watched this match from the best place in the ground, the then open press box of the Chinnaswamy Stadium. When the last Indian wicket fell, and the Pakistani team walked off, I saw a little boy run out from the pavilion under me. The victorious captain picked up the kid with one arm and cradled him off the ground, as his team behind him, and us press folks in front of him, applauded vigorously. That sight of Inzamam with his son at the end of a Test match remains one of the most affecting I have ever witnessed, in cricket or in life.

That was the last time I saw Pakistan's Walter Hammond, the last time, in fact, I ever saw any of his countrymen play cricket live, on the ground. For three years later terrorists from across the border attacked the city and citizens of Mumbai. Although

Pakistan played in the 2011 World Cup, no Pakistani team has played a Test series in India for more than a decade, and, with relations between our countries being what they are, I shall probably never see them play in Bangalore again.

VIII

If I restrict myself to those cricketers I have seen play in the flesh (thereby, sadly, excluding Hanif Mohammad), then my eleven favourite Pakistani cricketers would read:

1. Saeed Anwar
2. Younis Khan
3. Zaheer Abbas
4. Javed Miandad
5. Inzamam-ul-Haq
6. Imran Khan
7. Rashid Latif
8. Wasim Akram
9. Abdul Qadir
10. Mushtaq Ahmed
11. Waqar Younis

To be juxtaposed to my eleven of Indian cricketers I have seen in the flesh, as under:

1. Virender Sehwag
2. Sunil Gavaskar
3. Rahul Dravid
4. Sachin Tendulkar
5. Virat Kohli
6. Kapil Dev
7. S M H Kirmani

8. Anil Kumble
9. E A S Prasanna
10. Zaheer Khan
11. Bishan Bedi

Having constructed these Dream Teams, one might as well dream a bit more about how a match between them might pan out. It shall have to be played at a neutral venue, of course. At Lord's, with some green on the wicket and a wind blowing around the ground, Pakistan – with their marvellous swing bowlers – must start favourites. At Sydney, with dust on the pitch, Kumble, Bishan and Pras would have the edge over Qadir and Mushy. I'll leave it to the International Cricket Council to choose the umpires, but I must insist on nominating the commentators – who shall be Michael Atherton and Shane Warne.

IX

I'd like to end this chapter by recalling an encounter with a Pakistani cricket fan. It happened, in all places, on the outskirts of the city of Copenhagen, after the Davis Cup match between Sweden and Denmark that I have alluded to earlier in the book. Once the tennis had ended, I walked back to the suburban station to take a train back to town. I bought my ticket and ascended the steps to the platform; when I reached there, I saw a man of my complexion, somewhat older than myself, holding a cricket bat. I silently went up to him and took the bat from his hand, checked the grip and balance and played (as I recall) a cover drive in the air. As I handed the bat back to the stranger, the train arrived at the platform, and we both got in.

After the train began moving towards Copenhagen we introduced ourselves. He was Ali, from Lahore; I was Ram, from Bangalore. I was merely visiting Denmark, whereas he had lived here for twenty years, coming originally as a guest worker. Ali had laboured in a textile factory for a decade, acquired Danish citizenship, made himself eligible for social security, quit his job, and devoted himself to his one and only passion – the game of cricket. Every weekend he played a pick-up match with other former Pakistani guest workers in a ground that lay in this sporting suburb of the city. During the week he watched cricket at home, as it was telecast from around the world.

It was Sunday evening, and the compartment was empty. We had an hour to chat, and it was mostly about cricket, with some stuff about family thrown in. Ali had four sons; two worked part-time in the mills; two others lived, like the father, on social security. All were keen on cricket. The patriarch was the keenest of them all.

As the train trundled its way towards the city, Ali told me about the rich collection of video casettes he had acquired by mail order from England, Australia, and the Gulf. He had, he said, watched Viv Richards' double-century at The Oval in 1976 and Azharrudin's century at Lord's in 1990 over and over again. But then tragedy struck; when he and his family had gone to Pakistan on holiday, their home was burgled. The thieves took away many things, including the videos (not just cricketing) the family had collected over the years. However, when Ali made an insurance claim he was promptly and fully compensated. For, as he told me, in Hindustani, 'yahan ki Sarkar hamari jaisi nahin hain; poori imandari sé kam karti hai.' *The Government here is not like ours; it works with absolute and scrupulous honesty.* But while the burglary had not left Ali out of pocket, it had nonetheless left him spiritually bereft. As he said, in anguish, 'Wo Azhar aur Viv ka tape ab kahan sé laoon?' *Where can I ever get replacements for the tapes of those glorious innings by Azhar and Viv?* I suppose his wife felt the same sense of loss about the Bombay films of the 1950s and the Lahore dramas of the 1970s she would never be able to watch again.

When the train reached the Copenhagen main station we went our separate ways, he to his fully insured home, I to my hotel. It had been one of the most enjoyable conversations I had ever had with a fellow cricket fan; as well as by some distance the strangest. I already had many reasons to admire the Scandinavian welfare state; here was yet another, that it had allowed my new friend to so wholeheartedly devote his time and energy to what, whether home or away, would always be his favourite sport.

I write this some twenty-five years after I picked up a Pakistani's bat at Brøndby Station in Denmark. In memory of that meeting, and in tribute to my fellow cricket fan, I wish now to offer a joint All-Time Indo–Pak XI. There are six Indians; this is compensated for the fact that the captain is a Pakistani. Ram's Team for Ali, in batting order, reads:

1. Sunil Gavaskar
2. Saeed Anwar
3. Rahul Dravid
4. Sachin Tendulkar
5. Javed Miandad
6. Imran Khan (captain)
7. Vinoo Mankad
8. Kapil Dev
9. Syed Kirmani (wicketkeeper)
10. Wasim Akram
11. Anil Kumble

The solidity of Gavaskar and Dravid nicely matches the stroke-play of Sachin and Anwar, with Miandad playing builder or butcher as the situation demands. The terrifying pace of Imran and Wasim nicely matches the artful spin of Kumble and Mankad, with Kapil providing the leavening with his subtle control of swing and cut. The side has three of the greatest all-rounders in the history of the game. The batting has fabulous depth; number ten has a Test double-century to his credit, and even number eleven has a Test hundred. My great fellow towns-man, Syed Kirmani, would keep expertly to Wasim and Kumble, Imran and Mankad, but perhaps best of all to his captain in the 1983 World Cup winning side.

If they were playing at Eden Gardens or the Gaddafi Stadium, I'd back Ram's Team for Ali to take on an eleven of Anglo–Australian cricketers chosen from across the generations. I'd be slightly less confident with regard to an all-time team of West Indians led by Garry Sobers, though. But then, in the spirit of anti-colonial solidarity, I wouldn't really mind if we lose to the latter, even at home, so long as we defeat the former.

9

Accidental Administrator

I

I am by nature and instinct an anti-Establishment man. I left the academy thirty years ago, and have since had no allegiance to a formal institution. I could not cope with working in a university, and would have found it impossible to work in a newspaper or corporate office. I have never been a member of a political party.

The Friends Union Cricket Club is an exception to this rule, but there is nothing formal about this lone institution to which I belong. FUCC has no office, owns no property, and has no paid employees. Besides, allegiance to my club has always run hand-in-hand with opposition to the larger, more handsomely endowed, and less principled cricketing organisations that lie above it. I have already spoken of my decidedly mixed feelings about the Karnataka State Cricket Association. And there was no trace of ambivalence in how I saw the apex body of the game in India, the Board of Control for Cricket in India. I had long detested the control over the BCCI of scheming politicians and self-important ex-Maharajas. The shady nature of its financial operations stank. Then the Indian Premier League began, and the BCCI's operations became even more dodgy.

In 2013, after the match-fixing scandals and the exposure of rampant conflicts of interest, a pile of Public Interest Litigations were filed before the Supreme Court of India, asking it to intervene and clean up Indian cricket. The Court set up a one-man committee of Justice Mudgal, formerly of the Delhi High Court, who found clear evidence of wrongdoing by the son-in-law of the BCCI's former President, N Srinivasan, in the functioning of an IPL team owned by Srinivasan himself.* The Supreme Court then set up a three-man committee, headed by R M Lodha, a former Chief Justice of the Supreme Court, to recommend reforms in cricket administration.

The Lodha Committee travelled around the country meeting (as the term went) the game's 'stakeholders'. As a writer on cricket, I was also asked to meet the Committee. I did, in a room in the Gardenia Hotel in Bangalore, built on the ruins of the ITC Officers Colony in which my former clubmate, the Yorkshireman, Chris Hardinge, had once lived. Here I offered the three Justices my views on, among other things, cronyism in team selection and the neglect of domestic cricket.

In January 2016, the Lodha Committee submitted a report advocating wide-ranging reforms in the functioning of the BCCI and its member associations. They recommended term limits for office-bearers, curbs on conflict of interest, transparency in financial matters, a restructuring of membership rules for state associations, and the professionalisation of management. The Supreme Court accepted the report, and asked the BCCI to implement it. The BCCI, no doubt under the (probably accurate) impression that powerful politicians were on their side (and against Lodha's), stalled and prevaricated. The Supreme Court then dismissed the President of the BCCI, the BJP MP Anurag Thakur, for having made false statements and 'obstructed and impeded the orders of

---

* https://www.firstpost.com/sports/ipl-spot-fixing-full-text-of-the-mudgal-committee-report-1382627.html

this court as well'. Insisting that 'the turf of the cricket field is not a personal turf or fiefdom', the Court decided to appoint an interim 'Committee of Administrators' in their place, which would run Indian cricket until a new set of officials were elected following the Lodha guidelines.

I had been following these developments, but not closely, since I was not writing very much on cricket any more. On 13 January 2017, I was attending the twenty-fifth anniversary celebrations of the National Centre for Biological Sciences in Bangalore. While some top biologists, including two Nobel laureates, were speaking, I got a series of missed calls, followed by a message saying that Gopal Subramanium wanted to speak to me urgently. I had never met Subramanium, but knew of his high standing as a lawyer, and knew also that in the opinion of many learned jurists, he would have made an excellent Judge of the Supreme Court himself.

In the tea break I called back, and spoke to Gopal Subramanium. He said he was the *amicus curae* in the Lodha case, and the Court had asked him to suggest names for this new 'Committee of Administrators' (COA). He wanted to include mine. I asked who the other people in his list were. He named a few: the great, now retired, cricketers Bishan Bedi, S Venkataraghavan, and Diana Edulji, the retired civil servant Vinod Rai, and the banker Vikram Limaye.

I asked for twenty-four hours to think it over. The next day I wrote to Gopal saying that I was happy for my name to be put forward. But I suggested he also include the name of Sharda Ugra, whom I termed 'the leading writer in cricket's leading media outlet, Cricinfo', 'a person of total integrity and deep knowledge of the game as it is run (or not run) in India', and who 'knows the functioning of the current Board and various state associations at a day to day level far better than any of the cricketers who will be on the committee. And she knows the pulse of the younger generation of cricket lovers very well too.'

Meanwhile, the state associations and the Government of India demanded that they also be allowed to submit names for the COA. The Supreme Court looked at their suggestions, and eventually chose four names, all from Gopal's list. These were Vinod Rai (as chairman), Vikram Limaye, the former women's Test captain Diana Edulji, and myself. The two former captains of the Indian team whom Gopal had recommended, Bedi and Venkat, were ruled out as being too old. Justice Lodha had recommended that office-bearers of the BCCI and its constituent units retire at seventy; and that meant the COA had to follow this age limit as well.

The Supreme Court announced these names on the afternoon of 30 January. That day I was in Tirur, in Kerala, due to speak the next morning at the Thunchan festival, held in memory of the medieval Malayalam poet of that name. I received a continuous stream of phone calls and messages, from friends, acquaintances, and, most of all, from the press. In the former category was a warm and generous call of congratulations from Bishan Bedi, who noted wryly that while Venkat and he had been excluded by the Supreme Court since they were over seventy, the Court could not find, in his words, a single senior male cricketer of integrity below that age limit.

Meanwhile the Twitterverse had been abuzz. Through that evening and night, as I watched a Kuchipudi performance in Tirur, I got a great deal of abuse on my timeline from devotees of the Indian Prime Minister, Narendra Modi, or Modi *bhakts* as they are known. They were enraged that the Supreme Court, technically a government body, had given me a position of prominence. My Twitter bio described me as a 'failed cricketer'; this self-deprecatory joke was now thrown back at me, with dozens of bhakts demanding to know how a professedly 'failed cricketer' could presume to run Indian cricket. Some cricket lovers worried that with me in the Committee of Administrators, the Indian Premier League was in peril. I was known to be a partisan of Test cricket, and had harshly criticised the IPL in several newspaper columns.

Among the trolling and the abuse there was also some humour. In the Twitterverse I was stereotyped as a left-wing scholar and admirer of Jawaharlal Nehru, so one fellow tweeted that 'With Ram Guha in BCCI [the fast bowler Ashish] Nehra is one vowel from captaincy.' This was genuinely funny, so I retweeted it. I also tweeted a link to a satirical blog on my appointment, laboured in parts, as for example this paragraph:

> Given this development [my appointment to the COA],
> right handers – both bowlers and batsmen in the Indian
> team and its fringes – are now practising batting and
> bowling left-handed to save their spots in the team.
> Someone tipped them off that a culling of the right-handed
> was coming up.

But with at least one good joke, as under:

> Meanwhile, Mahendra Singh Dhoni, being the proactive
> cricketer that he is, apparently called Guha for some advice.
> 'Sir. I'm not sure which batting combination is right. Is it
> Raina before Yuvraj or Raina after Yuvraj?'
> 'Mr Dhoni, are you trying to make fun of my iconic book
> titles? If you behave like a paid troll, I'll get you fired!' shot
> back Guha.*

After giving my talk in Tirur, on 31 January I drove to Coimbatore, to take a flight to Delhi, where a meeting of the new Committee of Administrators had been called for the afternoon of 1 February. Through the long (and lovely) drive through

---

* http://www.opindia.com/2017/01/why-ram-guha-deserves-place-in-bcci-and-the-changes-that-are-already-happening.

northern Kerala, the messages and phone calls of congratulations continued to pour in, as did the abuse and anger on social media. I hadn't realised, or rather had forgotten, how much cricket meant to India and Indians. I had lived a fairly public life for the past two decades – articles, talks, books, TV shows, controversies – but nothing I had ever done (in this case hadn't even done yet) had attracted remotely as much attention, or excitement, as this appointment.

In Tirur, I had erratic access to email. When I reached Delhi, I opened my InBox, and read the flood of mails more fully. An entrepreneur-friend in Bangalore said it was 'nice to finally have somebody at BCCI who will obey nobody'. My old teacher and cricketing team-mate, R P Devgan, remarked it had been 'quite a journey from Cricket at the FRI, IMA and the Doon School Dehradun to St Stephen's in Delhi and now on to the controller of cricket in India'. He added: 'Wonder what Durai feels about it? A proud Uncle!'

The political theorist Partha Chatterjee, who gave me my first job, wrote, 'Dear Ram, I have never been more pleased with any appointment as with this one. You are our man. "Ram Guha tum aage barho, ham tumhare saath hai!"'* The greatest of modern cricket writers, Gideon Haigh, dryly remarked, 'You're running the BCCI, Ram? Have I entered an alternative universe?' Haigh's friend and mine, the editor of *Cricinfo* Sambit Bal, heard the news in Melbourne airport, shortly after watching Roger Federer defeat Rafael Nadal in the final of the Australian Open. Calling me on landing in Mumbai, Sambit said if Federer winning another Grand Slam at the age of thirty-five was unlikely enough, Ram Guha running BCCI (after the names I had called the organisation) was even more startling.

---

* A play on a widely used exhortation used by followers of political leaders in India, here roughly translated as: 'Ram, go ahead and lead by example, we are with you all the way!'

It was forty years since I had played cricket for St Stephen's. But, perhaps not surprisingly, I got several calls from cricketers I had played with or against back then, these retired Ranji (and in one case India) players asking me to use my newfound position of prominence to get them consultancy or coaching contracts with the BCCI. However, one old cricketer characteristically put the game above himself. This was Bishan Bedi, who had followed up his phone call with this message, 'Can I please send you some viable suggestions which could come in handy in discharge of your duties as newly appointed administrator … More strength to your very conscientious cricket involvement! Take care Ram of yourself and Indian cricket!' I asked Bishan to send the suggestions by mail. To which he replied, 'Sure, Ram, definitely … Meanwhile keep your cool, will ya?' (something that had been hard for him always, and, as he knew, was hard for me, too).

A day later Bishan Bedi sent me his suggestions, which must be quoted *in extenso* since – the SMS language notwithstanding – they reveal a depth of knowledge and a sincerity of intent rare and possibly unequalled in the world of Indian cricket:

I've honestly tried to put myself in yur shoes lately & discovered how uncomfortable the seat is that of an 'administrator' as appointed by the SC of India but then not all 'onerous' responsibilities are cushy & customised … so we must 'want' to do a job as against 'have' to. May God give U calm & patience to clean up a mess of nearly eight decades in few months … tough really Mate!

Point wise we can follow the dictates of Lodha Panel & get on with it … using a little common sense will help!! As I've been saying from my playing days 'Control' bit in bcci is hugely superfluous & undesirable, this term has given unfair authority to many a nincompoop, let's work on 'Cricket India' or 'Indian Cricket Board' … to be strictly followed by Uniform code by State Associations … no more 'Ltd

Companies' please ... these are highly legal steps, which, I hope are within yur purview!

Money as we all know is the bane of all problems, either lack of it or excess of it, in the case of Crkt Ind it is the latter! I reckon this distribution of 'funds' to State units must be stopped with immediate effect & disbursed only when required ... just about all State Units were availing of this filthy facility & falling 'in line' with whoever was at the helm, just ask fr the latest accounts & U'll get a good idea ... I'm very wary of bcci tv ... this too is hub of all corruption whence leading lights of Indn Crkt divulged in issuing certificates of merit to all & sundry in a bottomless administration!! No other Crkt set up in the world has tv co of its own!!

I'm enclosing few suggestions as I've received keeping DDCA in view especially! This business of 'Ltd' company is DDCA's legacy to entire North Zone. Punjab, Himachal, Haryana are registered as Companies & not as Societies which the Parent body is!!

Now, I'm slightly perplexed, do we touch the 'top' to ascertain 'culture' or get to the 'bottom' to locate 'grassroots'?! Your foursome may have to touch upon both simultaneously! When we played there was [a] School tournament called 'Cooch Behar' & any bonafide student of a school could play; but now we have under age tournaments where ages are fudged with impunity & with the connivance of State bodies & despite the best efforts of the system this malaise of 'over age' persists!

We need to revive 'Rohinton B[aria]' University's tournament to keep alive the importance of higher education in Crkt!! A kid who plays max two years in schools & four years in University can be trusted to have strong basics of Crkt. Today we see so many youngsters making a hefty pay cheque & entirely dependent on 'managers/agents' or parroting the language of 'support staff'!!

Now that Women's Crkt falls under the aegis of Crkt board it needs proper nourishing to be seen to be done. I hope Diana would do the needful on this count!! Some more suggestions soon Ram ... pl bear with me & God Bless U Mate ... Fondly ... Bishan

II

The day before I attended my first meeting of the COA, I wrote an email to my colleagues – none of whom I had previously met – urging that we 'incorporate into our committee of administrators, either as a full member or as a special invitee, a senior male cricketer with the distinction and integrity that Diana has. That will greatly enhance both our credibility and our ability to make informed decisions.'

The 'absence of a respected male cricketer in the COA,' I remarked,

is a glaring deficiency that has attracted a great deal of just criticism already, much of it from important stakeholders in Indian cricket. It must be addressed and remedied. The amicus curae had suggested two outstanding names, Venkat and Bedi, both of whom were rejected because they are over seventy. However, there are some cricketers of the right age and experience who fit the bill. Based on my knowledge of the subject, I would say Javagal Srinath would be an excellent choice. He is a world-class cricketer, was a successful and scandal-free Secretary of the Karnataka State Cricket Association, and is an ICC match referee, and comes from an educated technical background to boot. I strongly urge the Chairman and the other members to consider approaching him in this regard. He would complement Diana perfectly, and the combination of these two respected and top-class former cricketers would enhance our credibility and effectiveness enormously.

While Srinath is in my view the best choice, there are other alternative names too. I hope we can set aside some time at our meeting to discuss and resolve this issue.

I ended my email with this postscript: 'Needless to say, I have not discussed this with Srinath or with anyone else.'

When I brought this proposal up at the meeting itself, the other members of the committee were noticeably unenthusiastic. I was told that the Supreme Court had appointed us alone; and thus we could not get Srinath or someone else of his stature to join us. I said that there was nothing to stop us from having a respected male cricketer under seventy attend meetings as a 'special invitee'. That proposal was vetoed too. Then I suggested that at least we could get Srinath to make a presentation to us. The Chairman, Vinod Rai, was lukewarm about this as well.

The press coverage of the COA's constitution had been extraordinarily intense, as well as extensive; with cricket being what it was in India, a retired bureaucrat, a retired woman's cricketer, a banker and a historian had overnight become major national figures, our photos featuring on the front pages of newspapers and television anchors hounding us for 'exclusive' interviews. It seemed to me that this publicity had got to my colleagues, who did not want to open this exclusive club of four to other (even if extremely well-qualified) members.

At this meeting of the COA there were two presentations. The BCCI's Chief Financial Officer spoke on their accounts and their tax status; while the BCCI Manager in charge of the Indian Premier League made a much longer presentation on the Board's showpiece tournament and cash cow. This was a super hard-sell of the product, making fantastic claims for its contributions to cricket and to society. Corporate boxes, those testimonies to greed and cronyism, were described gushingly as taking cricket-watching to a higher level, through the 'new and unique experience' they allegedly facilitated. A slide displayed early on had the CEO of Apple, Tim Cook, being interviewed (significantly, by a white TV anchor) at an IPL match, and saying excitedly, 'IT IS INCREDIBLE … I HAVE NEVER EXPERIENCED ANYTHING LIKE THIS, THE CROWD'S EXCITEMENT IS AMAZING … IT SHOWS HOW IMPORTANT CRICKET IS.' Now middle-class Indians love Western certification; but it was evident that Tim Cook was merely flattering his hosts, preparatory to exploring the growing market for iPhones and Apple Macs in a country of a billion-plus people.

Through this presentation the Board official looked largely at me, perhaps because of my reputation as an IPL baiter. The reputation was not undeserved; in an op-ed in *The Hindu* in 2013 I had written that

The Indian Premier League is decidedly on the crony rather than creative side of the ledger [of capitalism]. The original auction for teams was shrouded in secrecy – the allocations were not made on the basis of bids transparently offered and assessed. Player prices do not accurately reflect cricketing worth either. Thus foreign players are paid a fraction of what Indian players of comparable quality are paid. The most egregious form of cronyism, however, is the ownership of an IPL team by the current president (and former secretary) of the Board of Control for Cricket in India. It is as if Alex Ferguson was simultaneously manager of Manchester United and the president of the English Football Association. Tragically, the cronyism runs down the line. The current chairman of selectors is the brand ambassador of the team owned and run by the Board president. The famous former cricketers who cover Indian cricket on television have been consultants to the IPL. Other commentators have accepted assignments from IPL teams. To put it bluntly, their silence on this (and some other matters) has been bought.

The 2017 IPL season was fast approaching. With the sacking of the BCCI's President and Secretary, there was a sense of worry and uncertainty among franchise owners, cricketers, support staff, and fans. The IPL contributed some 60 per cent of the Board's revenue, and was (whether I liked it or not) watched by hundreds of millions of Indians. So clearly the COA had to facilitate its smooth conduct, and it did. As the professional writer/editor in the Committee, it fell to me to finalise the press statement issued after our first meeting, which read:

New Delhi: 1 February 2017
The Committee of Administrators (COA) met the concerned BCCI officials today to take stock of the urgent and important matters mainly concerning the successful conduct of IPL 2017.

The COA has issued directions that the existing processes for availing the services and the appointment of the vendors for IPL will continue for this season.

The COA further assures the Franchisees and all the stakeholders that all the IPL preparations will be promptly dealt with under the supervision and directions of the COA by the BCCI/IPL management team.

The IPL operational timelines for 2017 season will be communicated shortly by the BCCI/IPL management team.

The IPL 2017 season will commence as scheduled from 5 April 2017.

So, ironically, my first consequential act as a BCCI administrator was to assist in giving the go-ahead to the IPL, despite my detestation of the tournament and all that it stood for. But in my mind some questions remained, which, I thought, I might, with luck and persistence, be able to place on the table before the 2018 season of the IPL. These were:

First, that the IPL was pure *tamasha*, not really cricket, despite claims by the BCCI that it was the beltway to the Indian team. (In fact, it was the Ranji Trophy which still largely played that role.) There remained doubts about matches being fixed, or so arranged as to ensure artificially close finishes. Admittedly the tournament had become a money spinner, but should the ends so completely define the means? The Board's presentation to us had emphasised the need to please and placate franchisees and sponsors of different kinds. Given what we knew of these people – the Mallyas and the Ambanis and the like – why was flattering these fat cats so important to the BCCI?

Second, that the tournament was inegalitarian in a social as well as geographical sense. Why was it that the densely populated and cricket-mad states of UP, Bihar, and MP did not have a single team between them? While Maharashtra had (at the time) two teams, and the neighbouring states of Karnataka and Tamil Nadu one apiece? Only because the first set of states were poor, and the second set of states rich. Why couldn't the BCCI consciously create franchises in states like UP and Bihar, or at least mandate that some matches be played in smaller cities, in far flung parts of the country?

Third, why couldn't revenues from the IPL be used to greatly enhance fees and prize money for players in the Ranji Trophy, and be used to fund and promote women's cricket too? There were many more Indian cricketers who made their living via the Ranji Trophy than via the IPL; besides, for us to have a consistently strong Test team (especially overseas) we needed a robust inter-state competition and therefore had to compensate domestic players better. And yet, as I found in my first weeks in the BCCI, Ranji match fees had remained at a very low level (a mere Rs 30,000 for each day of play). And complaints were pouring in about cheques for match fees sent by the BCCI not being passed on by state associations to their Ranji players.

The COA's go-ahead to the IPL made the front pages of the newspapers, prompting this amused letter from an Andhra cricket writer of my acquaintance, C Venkatesh:

Dear Sri Guha,

Involuntarily a smile escaped my lips on seeing the headline in TOI. It's about CoA's nod to IPL 2017 and you know why. The news item even had a mention of your celebrated hatred of the shortest of all formats. Ever since I heard the news about your presence in the CoA, I had two things in mind. The first one was actually a worry! Yes because the romantic in you might be lost, if you get down to the brass tacks and start administering the game, even for a brief while. I think it was Mukul Kesavan, who said that distance gives perspective. How true. I have been finding all the sports journalists to be very cynical since they cover the game day in and day out. But as an outsider, you retain the flavour for the game. Your writings like 'that is the first time I shook hands with a Test cricketer,' connect you with the readers. Now my worry is that you may lose that fascination, once you get into the murky world of cricket administration where everyone is a sinner. Proximity breeds contempt. So please don't take things to heart and let this stint affect your writings in anyway.

My second feeling was of curiosity ... As a professional writer you write only what you like, but I think the new role is going to make you do things which may not be to your liking. But IPL with all its minuses has a huge plus in providing a huge platform for the fringe players and contributes in a big way to the talent pool. So please pardon the sinners, they don't know what they are doing.

IPL 2017 was on track, but supporters of the tournament worried that, with me in the COA, I would seek to undermine future editions. The journalist Anand Vasu, writing in the *Economic Times*, spoke of my 'pathological hatred for the Indian Premier League (IPL), one of the most anticipated fixtures in the international cricket calendar', and further claimed that I 'panned the tournament at every chance'. This alarmist tone betrayed some deep insecurity; in eight years I had written two pieces on the IPL, this when I had a weekly column translated into several languages as my pulpit. My dislike of IPL and its excesses, its cronyism and corruption, had been manifest here, but scarcely in a pathological manner! But even my episodically expressed reservations had created fear among the cheerleaders.

Vasu then offered this apologia for the way the IPL was run, or mis-run:

> The rules of engagement in India are something each of us is born with and grow into; the conventions that our lives are ruled by are in our blood; the way we do things is by no means black or white. If, in every walk of life, we are uniquely Indian, for better or worse, why do we expect cricket, and how it is run, to be any different?

That is to say – We are Like That. The IPL was poorly run and corrupt because India was poorly run and corrupt. This peculiar defensiveness went hand-in-hand with, and was a product of, a vulgar anti-colonial nationalism. English and Australian journalists had been condescending towards Indian scribes for decades; now, post IPL and the rush of foreign players to our country, the balance had been redressed. With India as the centre for world cricket, with the BCCI's growing clout in the International Cricket Council, no longer could foreign cricket correspondents talk down to their Indian counterparts. This also explained why even senior newspaper editors had become cheerleaders for the

IPL, celebrating it as a great global brand produced in India. Thus Shekhar Gupta had written in the *Indian Express* in 2011 that the IPL had 'produced more young talent in one year than our domestic cricket would have normally done in five ... The IPL has also monetised the game of cricket as no idea has done, even the advent of other short versions of the game in the past three decades. What is even better, these new riches are enriching, besides cricketers, the media, sponsors, event managers, the hospitality industry and so on. For a game dying because of spectator apathy this has been a brilliant economic stimulus with pretty effective trickle-down.' The exuberant hyperbole (for in fact it was still the Ranji Trophy that produced the best talent, both for the Indian team and even for the IPL) was characteristic; unmentioned was the fact that the two most prominent faces of the IPL, Lalit Modi and Vijay Mallya, had run away to London to escape going to jail. Corruption, cronyism, match-fixing, conflict of interest – these too were intrinsic to the IPL, but the flag-wavers would not mention them.

III

On the international front, the first challenge before our new Committee of Administrators was the growing pushback by other countries against the bullying tactics of the Indian Cricket Board. Some years previously, the BCCI had got together with Australia and England to take control of the International Cricket Council. These three countries awarded themselves a disproportionate amount of the game's revenues (with India getting the most money), while also manipulating the international cricketing calendar such that they played each other regularly, leaving other countries out in the cold.

This so-called 'Big Three' model was the handiwork of N Srinivasan, who had headed both the BCCI and the ICC.

Srinivasan was a textbook case of the authoritarian personality. He was accustomed to getting his own way; and had bulldozed other Indian cricket administrators as well as the Indian press into submission. But then his family got implicated in the match-fixing scandal, which led to fingers being belatedly pointed at his own conflicts of interest.

In November 2015, Srinivasan was replaced as Chairman of the ICC by Shashank Manohar. Based in Nagpur, and the long-time head of the Vidarbha Cricket Association, Manohar was less authoritarian than his predecessor, somewhat more open to hearing other points of view. With him at the helm, the smaller, less financially privileged members of the ICC asked for a rollback of the Big Three model. A new revenue-sharing agreement was drafted, under which India's share would be reduced from $570 million to $290 million, with the money going to develop the game in other, less well-endowed parts of the cricketing world.

This new model was fairer than the one it sought to replace; yet it evoked much outrage in an increasingly jingoistic Indian press. Why should we not continue to dominate world cricket, asked writers, commentators, retired cricketers, and now out-of-work administrators? Shashank Manohar was denounced as a traitor, and a toady of Western imperialism. He was compared to Mir Jafar, a Bengali nobleman who, back in the eighteenth century, had helped the East India Company secure its first bridgehead on the Indian subcontinent.

In February 2017, this new model was discussed at a meeting of the ICC in Dubai. As the financial expert in our Committee, Vikram Limaye was deputed to attend it on behalf of the BCCI. He came back saying that while we could perhaps lobby successfully for a smaller reduction in India's share, there was no doubt that, as he put it, 'the relationship between the BCCI and the ICC is very poor – no trust at all'.

In a long email to my COA colleagues, I explained the historical background to this lack of trust. Test cricket began in 1877.

For a full century thereafter, the MCC and hence England presided over how international cricket was played and regulated. They unilaterally decided schedules, laws, and other matters. In 1977, with the advent of World Series Cricket, power began shifting to Australia, which by the time of the World Cup held Down Under in 1992 had become the acknowledged centre of international cricket. Their summer (winter for us and for England) was made inviolate; the Australians stayed at home, while visiting teams were compelled to adjust their schedules and go there (and usually get thrashed, to the gloating of the home media). The power of Channel 9, and the fact that Australia in the 1990s and beyond were far and away the best side in the world, consolidated this dominant position.

Resenting this (not always benign) imperialism of the Brits and the Aussies, Asian countries began asking for a more equitable ordering of world cricket. This was both necessary and overdue. This movement was led by India, working in alliance with Pakistan and Sri Lanka, and in time, Bangladesh. But post IPL and its commercial success, hubris overcame the BCCI, and under N Srinivasan especially, other Asian nations were cast aside, and India bid to become the sole hegemon of world cricket, flexing its money and muscle to achieve this. Tragically, this bid was encouraged by the Indian media, partly out of a sense of revenge: having been so long condescended to by the Western media, they now wanted to lord it over them in turn.

I told my colleagues in the BCCI that English and Australian hegemony had often worked against the larger interests of cricket worldwide. But, I added, so would Indian domination. India, I argued, must not become to international cricket what the United States was to international politics; setting the rules, and disregarding otherwise fair international treaties when it did not suit them. An example of BCCI bullying was our refusal to accept the Decision Review System, because of pressure from our shorter players (such as Sachin Tendulkar and M S Dhoni), for it would make them more vulnerable to lbw decisions, rather than for any more logical reason. Another was the foisting of L Sivaramakrishnan as the international players' representative to the ICC, not on the basis of his cricketing record or cricketing intelligence, but merely because he was a long-term loyalist of N Srinivasan. The Big Three model was another instance of how Indian bullying worked against the interests of the international game as a whole.

My colleagues largely agreed with me, but, as the nationalist hysteria rose higher, and grew more shrill, they found it difficult to articulate this egalitarian position in public. Meanwhile, N Srinivasan was seeking to make a comeback to the BCCI on the back of such jingoism. Although he was clearly disqualified under the Lodha guidelines – being over seventy and having served more than nine years as an office-bearer – he attended meetings of the BCCI's state associations, where he dominated proceedings. I urged our Chairman, Vinod Rai, to issue a public statement saying this was illegal, but he was too nervous to do so. His silence emboldened the Old Guard further. They now called for a boycott of the Champions Trophy, due to be played in England that June.

The scoundrels who now sought to wear the garb of patriotism found support in the hyper-nationalistic press. The editor of *Swarajya*, a magazine of Modi bhakts, demanded that the Committee of Administrators be sacked. Just as Jawaharlal Nehru had (allegedly) bargained away a seat at the UN Security Council, he wrote, now, we Nehruvians were now 'happily hand-ing over our dominance [of World cricket] without a second thought or even a *mea culpa*'. He claimed that 'India has the clout to let ICC go to hell and start its own World Cricket Council (WCC), if it chooses to do so'. This writer had me in mind without mentioning my name; meanwhile, one reader posted this comment on his article:

After a long long time, a non-white cricketing nation has come to the fore & we have the stupid Supreme Court destroying that structure. It can happen only in India that we give up power. I believe this SC intervention to straighten BCCI affairs is nothing but a project bankrolled by some outside forces. What the f*ck is a biased historian doing in the CoA? Is this some kind of a joke? BCCI is screwed for sure here. If BCCI has any self-respect they should just put the foot down.

The jingoists found further support from the great former opening batsman Sunil Gavaskar. In a column with the remarkably paranoid title, 'Cricketing world is against India', he asked the BCCI to demand that the Big Three model be retained in its entirety. Gavaskar then continued, 'We in India are champs at cutting our own noses and limbs just to spite some other fellow Indians whom we rightly or wrongly don't like. For close to nine years there are some who have tried to finish off the Indian Premier League (IPL) simply because they are not part of it or are not benefitting from it.'

Gavaskar's screed raised this obvious counter-question: If those attacking the IPL were doing so because they were not benefiting from it, were those defending the IPL through thick and thin – to the extent of boosting fugitives like Lalit Modi and Vijay Mallya – only doing so because they benefited from it? Further, it was hard to take a sermon on patriotism from someone who – whatever his past achievements as a cricketer – loved his country so much that for many years now he had avoided paying taxes in India.

Gavaskar followed up his article with a television interview where he suggested that if the Big Three model was tinkered with, India should not send a team to the Champions Trophy. The remaining office-bearers of the BCCI were also inclined towards this view. The Indian team for the tournament had not yet been announced, prompting an anxious email from the ICC, since the deadline had long passed, and the other participating countries had named their teams.

It was now late April. The prestigious Champions Trophy would start in just over a month. Our team had still not been selected. Our participation was not yet confirmed. The BCCI Old Guard and their acolytes in the press were seeking to black-mail the ICC into submission. I found this appalling, and urged our Chairman, Mr Rai, to order the selectors to convene to select the team. He would not do so. So I told my colleagues that I was going to tweet, in my personal capacity, that India should not boycott the Champions Trophy.

On 30 April, I issued these two tweets:

Speaking in my personal capacity, as a cricket fan, I believe the Indian cricket team absolutely must take part in the Champions Trophy.

Boycotting or threatening to boycott a prestigious international tournament does not become a great cricketing nation.

Meanwhile, while some newspapers had gone along with the prevailing chauvinism, the *Indian Express* had published an excellent editorial asking the BCCI to stand for decency and justice. So I issued a third tweet:

The choice before the BCCI: 'It can be the popular king of a growing game or the despised don of a dying sport.' http://indianexpress.com/article/opinion/editorials/ bccis-choice-4632391/.

The state associations had scheduled a BCCI Special General Meeting for 7 May. The worry was that N Srinivasan and his acolytes might here press for a boycott of the Champions Trophy.

Senior journalists were on their side, calling me a traitor for my tweets. But then the tide decisively turned against the Old Guard when, on 4 May, a dozen former cricketers issued a statement saying that India must send a team to the Champions Trophy. They included Rahul Dravid, G R Viswanath and Sachin Tendulkar. The statement had been drafted by Sanjay Manjrekar, a cricketer-turned-commentator keen here to do the right thing. Manjrekar did not sign himself, but his intervention was decisive. Dravid, Vishy and Sachin were three of the greatest names in the history of Indian cricket. Their voices, at once credible and convincing, silenced Srinivasan and Gavaskar and their cronies. A selection committee meeting was now convened, and India sent a team to the Champions Trophy.

IV

Our Committee of Administrators met two or three times a month, usually in Mumbai. In between meetings there were lots of mails to answer and documents to read. The various state associations had filed caveats before the Supreme Court, and we had to file responses to them.

At one of our first meetings, in Delhi in mid-February, the auditing firm of Deloitte made a presentation. When Shashank Manohar was President of the BCCI, he had commissioned a series of reports on the finances of state associations. However, the findings were so damaging that they were suppressed. Invoking a confidentiality clause, Deloitte would not share the reports with us either; but they agreed to give an overview of what they had found.

I took notes as the Deloitte team spoke. They had found all kinds of malfeasance in the state associations. Thus, under the head of 'Cricketing Infrastructure', one association had bought as many as eighteen private cars. Some associations maintained

271

handwritten accounts. Travel, building and consultancy contracts to relatives and proxies were rife. Annual grants to affiliated clubs were not passed on, nor was one meant for retired Ranji and Test players. Deloitte even found cheques from five and more years ago, kept by the association and withheld from the beneficiaries. Some associations held their funds in personal accounts, others in banks and co-operatives where the officials themselves had a stake. Flats had been bought for officials from BCCI funds. Reimbursement had been paid for travel on flights for routes which did not exist. A staggering 220 crores* was locked up in land purchased by different associations where nothing had come up at all, not even a practice pitch. In one case, crops were still being grown on land transferred years ago for the construction of a cricket stadium; in another, the property deeds for the purchase of the land had gone missing, opening up the possibility of damaging litigation. More than 100 crores had gone in advance payments for land not transferred to associations. Cost over-runs for the construction of stadia amounted to hundreds of crores.

Indian cricket had been badly run for decades, and it had become even worse run since the start of the IPL. More money meant more opportunities for cronyism and corruption. The consequences of this maladministration were borne by players, both active and retired, and by the fans. After I became a COA member, correspondence came pouring in from interested parties in the world of Indian cricket. These conveyed details of how the game was being mismanaged in different parts of the country. The Resident Editor of the *Times of India*'s Nagpur edition wrote to say that the Vidarbha Cricket Association, long run by Shashank Manohar, had prohibited entry of all journalists from his paper in their stadia, because of some critical stories the paper had run. (Manohar not crooked, as some of his peers were, but

---

* A crore is 10 million rupees.

he was easily as vindictive.) Former Ranji and Test players from Goa, Tripura, Uttar Pradesh, Madhya Pradesh and Jammu and Kashmir wrote of how their associations had been captured by corrupt cliques, who allocated lucrative contracts to their cronies and also manipulated team selection to favour their family or friends.

Ordinary fans also sent their complaints. One asked the COA to instruct TV channels to show fewer advertisements between overs, as because of these ads 'the whole flow of watching cricket dissipates and also causes irritation'. A second, writing from the temple town of Moodbidri, asked, 'Do we really need the dances and cracker shows used in limited-over matches, which really disturb and destroy sports taste, besides prompting other ills? Simply because other countries are indulging in that should we follow everything they do?'

And a third wrote of watching a Test match at the KSCA's Chinnaswamy Stadium, to find:

The same old story:
1. Leaking Toilets.
2. No safety – Electrical points – No MCB Switches – Direct wiring.
3. Unhygienic food being sold – Cut fruit and Shivajinagar Samosa's.
4. No Fire Fighting equipment in the stadium, No safety exit route.

Who is responsible for this?
Why do paying spectators get treated like shit?
Will be forwarding you emails that I sent to KSCA complaining about the very same lack of facilities during the recent world cup matches too.
It's time to crack the whip.

V

In our COA meetings, legal, administrative and financial matters figured far more than cricket and cricketers. There were exceptions, as in a meeting in the last week of February which began with a consideration of the annual C K Nayudu Lifetime Achievement award. The jury normally consisted of the BCCI President and Secretary, and an eminent journalist. This year, since there was no President or Secretary in place, Diana Edulji and I substituted for them. The BCCI's *babus* already had a name on file; it was that of Ravi Shastri. Apparently the now dismissed President and Secretary were keen that Shastri be given the C K Nayudu award. I protested vigorously, for Shastri's own cricketing record was moderate, not outstanding. It was some distance short of Gavaskar, Bedi, Viswanath, Kirmani, Kapil Dev, and other previous awardees. Giving him a prize he did not deserve would be seen as a reward for being an apologist and propagandist for the BCCI Old Guard. Shastri had once described Lalit Modi as the 'Moses' who showed Indian cricket the Promised Land. And he had been extremely close to N Srinivasan as well.

Instead of Shastri, I suggested that the award be given jointly to Rajinder Goel and Padmakar Shivalkar. They were both great cricketers, great servants of Indian cricket, who had tragically never played Test cricket because their careers overlapped with that of their fellow left-arm spinner, Bishan Bedi. Honouring them would also celebrate our premier domestic tournament, the Ranji Trophy, that for some eighty years now had sustained the game in India. Diana Edulji endorsed my suggestion, and the journalist who made up the jury was on board too. We also proposed an annual lifetime award for a woman cricketer, and chose Shantha Rangaswamy as the first recipient.

The BCCI's annual awards ceremony was held on 8 March 2017, in my hometown, Bangalore. Apart from the lifetime awards, prizes for the best batsman and bowler in different age categories were also presented. Farokh Engineer delivered the annual Pataudi lecture. Ravi Shastri was the master of ceremonies; he had to be somewhere, even if not as an awardee. In their acceptance speeches, both Shivalkar and Goel praised Bishan Bedi lavishly. In attendance were the Indian cricket team, fresh from winning a Test match against Australia at the Chinnaswamy Stadium. Despite the KSCA (still run by N Srinivasan loyalists) asking for a boycott of the ceremony, many former Karnataka and India cricketers attended. When G R Viswanath entered the room a hush fell over it; all eyes, young and old, following the littlest and most beloved of Indian cricketers as he made his way to a seat in the front row, stopping to acknowledge salutations from fans and former team-mates.

On this evening I did something I almost never do – I took a selfie, with Bishan Bedi and the coach of the Indian team, Anil Kumble. *Cricinfo*'s man on the spot began his report on the event with this paragraph:

> Ramachandra Guha is clapping wildly as Bishan Bedi is invited onto the stage. There are several other hands coming together in applause but Guha's stands out, accompanied by a violent bobbing of the head. Guha is a writer, historian and now, of the volition of India's Supreme Court, a cricket administrator, if only temporarily. But on Thursday evening, at the fifth MAK Pataudi memorial lecture and the annual BCCI awards, he better resembles the awestruck teenager who had met a whiskey-guzzling Bedi for the first time in 1974.

It was a happy affair, in many ways the highlight of my months as an accidental cricket administrator. But there were two sour notes. First, at various times in the evening, several former cricketers asked me for jobs with the BCCI (as IPL consultant, NCA

coach, talent scout and consultant, etc). Second, most state associations boycotted the ceremony, as instructed by N Srinivasan.
One of them was my own association, the KSCA. This saddened
me, and I made my upset public, writing in the local edition of
the *Times of India*:

> My assignment as a cricket administrator is temporary; my
> status as a fan of Karnataka and Indian cricket, absolutely
> permanent. I hugely enjoyed watching the recent Bengaluru
> Test with other fans in the N Stand and delighted in, among
> other things, [the Karnataka player] K L Rahul's two superb
> half-centuries.
>
> It was as a long-time lover of Karnataka cricket, and as a
> long-time member of the Association myself, that I was
> saddened by the KSCA's boycott of the BCCI Awards
> function. I wish that the office-bearers of the KSCA had
> accepted the invitation to attend the BCCI Awards, which
> were a true celebration of cricket and cricketers, with living
> legends like Bishan Bedi and Farokh Engineer rubbing
> shoulders with current greats like Virat Kohli and R Ashwin.
> Proudly present in the audience were many of Karnataka's
> iconic Test players, such as G R Viswanath, E A S Prasanna,
> Anil Kumble, Javagal Srinath, Venkatesh Prasad, Sadanand
> Viswanath and Sunil Joshi. And Karnataka's own Shantha
> Rangaswamy was the first winner of the Lifetime Award for
> contributions to women's cricket.
>
> Among the nicest things about the BCCI Awards
> function in 2017 was that, for the first time in the history
> of the event, the awards were given out by former
> cricketers, not by administrators. That is how it should be;
> with cricketers first, always (and fans next). The BCCI
> Awards were a high point of a great season for Indian
> cricket, and a heartfelt salutation to superb cricketers of the
> past, present, and future. That is why I believe that my own

Association, the KSCA, should not have boycotted this
wonderful event.

VI

I was pleased with helping in getting Rajinder Goel and Padmakar
Shivalkar recognition by the BCCI. Sadly, I failed in my attempt
to honour an even more accomplished left-arm spinner. This was
Vinoo Mankad, who – Kapil Dev, Sachin Tendulkar, and Virat
Kohli notwithstanding – is in my opinion the greatest cricketer
ever produced by India. Mankad was born in Jamnagar on 12
April 1917. In the third week of February 2017, the cricket
writer and coach Makarand Waigankar sent me this SMS:
'2016–17 is a birth centenary of one of the greatest all rounders
Vinoo Mankad. BCCI ignored it. COA can surely do
something.'

I replied to Waigankar as follows: 'Completely agree with you.
He and Merchant and Hazare were our first great Test cricketers
– and must never be forgotten.'

On 23 February, I wrote to the BCCI's CEO Rahul Johri,
copying my COA colleagues:

Dear Rahul,
12 April 1917 marks the one hundredth birth anniversary
of the great Vinoo Mankad. Mankad was not only one of
our first truly great cricketers, he was absolutely the first to
stand up for the rights of players. He was the best all
rounder of his generation, who played a critical role in
India's first Test and series wins. In fact, so crucial was he to
India's early successes that in the Tests that India won when
Mankad was in the team, he averaged over a hundred with
the bat, while taking more than eight wickets per Test at
some 13 runs apiece. And, as I noted, he was also the first

to argue that players must have the right to be professionals, and make a honest living which the Board at the time denied them.

Incidentally, since the Australians are now here, on our first tour of Australia in 1947, Mankad scored two brilliant hundreds against the fearsome fast bowlers Lindwall and Miller. He had a fantastic record in England too (his performance in the Lord's Test of 1952 is the stuff both of history and legend), and also played well in West Indies and Pakistan. He was the first to show that Indian cricket could hold its own anywhere in the world.

Without Mankad there would have been no Gavaskar or Kapil Dev, no Kohli or Ashwin either. He showed the way to them. I strongly urge the BCCI to commemorate his centenary in some proper and fitting way.

Yours
Ram

There was no reply. I raised the matter at the next COA meeting, suggesting that the commemoration be done in one of the IPL matches. Mankad was a brilliant attacking batsman, an extremely restrictive bowler, and a fine fielder anywhere – that is to say, a cricketer who would have commanded the highest price at auction had the IPL been around in his days. But no one was willing to entertain the suggestion: my fellow members of the COA because they were indifferent to history, the officials of the BCCI because they were too nervous to tell the tournament's sponsors that for a single IPL match the name of the greatest of all Indian cricketers would shine as brightly as their own.

10

Exiting the Establishment

I

In February 2017, barely a week after I was appointed to the Committee of Administrators, I got a call from a cricket journalist, alleging that some members of the India Under-19 side had been diverted from an ongoing series against England to try out for an IPL team, the Delhi Daredevils. Rahul Dravid was in charge of the India Under-19 and A teams while continuing to be the mentor of the Delhi Daredevils, a fact that had escaped my IPL-resistant cricketing brain. To coach a private franchise and a national side simultaneously, and to be paid for both jobs was not permissible under the Lodha guidelines. I at once dashed off a letter to my fellow COA members, under the subject heading: 'India vs IPL?' Here I said:

> Wikipedia informs me that the current Under-19 coach of the Indian team, is listed as a mentor for the Delhi Daredevils. If true, this surely is a conflict of interest and should not be permitted. But beyond this personal issue, there is a larger institutional question here. The Under-19 team has over the last decade produced some of our finest international players, including Virat Kohli himself. This

process can be furthered only if these youngsters are groomed and developed, rather than have them hastily diverted by the IPL, whose interests are entirely commercial. Making these still developing youngsters prone to such blandishments at this early stage of their lives and careers, and asking them to put IPL before country, is not appropriate.

Since I knew Rahul Dravid personally, I also wrote directly to him, pointing to this conflict of interest. I urged him to give up either his IPL job or his assignment as coach of the India Under-19 and A teams. 'You should not continue with both,' I wrote. Dravid wrote back saying that he was on a ten-month contract with the BCCI for his India duties, leaving him free to spend two months of the year with an IPL team. He said that his case was not unique; noting that other 'coaches and support staff in the Indian team and even overseas coaches have the two months of the IPL free in their contract'. He also enclosed the BCCI guidelines, which seeemed to allow this double-dipping. Dravid said that if the guidelines changed and he had then to explicitly choose between the IPL and national duties, he would do so.

I wrote back to Dravid saying that 'the BCCI policy you mention was framed before the Lodha Committee report. I believe that this is indeed a conflict of interest, but of course I shall put the whole matter before the COA so that we can come up with a standard policy on the subject, to apply to all, administrators as well as cricketers, retired and still active.'

I raised the issue at our next COA meeting, held on 17 February. I had meanwhile got to know that some other national coaches had been forbidden from taking up IPL contracts. There was no consistent policy, with the administrators choosing whom to favour and whom not to. The BCCI's CEO, Rahul Johri, was keen to allow such flexibility, arguing that it was necessary to keep great former players in good humour. Evidently the BCCI management, as well as office-bearers, liked to have the powers to offer lucrative IPL contracts to coaches, support staff, commentators and even journalists. This was done with an eye to the perpetuation of their own power; for handing out such favours ensured loyalty and subservience. However, a reading of the Lodha guidelines made it clear that for the same person to work for the national team, and for an IPL side, constituted conflict of interest.

In the second week of March, it was brought to my notice that a camp was on for the India Under-19 team at the National Cricket Academy in Bangalore, but their coach, Dravid, as well as their physio, Andrew Leipus, would not be in attendance as they were busy with the IPL. On 11 March, I wrote to my colleagues that:

> This is an issue I have flagged several times already. No person under contract with an India team, or with the NCA, should be allowed to moonlight for an IPL team too.
>
> BCCI in its carelessness (or otherwise) might have drafted coaching/support staff contracts to allow this dual loyalty business, but while it might be narrowly legal as per existing contracts, it is unethical, and antithetical to team spirit, leading to much jealousy and heart-burn among the coaching staff as a whole. ...
>
> I would like an explicit and early assurance from the BCCI management that such manifestly inequitous loopholes in coaching/support staff contracts will be plugged forthwith.

Unfortunately, no such assurance was forthcoming. Meanwhile, it was brought to my notice that a company that Sunil Gavaskar headed, the Professional Management Group, represented current India players. On 19 March, I wrote to my colleagues pointing out that 'this is a clear conflict of interest. Either he [Gavaskar] must step down/withdraw himself from PMG completely or stop being a commentator for BCCI.' I added:

> I think prompt and swift action on this matter is both just and necessary. COA's credibility and effectiveness hinges on our being able to take bold and correct decisions on such matters. The 'superstar' culture that afflicts the BCCI means that the more famous the player (former or present) the more leeway he is allowed in violating norms and procedures. (Dhoni was captain of the Indian team while holding a stake in a firm that represented some current India players.) This must stop – and only we can stop it. The BCCI CEO on his own will be too nervous and insecure to do anything about it.

Sunil Gavaskar in fact had multiple conflicts of interest. And journalists had written about them before. An article in *Mint* newspaper from 2014 noted that:

> Gavaskar is an administrator, commentator, possibly the BCCI's covert representative on TV, and agent of Indian cricketers, all at the same time. If this is not conflict of interest, what is? In addition, he is an NRI based in the United Arab Emirates, where, coincidentally enough, the first phase of IPL7 is going to be played. The choice of the UAE as venue has been controversial, since India has avoided playing there for years because the region is the global headquarters of illegal cricket betting, and IPL6 was hit by a huge betting scandal which led to the whole Supreme Court business.

The BCCI Old Guard had winked at these conflicts of interest, because their own violations of the law and of ethical standards had been even more extreme. As that same article in *Mint* observed:

> N Srinivasan's conflicts of interest as President of the BCCI are well-known. He is the head of the administrative body, his company India Cements owns IPL team Chennai Super Kings, whose captain M S Dhoni is India's captain, who has also been given the post of vice-president in India Cements, and as long as Krishnaswamy Srikkanth was the chairman of the Indian team selection committee, he was the paid mentor of the Chennai team. Quite amazing, really. Srinivasan changed BCCI's Constitution, bought over, bullied and blanked out state cricket associations to stay in power.*

As Board President, Srinivasan would not hold Gavaskar to account for his violations. As commentator and columnist, Gavaskar would not hold Srinivasan to account for his violations. But while Indians apparently did not understand the concept of 'conflict of interest', other cricketing nations clearly did. Thus Michael Atherton would never dream of becoming a player agent. This was in part because he may have had a keener ethical sense than other opening batsmen-turned-commentators, or perhaps because Sky Sports would never permit what the BCCI so routinely allowed.

I had hoped that, with the Supreme Court backing us, we could get Indian cricket administrators to adopt the best practices worldwide. But it was not to be. While Diana Edulji endorsed my suggestion, the other members of the COA were reluctant to initiate remedial action, perhaps because Dravid and

* See http://www.livemint.com/Opinion/1BOv0r0U3wRkCtut8Dq1fK/
Interests-conflicts-and-Sunil-Gavaskar.html.

Gavaskar were two of the greatest names in the history of Indian sport.

I could understand why the BCCI's officials were overawed by the aura around former and current superstars. But that our Chairman, a distinguished civil servant, was similarly cowed by sporting reputations puzzled and dismayed me. In March, the BCCI put up for our consideration a list of players offered central contracts. I was shocked that Mahendra Singh Dhoni had been offered an 'A' contract despite his not being willing to play Test cricket. This sent absolutely the wrong signal to younger players. Having retired from Tests, Dhoni was on duty for the national team at most for about three months in the year. And he didn't need the money either. The national selectors, I told the BCCI management, were here 'succumbing to the superstar culture; they are either too afraid of offending Dhoni, or insecure because they themselves have a modest international record, or both'. However, in the absence of support from the COA's Chairman, Vinod Rai, I was unsuccessful in having this craven currying of favour reversed.

In the second half of May, the superstar culture manifested itself once more. The Indian team had just completed a very successful home season, winning Test series against New Zealand, England, and Australia, and sweeping the one-day series against these sides as well. Much of the credit for this had gone to the captain, Virat Kohli, and his players, but the team's coach, Anil Kumble, had garnered some praise too. Kumble's cricketing intelligence and professional discipline were well known, the former strikingly demonstrated when, against Kohli's advice, he picked the left-arm wrist-spinner Kuldeep Yadav for the crucial final Test against Australia, and the debutant took four wickets on the first day, swinging the match and series in India's direction.

Kumble had been appointed in June 2016 by a 'cricket advisory committee' consisting of Sourav Ganguly, V V S Laxman, and Sachin Tendulkar. The Board President at the time, Anurag Thakur, had chosen to offer Kumble a one-year contract in the first instance, while telling him that it would in time be extended to three years. In the twelve months that Kumble had been in charge, his team had a fantastic record. Yet, as the end of his one-year term approached, there was no word of an extension.

On 12 May the IPL final was held in Hyderabad. Before it began, the COA had scheduled a meeting with Anil Kumble. I had a prior commitment to release a book that morning in Bangalore, so could not attend the meeting with Kumble, which I minded, or the IPL final, which I minded not at all.

At the meeting with my colleagues, Kumble made a presentation on the future of Indian cricket, and also discussed the renewal of his contract as head coach. The Indian team were about to leave for the Champions Trophy. Kumble was worried (understandably) about the uncertainty, and thought (again understandably) that since his team had done so well his contract should be renewed. However, he was told by my COA colleagues that it could not be renewed automatically, and other people would also be asked to apply.

When I heard that Kumble's contract was not being extended, I phoned Vinod Rai. I learnt that the Indian captain, Virat Kohli, had told Rai that he found Kumble too domineering. Kohli also claimed the team was winning only because of the players, and the coach had nothing to do with it. The captain wanted another coach. Meanwhile, Ravi Shastri was lobbying for the job, intriguing with the BCCI officials.

I told Rai that this was outrageous. He mumbled something about 'procedure' and 'due process'. In that case, I asked, why was the extension not discussed during April and May, when the IPL was on? If the captain and the head coach were not getting along, why was this not brought to our notice earlier? A major international tournament was imminent, and the uncertainty would undermine the morale and ability to focus of the coach, the captain, and the team. Above all, I told Rai, giving the Indian captain a veto power over the coach was a shocking example of the superstar culture gone berserk. In no sporting team anywhere in the world was the captain encouraged or permitted to choose the coach.

Rai heard me out, but then went ahead and did what Kohli and the BCCI Old Guard wanted. He asked for applications for the head coach's job to be made afresh. Kumble, feeling humiliated, understandably did not apply. While some excellent candidates did apply Kohli insisted that he wanted Shastri, who was duly appointed head coach of the Indian team.

II

My work at the BCCI was intense but also educative. But as the months dragged on, and my own proposals were steadily put aside, I began to feel disenchanted. My colleagues in the COA were all well-regarded professionals, and I respected their ability and track record. However, I found Rai and Limaye excessively cautious in effecting reform, and Rai and Edulji too keen to talk to the press. My colleagues were also not immune to the publicity that went with the job. They availed of VIP treatment at IPL matches, and Vinod Rai even released a book about Tendulkar, with the superstar sitting next to him – perks that would not have ever come our way had the Supreme Court not appointed us, and thus perks that we should have rigorously eschewed. But since Rai and company did not, the wily BCCI management plied them with more photo-ops, further defanging our Committee.

On 5 April – a little over two months after the COA was constituted – I wrote to Gopal Subramanium saying that I was thinking of resigning from the Committee to which he had so graciously recommended me. I adduced two reasons: the COA's failure to stop the intriguing of the BCCI Old Guard, and the fact that, as I put it, the Supreme Court itself, 'after taking a strong stand in favour of the Lodha Commission reforms when Justice Thakur was in charge, seems now to have backed off'. Gopal wrote back saying that while he understood my position 'completely', I should not resign yet.

Through April and May, I stayed on, attending meetings, writing mails, reading and commenting on documents. I found myself pushed even more to the margins. The issues I raised continued to be ignored. In the last week of May, with the IPL behind us and a new twelve months commencing, I wrote once more to my colleagues on the conflict of interest issue. I said here, as I had said in the past, that 'coaches and support coaches and support staff for national teams should not take up IPL assignments, but BCCI can/should pay them an enhanced salary/ compensation package'. I added that the practice of 'BCCI contracted commentators being player agents ... should be stopped forthwith'.

Diana Edulji replied to my mail saying 'I concur'. However, our two other colleagues were conspicuously silent. While they said nothing at all, the BCCI's CEO, Rahul Johri, who had also been copied into the mail, wrote suggesting that 'this could be an agenda item in the next COA/Office bearers meeting to discuss threadbare and till then let there be status quo'.

When I saw that telling phrase, 'let there be status quo', I decided that there was no point my continuing any more. The next day I talked to two lawyer friends, and then wrote to Gopal Subramanium saying that I was resigning from the Committee of Administrators. My decision, I told him, was 'in part because of the change of orientation of the Court; but in larger part because of the fact that I am not on the same page as the other members of the committee. For four months now I have found myself isolated on most questions I consider important when it comes to the reform of cricket administration. Rather than waste any more of their time or mine, I feel it best if I resign and allow them to get a more like-minded substitute.' Gopal graciously wrote back saying, 'I respect your decision under the circumstances and will always be keen to further our association in every way.'

On 1 June, I asked the Supreme Court to relieve me of my membership of the Committee. I also wrote a formal letter of resignation to Vinod Rai, where I foregrounded the COA's failure to address the conflict of interest issue, to assure a fair deal for domestic cricket and Ranji Trophy cricketers, to stem or reverse the superstar culture, and to keep the discredited and disqualified Old Guard from attending BCCI meetings. I ascribed these failures in part to 'the absence of a senior and respected male cricketer on our Committee'. I quoted my letter of 1 February suggesting that such a cricketer be asked to join the Committee, recalled my mentioning it in a formal meeting of the COA, and deplored the fact that the proposal was not acted upon. 'We should have', I wrote,

approached the Court to take the necessary action, or else incorporated a senior, respected, male cricketer as a special invitee. With such a person on board the COA would have gained in experience, knowledge, understanding, and, not least, credibility. Indeed, had we had such a person on board, the BCCI management and the office-bearers would have been compelled to be far more proactive in implementing the Lodha Committee recommendations than they have been thus far. As the only cricketer on the COA, Diana's contributions have been invaluable; on many issues of administration and the rights of players she has brought a perspective based on a first-hand experience that the rest of us lacked. A male counterpart would have complemented and further enriched her contributions; but perhaps it is not too late to make amends.*

The first draft of my resignation letter had a paragraph which I excised from the version I sent Vinod Rai. I reproduce the para here:

As I see it, cricketers (both international superstars as well as workaday professionals of the domestic game) should come first, and fans should come second. Administrators are there merely to facilitate the careers of the first and the viewing pleasure of the second group. Yet, as we know, in the past Indian cricket administrators acquired a great amount of power and prestige, which they did not use wisely or well. I do not have in mind here the financial malfeasance documented by the Deloitte reports (though that also needs to be addressed), but rather the attempts by publicity-hungry administrators to have some of the glory of cricket and cricketers reflected back on them. Unfortunately, the COA has not done enough to check or reverse this trend. The excellent start made at the BCCI Awards, where great retired cricketers rather than administrators gave away the awards, was not followed up on. I believe all members of the COA should have eschewed VIP treatment at IPL matches and at star-studded cricket book events, so as to set an example. Because they didn't, the office-bearers took this as a signal to promote themselves at every photo-op as well, and in time start once more to intrigue in player and team politics, as witnessed most recently in their interference in the re-selection of the Head Coach by their underhand

---

* The full text of my letter is available here: https://indianexpress.com/article/sports/cricket/full-text-ramachandra-guhas-resignation-letter-to-bcci-vinod-rai-4685575/.

attempts to substitute the incumbent with someone more pliable to their wishes.

III

In the interests of transparency, and because I owed it to the wider cricketing fraternity, I released my formal letter of resignation from the COA to the press. But, I assured Vinod Rai, I would not tweet about the matter or speak to the press or on TV. I sent the letter off to one newspaper and one website, declined to answer calls or reply to messages from unknown numbers, and went off to the Nilgiris for a week.*

My resignation provoked a torrent of commentary on television and in the press. A piece I especially liked was written in the *Hindustan Times* by a sociologist of sport, who thought my letter showed that Indian cricket had been let down most of all by its top cricketers. 'It took a historian and an academic to articulate the problems that everyone has been side stepping', she wrote, adding:

> But the thing that bothers me the most is the support he absolutely did not get from our heroes. Why have they all been so silent?
>
> Why do our vocal cricketers who think it worth their while to encourage trolling a woman on Twitter [which one famous former cricketer had done] or suggest that Kashmiris who oppose the Army should be killed [which another famous cricketer had advocated] lose their voices while they

---

* The one exception were two calls from an unidentified number, followed by a message saying 'This is Kapil Dev.' I called back, and talked to the captain of our 1983 World Cup winning side, who told me that (a) he agreed with what I had done and written, and (b) that nothing would come of it, since the BCCI was incapable of reforming itself.

stuff their own pockets? Why did no one say anything? Did they not know that those who were paid to represent certain players were also responsible for commentating on their game and selecting them for teams?

There is absolutely no reason why the silence of our 'Superstars' should not be construed as tacit support for all the 'conflicts of interest'. Even if they haven't fixed matches and sent hints to bookies with towels on their pajamas; they are guilty. Guilty of condoning the corruption by their silence.*

Meanwhile, a piece in *Cricinfo* remarked that 'in showing no bias in pointing out the conflicts of interest, in naming names, and in the clarity with which it does so, this is a bold and unprecedented letter. It says a lot that such a brave assessment can only be made by someone on the outside and with no designs of gaining materially from Indian cricket.'†

Another piece commented that my resignation had created a stir 'primarily because he has dared to reiterate the conflict of interest in [the] cricket establishment about which many know but few want to speak about'. This writer spoke of how politicians cutting across party lines had ensured 'the BCCI's virtual immunity' from public scrutiny; while the retired players 'remained an obedient lot because they financially gained by remaining on the right side of the cricket establishment. They knew that any discordant voice on their part would squeeze out the financial largesse that the cash-rich BCCI offered them.' The piece specifically mentioned Sunil Gavaskar and Ravi Shastri, who had both 'been given an annual contract of Rs 3.6 crore

---

* See http://www.hindustantimes.com/cricket/opinion-ramachandra-guha-s-resignation-letter-proves-our-cricketing-heroes-have-betrayed-us/story-fnTuB0NIUTAGu7yGKwCO6M.html.

† http://www.espncricinfo.com/india/content/story/1100724.html.

each by the BCCI to ostensibly serve as commentators but actually to buy their silence'.*

To my great delight, I found myself the subject of a poster issued by the iconic Indian milk co-operative, AMUL, which had made it a practice to print cleverly worded cartoons to comment on current affairs.† A few days after I left the BCCI's Committee and Administrators, a cartoon issued by AMUL had me, pen in hand, writing my resignation letter, against a background of cricketers holding bats as if they were weapons. The words on top punned on a famous Hindi song that ran 'Ye Kua Hua? Kaise Hua?' (*What the hell has happened? How the hell did this happen?*) – with 'Guha' replacing 'Hua'. The words at the bottom played on Vinod Rai's discomfiture: 'Rai ho ha fry ho!' – for which an idiomatic translation might be, *Rai's goose has been cooked.*

The public commentary on my resignation was largely sympathetic. The private mails I received were more mixed. Many cricket fans wrote to congratulate me on my boldness and on exposing corruption in public; others thought I should have stayed in the COA and fought on. Some letters juxtaposed praise with condemnation, as for example this one:

---

* http://www.firstpost.com/sports/ramachandra-guhas-resignation-must-make-sc-harden-stance-against-conflict-of-interest-in-cricket-3520205.html.

† These Amul posters were originally conceived in the 1960s by the Bombay advertising legend, Sylvester D'Cunha, and now come out under the supervision of his son, Rahul D'Cunha.

Dear Mr Guha,

I admire and congratulate you on your frank, open, insightful, truthful, and courageous letter to COA …

There is so much hope (indeed last hope) of a true cricket lover to clean up Indian cricket and set clear guidelines of laws, rules, regulations, and oversight.

If corruption and selfishness are removed, and people of character and integrity are brought in to run Indian cricket, Indian cricket can create jobs, inspire a nation, and bring in talent to give pure joy to billions.

Nevertheless, I am deeply saddened that you 'ran away from [the] battlefield' instead of staying put and ensuring Indian cricket is cleaned up. You had a great opportunity, but you ran away. Of course, every word you have written to Vinod [Rai] is golden and you have laid it out perfectly. But remember, criticism is easy, doing a perfect (or the near perfect; because nothing in life is ever perfect) job is infinitely complex.

However, I am immensely thankful to your insights and the letter to Vinod Rai. I just wished you stayed on and did the job.

Just praying for Vinod Rai and team to clean up Indian cricket – hopefully, they can move faster, with clarity and vision …

There was also the odd abusive letter, as for example this one:

What you did is a deed of coward persons. You quit the Committee and then started slamming the Indian Captain and the wicket keeper for apparently no fault of theirs in the eve of such an important tournament. Shame on you!!!

And yes the Indian captain is the ultimate post in Indian cricket. He has the veto power to chose coach. So Mr. Guha, Just keep your mouth shut.

Meanwhile, I received a charming mail from an astrologer, providing a link which explained why I had acted as I did. My correspondent had cast a horoscope extrapolated from my date of birth, whose 'most noticeable feature is a Sun-Uranus square both in hard aspect to Saturn'. The astrologer helpfully explained that:

> It is natural for those born under the Sun-Uranus aspects to question tradition. These are individualists. They naturally rebel against that which is established. It doesn't mean that they consistently break all the rules, but they definitely do question some of the rules, especially those that simply don't make much sense to them. The hard aspects to Saturn increases the chances of a conflict with authority.

Having just turned fifty-nine, I was apparently having my 'second Saturn return'. In the days before my resignation, it seemed that 'transit Mars [25ge]' had 'formed an opposition' to my 'radix and transit Saturn [25sa]'. The behaviourial consequences of this opposition were as follows:

> This is a time in which you are especially sensitive to the limitations or blocks in your path, which can point to frustration or stress. You may be especially impatient with protocol, red tape, traditional methods, superiors, and rules that seem oppressive.*

A man I had never met had now cast a horoscope to authoritatively confirm what I knew already; that I was an individualist who questioned authority, who didn't blindly follow rules, or unquestioningly obey superiors, these traits and quirks encoded

---

* See https://javed22.blogspot.in/2017/06/ramachandra-guha-flays-indian-cricket.html.

in me from the time of my birth, but apparently accentuated and intensified since my 'second Saturn return', which just happened to coincide with my spell as a cricket administrator. Had Vinod Rai been shown my horoscope, perhaps he would never have agreed to my being a member of his Committee in the first place.

IV

The day after my resignation letter appeared in the press, Sunil Gavaskar hit back at me. He told a television channel that he was 'very, very disappointed if anyone is doubting my integrity'. To my charge that Indian culture was afflicted with a 'superstar culture', Gavaskar responded, 'If there is a superstar culture, then there is also a jealousy culture. Jealousy culture at people who have done something for Indian cricket, continue to do something for Indian cricket that they should not be allowed to do something for Indian cricket and those who have not done anything for Indian cricket, who have got a peripheral connection with Indian cricket should be allowed to do something.'

The quotes above come from a web report* but the next day's *Times of India* reported the interview too, under the headline 'SUNNY HITS BACK AT GUHA', and with this extraordinary opening paragraph: 'New Delhi: Sunil Gavaskar dismissed Ramachandra Guha's "conflict of interest" charge and said that it was "baffling" to find that his integrity was being questioned when in reality "he had none"'.

The truth-telling here was entirely unintended, the work of a careless or incompetent sub-editor (Gavaskar meant he had no conflict of interest, not no integrity). A friend who, like me, had greatly admired Gavaskar the cricketer as distinct from Gavaskar

---

* http://www.freepressjournal.in/cricket/baffled-sunil-gavaskar-hits-back-at-ramachandra-guha/1079735.

the ex-cricketer, gleefully sent across a screenshot of this paragraph, with the subject heading of his mail being: 'I couldn't have put this better ...'

The other cricketing legend I had charged with conflict of interest, Rahul Dravid, also responded to me, albeit in more restrained language. He put out a statement via the BCCI that what he had done was within the rules as defined, so he was 'extremely disappointed as to how this has unfolded publicly'. Dravid copied me into this statement, whereupon we had an email exchange, in which I was constrained to tell him that the contract he had signed with the BCCI 'was not what any properly professional national sporting organisation would have allowed'. Then I continued:

As for this being 'a standard contract', I was told by other national coaches that they were explicitly disallowed from working in the IPL. It appears some were allowed, others weren't. There was also the issue of your unavailability for NCA camps when the IPL was on. There were other questions raised to me as a COA member about India under 19 players being called for Delhi Daredevil trials.

Your own commitment to Indian cricket and your own personal integrity may be total; but the very fact of your having dual loyalties opened up these questions. Besides, even if you were originally asked to take up national duties while still an IPL coach, surely for your second term you should have been asked to choose.

Sunil Gavaskar was a hero of my youth (my books on cricket are testimony to how much I venerated him). I am proud to have known you personally. But what he is doing and what you had done was not something the BCCI should have allowed or Lodha guidelines permit. Had I not pointed this out, I would have been guilty of succumbing to the superstar culture myself.

A few weeks after this exchange, Rahul Dravid signed a new contract with the BCCI as their Under-19 and A team coach. This was a two-year, twenty-four-month contract, which explicitly ruled out his taking an IPL assignment. So Dravid acted quickly and responsibly, whereas the other great cricketing legend, Sunny Gavaskar, took his time. On 12 September 2017, some four months after he had accused me of being jealous, the *Bangalore Mirror* carried a story headlined 'Sunny Days are Over'. Gavaskar's Professional Management Group, it reported, had shut its player management wing so that the former India skipper could continue as a BCCI commentator. The India players represented by PMG had been told they were free to look for new agents. The *Mirror* quoted from my resignation letter, as did the *Indian Express*, which noted that, 'In the wake of Guha's resignation, the BCCI tightened the screws on the issue – Rahul Dravid had to quit as coach of Delhi Daredevils to remain as the coaching head of the junior India teams', and now Gavaskar himself had, despite the bluff and bluster back in June, to accept that he was guilty of conflict of interest as well. In these two instances, if in nothing else, my resignation had served a purpose.

I knew Rahul Dravid fairly well, and wondered what this controversy would do to our friendship. Dravid is, by the standards of our cricketing greats, relatively publicity-shy. He was upset by the furore caused by my resignation letter, and the fingers (briefly) pointed at him. For some time our relations cooled. I invited him for a book event, and for a dinner; he declined even to reply to my mails. Then, on a tour of England with the India A side, Dravid met a mutual friend, the former England captain Mike Brearley, who advised him not to let his ego come in the way of sustaining human relationships. Dravid now wrote me a mail where he said that while he may not have agreed with some of my views, 'I have no doubt about your intention or your desire for Fair Play'. He added that it 'helps to have people who can tell you as it is and show you another side of the coin with your interest in mind'. I was naturally very pleased to get this reply, and wrote back that we must meet soon, to talk of things that interested us both: such as Karnataka, fatherhood, and, above all, Friends Union Cricket Club versus Bangalore United Cricket Club.

In the spring of 2019, Rahul Dravid's club celebrated its centenary. To my surprise, and pleasure, he asked me to speak at a commemorative function to honour its past and present players. I went, and said that while I could not gainsay that BUCC was founded earlier than us, my club had two distinctions our rival could not match. For one thing, it was FUCC that had produced Karnataka's first ever Test cricketer, the off-spinner V M Muddiah. For another, while BUCC had thought of having a club tie designed only for its centenary, our club had one specially made for its fiftieth anniversary itself. With red and brown stripes, and the FUCC crest, this was the tie that I was wearing that evening.

I had come however not to boast but to pay tribute, on behalf of a younger and lesser cricket club of Bengaluru to an older and greater one. At the entrance to the venue was a board displaying the names of the BUCC players who had represented the country. I pointed out in my talk that two of them were in the eleven that won India's first cricket World Cup, at Lord's in 1983. These were Syed Kirmani and Roger Binny. I added that while three Mumbai players were in that team, they played for three different clubs in their home city. BUCC had the even greater distinction, I said, of providing two players in an All-Time Indian Test XI. These were Rahul Dravid and Syed Kirmani. I added that, having made this assertion, I was not going to show my face in Ranchi (the home town of M S Dhoni) any time soon.

The star of this BUCC show was G R Viswanath, Dravid's boyhood hero and mine. A shy man, not partial to public speaking, he had nonetheless agreed to being asked a few questions on stage by an interlocutor. This man began by praising the Little Master for his courtesy, for never having sledged an opponent or questioned an umpire. Vishy answered that he had learnt to be polite the hard way. In his early years in club cricket, he came up against a fast bowler who lived in the same neighbourhood. As little kids, they had played tennis ball cricket together; now, however, they were playing for rival clubs in the KSCA's First Division. Vishy came in to bat with his side at 10 for two, and was rapped on the pads by the first ball he faced. His team-mate-turned-opponent roared an appeal for lbw; when it was turned down, he came down the wicket and pointed to the spot where it had hit the batsman's pads. Vishy asked him to address his anger to the umpire instead. Then, after he had hit the next ball past cover for four, the batsman advanced down the wicket himself, showing the bowler with his bat where the ball had gone.

Vishy, characteristically, did not tell us how many runs he got that day. But he did say that after the match ended, and the teams exchanged the usual courtesies, his childhood mate refused to shake his hand. For days afterwards, when they passed on the street the bowler would ignore the batsman; it took several months before they were on speaking terms again. Sledging was too costly, Vishy decided; life was too short and friendships too precious for one to be rude and offensive about a mere matter of bat and ball.

V

I knew Sunil Gavaskar, slightly, and knew that he would be very angry, at being exposed in public for his double standards. And so he was. In December 2017, six months after I left the BCCI, he was due to speak at an event in the Bombay Gymkhana to commemorate India's first Test captain, the great C K Nayudu.

When he arrived at the venue and heard that I was also one of the invited speakers, he stormed out in a rage.

In June 2018, Afghanistan played its first ever Test match, against India at the Chinnaswamy Stadium in Bangalore. I watched the first day's play, from the Members Stand. Here I sat alone; but after an hour was joined by my mate Suresh Menon, who had found out where I was and come over from the press box. We watched together until the end of the first session; whereupon he suggested we walk over to the press box for lunch. As we got into the lift to take up to the third floor, I joked to Suresh: 'I hope we don't run into [the Indian team coach] Ravi Shastri when we get out of the elevator.'

The lift took us up, slowly, and stopped at our destination. As the doors opened to let us out, a former cricketer I had criticised walked in. However, it was not Ravi Shastri but Sunil Gavaskar. I said hello, but he simply glared back and made his way to the bottom of the ground. That evening a friend rang to say that Gavaskar had complained in the press box about what this fellow Guha, supposedly now out of the BCCI, was doing there.

That, I thought, was that. Gavaskar's path and mine would never cross again. Then, on the evening of 11 February 2019, I got a call from the former Karnataka cricketer B Raghunath. Raghu was a close friend of G R Viswanath, and it was about him that he was calling. Vishy, he said, was turning seventy the next day, and 'Sunil' was throwing a surprise party for his fellow Little Master (who was also his brother-in-law). All the Karnataka cricketers would be there, of course, but said Raghu, 'Sunil' had particularly asked that Suresh Menon and I be invited.

Gavaskar is known in the cricketing world as 'Sunny', or, to those younger than him, as 'Sunny bhai'. It is only the Indian players of his own generation who call him Sunil. I understood whom Raghu was referring to, but wasn't sure I had heard him correctly. 'Sunil asked that *I* be invited?' I asked suspiciously.

'Yes, yes,' answered Raghu, 'he told me to make sure that Suresh and you come for Vishy's party.'

In my book *Spin and Other Turns*, there is a chapter on Sunil called 'The Two Gavaskars', and another on Vishy called 'The Best Loved Cricketer'. The first focuses relentlessly on cricketing technique, the second on character as well as batsmanship. I am reasonably sure that Vishy has read neither chapter, and absolutely certain that Gavaskar has read both. He thus knew how much I admired his brother-in-law, as a cricketer and as a human being. For Vishy's sake, he thought, I must be there.

The party was held on a rooftop restaurant opposite the Karnataka Golf Association, where G R Viswanath was often to be found after he retired, sometimes on the course itself, at other times at the bar. The honorand himself had no idea what was to happen. Sunil had intrigued with his sister – Vishy's wife Kavita – to keep it a secret. All Vishy knew was that he was to meet some friends somewhere near the golf course at 8 pm to celebrate his birthday.

Raghu and Sunil had told the guests to come an hour early. I arrived around 7.15 pm. The first person I met as I emerged from the lift was Sunil Gavaskar, who was talking with Suresh Menon. This time he was all smiles. I thanked him for including me in the party. We exchanged stories about Karnataka *v* Bombay matches he had played in and Suresh and I had merely watched. Then, thinking I must not monopolise him, I wandered across in search of others I could talk to. Of these there were plenty. So I chatted with Durai's old protégé Sudhakar Rao, with my own friends Venkatesh Prasad and Anil Kumble.

At five minutes to eight, Sunil came around, summoning us to the elevator, to await the birthday boy. He placed himself closest to the door, to greet him first. A video of what happened next circulated quite widely on social media. This began with Vishy emerging from the lift, blinking, looking around, to see his team-mate-turned-relative standing to await him. The video pans to the Karnataka cricketers waiting to greet Vishy, and then I too make a cameo appearance, saying, as I offered birthday wishes to this hero of my youth, that 'I first shook your hand when I met you with my uncle Durai on Nrupathunga Road in 1970'.

VI

From my four months in the BCCI, I reached this melancholy conclusion: were the game better administered in India, the Indian team would never lose a cricket match. Our population was twice that of the Test-playing countries combined. We had some thirty first-class teams, almost twice as many as England, and four times as many as Australia. In those other countries cricket was the second or third most popular sport, whereas in India it was always number one.

Cricket in India was the greatest, the most intense, popular passion in the history of the human race. There was a colossal fanbase, some several hundred million strong. There were ten times as many cricket-crazy Indians as there were football-mad Brazilians. The BCCI had huge cash reserves. With this demographic and financial base, India should always and perennially have been the top team in all formats of the game. If we still lost matches and series, then surely the fault lay with how the game was (mis)managed in our country.

That Indian cricket administrators were venal and corrupt I knew beforehand. What surprised and shocked me more was how amoral India's top cricketers were. Years ago, when I had written my first book on the game, *Wickets in the East*, Suresh Menon had remarked (in a review) that I could write so affectionately about the players because I did not follow them on tour or from the press box. More recently, when I joined the COA, my friend C Venkatesh worried that the romantic in me might be lost, and that proximity to cricketers might breed contempt.

And it did.

After I resigned from the COA, I wrote to a friend that:

There are four categories of cricket superstars in India:

1. Crooks who consort with and pimp for bigger non-cricket playing crooks.
2. Those who are willing and keen to practise conflict of interest explicitly.
3. Those who will try to be on the right side of the law but stay absolutely silent on … those in categories 1 and 2.
4. Those who are themselves clean and also question those in categories 1 and 2.

I also offered examples of which cricketers I thought fit into categories 1, 2 and 3 respectively. As for category 4, I said that in India at least only one cricketing great had remotely any chance of qualifying for inclusion. This was Bishan Bedi.

11

Varieties of Cricketing Chauvinism

I

When I was playing cricket for St Stephen's, in the 1970s, I batted well down the order – number ten, sometimes; number eleven, most times. Yet, every year, I harboured a fantasy of being sent in as a nightwatchman in the biggest match of the season – the Inter-College Final, against Hindu, a match watched by twenty thousand people, and written about *in extenso* in the capital's dozen English newspapers. The next morning's paper would – in my fantasy – have Hindu College at (say) 240 all out, and St Stephen's in reply at (say) 30 for two, with the last entry in the scorecard being: R Guha, 4 not out – this sending hundreds of *Dilliwalas* to the bus stand in anticipation.

Alas, the situation never arose. I never batted above number ten, and my highest score in a competitive (as distinct from friendly) match was 4 (out). But for at least a decade after I left college, I had a recurrent dream about my batsmanship. This had me sitting in the players' tent, when the captain's command to pad up drew me out of my dreaminess. I rushed to my kit, took out my abdominal guards and put them on first, before lovingly buckling my pads, one pad, one buckle, at a time. Then I sat on a chair, bat between my legs, watching the game. I ground my nails down to the finger bone until, finally, a wicket fell. I gathered my gloves (there were no helmets in those days) and strode to the wicket. Before I got there I woke up. I had been cheated of that newspaper entry once again.

The dream is easy to deconstruct. It is a variant of the court jester wanting to play Hamlet. For batsmen are the privileged elite of the game, bowlers the hardworking but under-recognised subalterns. The team's captain is, nine times out of ten, a batsman. Batsmen also garner 90 per cent of the headlines, 90 per cent of the Man of the Match awards, and 90 per cent (or perhaps even 95 per cent) of the sponsorships.

In my twenties (and thirties) I often had another cricketing dream. This involved books, or, rather, a particular book. Here, I was taking a long journey across India, which involved changing trains at a railway junction I had never visited before. I arrived on time, to find that the connecting train was three (or perhaps four) hours late. I asked the chap at the station's A H Wheeler newsstand (these were pre-Google days) for the name and address of the best bookstore in town. He wrote this out on a piece of paper; and I set off in search of an auto-rickshaw to take me there. I reached the store to find, to my delight, that it stocked old books as well as new. I went naturally to the used section, where, on a top shelf, beyond my reach, I spied a title in leather binding; surely once the prized possession of the town's greatest bibliophile. I asked the (dour) store-owner for a stool, which he reluctantly brought over. I got atop it, reached out for the book, and brought it down to the floor with me. I opened the fly-leaf to read: *'An Autobiography' By Neville Cardus. First Edition. Rupert-Hart Davis. London. 1949.*

My heart raced with ancticipation. However (in the dream) I was still a college student, with a purse to match. Surely I would not have the money to pay for this rare, *very* rare, book? So (in the dream again) I asked the shopkeeper, in as unemotional and disinterested a voice as I could command, its price. He said, ten rupees. I excitedly opened my wallet, handed over the money – and woke up.

This dream is less generic, more closely connected with this writer's personal biography. When – with my father's help – I was building my cricket library in Dehradun and Delhi, I was able to find books by many fine writers on the game – Jack Fingleton, Ray Robinson, A A Thomson, John Arlott, R C Roberston-Glasgow, Sujit Mukherjee. I owned a whole sheaf of cricketing autobiographies, by (among others) Keith Miller, Syed Mushtaq Ali, Denis Compton, and Garfield Sobers. I even had a copy (bought, as I have related, at the World Book Fair of 1978) of a book very scarce in India at the time, C L R James' *Beyond a Boundary*. I had all these, but nothing by the most celebrated of all cricket writers, Neville Cardus.

I had, however, seen a Cardus book several times. This was, in fact, his *Autobiography*. It lay in the possession of an older cousin who had been to Oxford. As a boy, I had spied the book in my cousin's bedroom in New Delhi; but been too shy to ask to borrow it. That is why, in my dream, I found it in some unknown bookstore in some obscure central Indian town. Only to be woken up before I could pay for it. Like that newspaper entry which had me batting at number four, Neville Cardus's *Autobiography* would remain forever outside my grasp.*

II

There are two fundamental axes of cricketing chauvinism: of nation and of generation. Every cricket fan almost without exception is born with them; and most cricket fans never outgrow them.

---

* I have since read Cardus's *Autobiography* (many times) and even come to possess several copies of the book. But never a first edition.

'There are no cricketers like those seen with twelve-year-old eyes.' Thus wrote the former England googly bowler Ian Peebles, second only to Jack Fingleton among players-turned-writers. I was twelve when I shook hands with my first Test cricketer (G R Viswanath), twelve when I saw my first active Test cricketer play in a match (Erapalli Prasanna, for his club City Cricketers). They remained, for many decades thereafter, great personal favourites, almost the first two names entered in any All-Time India XI that I constructed.

Thus the chauvinism of generation. As for the chauvinism of nation, let me quote my uncle Durai: 'If Sunil Gavaskar had been born an Englishman, he would have been made an Earl by now.' The reference here was to the memorialisation in cricketing literature of the odd century that those Englishmen, Graham Gooch and David Gower, had made against the fearsome Caribbean fast bowlers of the 1980s and 1990s. Now Gavaskar had scored no fewer than *thirteen* hundreds against the West Indies, seven of them in the Caribbean. Had he been an Englishman, how many books might have been written about this?

When I was young, I desperately wanted India to win; every match, against every opponent. These victories came erratically, especially overseas; which is why '1971' was (and remains) a set of sacred digits for me. As I grew older, Indian cricket teams became more competitive abroad, and virtually unbeatable at home. Now, I still wanted India to win, but what I wanted even more was a good match. I became disgusted by the cricketing jingoism around me, as in the refusal of my fellow fans in the Chinnaswamy Stadium to honour the great Javed Miandad when he exited the stage as an international cricketer. I began to enjoy, more and more, matches in which India was not playing, in part because the investment was aesthetic rather than emotional; in part because Indian commentators are both loud and partisan, and take the fun away from watching cricket on television.

The embracing of cricketing internationalism happened slowly, over a period of time. The shedding of generational chauvinism I can date more precisely; it occurred in a flash, on the late evening of 27 March 2016. India were playing Australia in what was effectively the quarter-final of the World T20 Championship. While wickets fell around him, Virat Kohli played an innings of breathtaking brilliance to keep his side in the game. I had first been impressed by Kohli when he scored an assured hundred before my eyes in a Bangalore Test, against an excellent New Zealand attack which had Sachin Tendulkar in all sorts of trouble. I had also seen, on television, Kohli play some superb one-day innings; it was clear that, especially when chasing, he was even better than Sachin in this version of the game. Now I was seeing him craft an innings of genius in the shortest form of all.

The Australians have a tradition of being brilliant at the death; in this match, their chosen exponent of this art was the left-arm medium-pacer James Faulkner. He was notoriously miserly, and when he began the eighteenth over India needed 39 runs off 18 balls. Kohli hit the first two balls for four, bisecting two fielders on the off-side boundary, exquisite cricketing shots. After the second of these I tweeted, 'There goes my boyhood hero G R Viswanath from my All-Time India XI. It now reads Sehwag, Gavaskar, Dravid, Tendulkar, Kohli …' As I clicked 'Tweet', Vishy's replacement hit Faulkner over mid-off for six. India won in a canter.

As I write this, some three years later, R Ashwin is on the verge of displacing E A S Prasanna as the off-spinner in that All-Time XI. In Test cricket, at any rate, Syed Kirmani still holds his place against M S Dhoni, but I might live long enough to see a replacement for Kiri emerge too.

III

I no longer care that much whether India wins or loses a Test match. I am prepared to allow that the cricketers I venerated when young may have been exceeded, in achievement and artistry, by those who came later. Other preferences and attachments remain. The first of these is to the Friends Union Cricket Club. In the 1970s, when I was just about good enough to play for the FUCC in the first division, I was playing in Delhi for St Stephen's College instead. In the 1980s, based in Bangalore, I played two matches for our B team in the second division. If a cricketing history of my club is ever written I shall have no place in it. My distinctions lie outside the field, in having been the club's youngest and (with the exception only of my uncle Durai) most long-serving and loyal member. I have supported this cricket club, emotionally, for more than fifty years, and of late have helped support it financially too.

One mark of my primary cricketing loyalty is this: the only tie I possess is that of the Friends Union Cricket Club. I have worn my FUCC tie at the National Defence College in New Delhi; at King's College, Cambridge; at Yale University in New Haven; at the Indian High Commission's Residence at Pretoria; and – with the greatest pleasure – in the pavilion of the Lord's Cricket Ground.

I once wore my club tie at a formal dinner at All Souls College, Oxford. Sitting opposite me was an Israeli scholar who had just been appointed to a new Chair at the University, and was extremely anxious to show us how well he knew its ways and mores. He dropped some names, of senior dons, and spoke of his familiarity with the manuscripts collection at 'Bodley' (the Bodleian Library). I nodded politely, while answering a rapid series of questions posed to me by the person to my left. This was the Warden of All Souls. The questions were (as it happens) about cricket; however, the Israeli could not hear them. All he could see was that the Warden had a greater interest in conversing with the unknown Indian to his left than with the freshly minted Professor on the other side of the table.

As the meal proceeded the Israeli scholar went silent, while looking ever more closely at my tie. After the port had been consumed, and the dinner had finally ended, he could contain his curiosity no more. He took my tie in his hand, looked at it one last time, and asked: 'Is this Magdalen?' I nodded, and walked off into the night. How could I tell the new Professor of the Study of Abrahamic Religions that the tie denoted membership not of a famous old Oxford college but of a little-known cricket club in southern India?

As I have grown older, my club has provided me with joy as well as consolation. In the first week of September 2017, the campaigning journalist Gauri Lankesh was murdered in Bangalore. I was then away abroad; but, since I had known Gauri for many years, I gave an interview and wrote a column about the climate of hatred and intolerance that surrounded us. I had faced threats to my life in the past; now, in light of my renewed criticisms of right-wing extremism, the state unit of the Bharatiya Janata Party said they would take me to court for defamation. The newspapers covered this harassment avidly, noting that while, in the wake of Gauri's death, many writers had been given police protection, I was not on the list, perhaps because the Congress was in power in Karnataka, and I had been as critical of them as of the BJP.

I came back to Bangalore in late September, thoroughly shaken by what had happened in my absence. I was alone at home; my wife and children were still overseas. Days after I returned, my uncle Durai called. Politics was not mentioned, but cricket was. Our club's second team was playing that weekend, in the final of the fourth division. The match was at the RSI ground, across the road from my house. Would I drop in at a time of my convenience? The boys would be pleased if I came.

On the afternoon of 23 September 2017, shaking off my jet lag, I left home, crossed M G Road, walked left on Cubbon Road and entered the Rajendra Sinhji Institute from a side gate. It was still the loveliest ground in Bangalore, ringed by the same trees that had stood while C K Nayudu and Frank Worrell had played there. That was before I was born; but it was also here, twenty years ago, that I had seen B Ramprasad almost bowl Kerala to victory over Karnataka.

On this day, the RSI was home to a lowly fourth division match. Walking in, I saw a left-arm spinner bowling, and recognised the action at once. It was of the former Karnataka cricketer Anand Katti. He had never played for my club, so FUCC must be batting.

I joined Durai, sitting as ever in a plastic chair outside the so-called 'pavilion', his boys and their kit sprawled on the ground. There was one other person seated, next to my uncle, who greeted me with a warm 'Hello, Sir!' Now aged thirty-three, this chap, S Karthik, had joined the club as a schoolboy. Back in the early days of this century, Durai had asked me to come see Karthik bowl in his first match for the A team. He had a lovely high action, and swung the ball away, and late; he also batted capably in the middle order. The boy captained the state at both Under-14 and Under-16 levels, but then his parents insisted that he get a good education. Durai concurred, so Karthik went off to engineering college and stopped playing competitive cricket (for the time being).

In 2009 I was in the capital of Uttar Pradesh, giving a lecture, when, to my surprise (and joy), an FUCC clubmate came up to to say hello afterwards. It was S Karthik, who had finished his engineering degree and was now at the Indian Institute of Management, Lucknow. Now, eight years later, I was meeting him at the RSI ground. On weekdays Karthik worked as a

Product Manager with Amazon, but on weekends he turned out in whites for the FUCC B team, seeking at Durai's command to bring them up to the third division.

As Karthik and I chatted, my uncle's phone rang. He picked it up, and we heard him say, among other things, 'You're in Bristol – that's in Gloucestershire, right? … Yes, we reached the final, so whether we win or lose the team will be promoted to the third division … Thanks for calling,' and then, before hanging up, 'All the best with your studies.'

I asked Durai who the caller was. Someone who had played for the B team, he said, and had just recently gone to England to study engineering. 'There is a 0.000001 per cent chance of becoming a Test player,' said my uncle, looking first at Karthik and then at me, 'so I tell my boys, play cricket but also study well, so that you can have a secure future.' That is just what this lad now in Bristol did, while staying in touch from far away with a club and a mentor who meant as much to him as his own parents.

My uncle Durai and I never talk about politics, and not just because we have cricket to talk about. In recent years he has turned steadily rightwards, and has even come to see in the authoritarian demagogue Narendra Modi the Saviour of the Nation. In this he differs not just from me but from my mother, his beloved elder sister. Brought up on and still committed to Mahatma Gandhi's idea of a plural and inclusive India, my mother despises both Modi's demagoguery and the demonisation of Muslims that his party practises.

Durai speaks to his only sister every morning; and, when she is living with us in Bangalore, visits her twice a week. My mother occasionally argued about politics with Durai, though I, wishing to keep the relationship based on our shared love of cricket intact, never did. But one day in December 2019, when I went to her room when her brother was visiting and he was saying something in praise of Prime Minister Modi, I said, impulsively,

'Maybe you'll change your mind about this Government when they come to arrest your nephew.'

The next morning my mother left for the town of Manipal, to spend some time with my sister. A few weeks later I was detained by the police, while protesting against new legislation proposed by the Modi Government that explicitly discriminated against India's large and vulnerable Muslim minority. During the day, while I was in police custody, my uncle was at a ground on the city's outskirts, where his – rather, *our* – club was playing a match. The news of my arrest made him very anxious, but duty demanded that he not leave his station. I was released at around five in the afternoon. Two hours later, my eighty-three-year-old uncle arrived at our house, still in whites, having driven many miles through Bangalore's traffic to get to where his sixty-one-year-old nephew was. He looked absolutely shaken. Luckily, I had the good sense not to remind him about my prediction, instead asking how the club had done on the day.

IV

One day, when my son Keshava was eight or nine, I came down for breakfast to find him reading the back pages of the newspapers. He looked up when he saw me and said, 'Appa, *we* have got the first-innings lead against Tamil Nadu.' Twenty years later, for all our disagreements on other matters, in this realm my son and I are still on the same side. When he is in town and Karnataka is playing we go off to watch them at the Chinnaswamy Stadium, sometimes the only people sitting in the upper tier of the Members Stand.

Another prejudice Keshava and I share is in favour of Test cricket. He laconically describes himself on Twitter as a '(Test) cricket tragic'.

My own views on the subject were more expansively set out, in an article I published in the *Telegraph* in 2008, the week before the inaugural season of the Indian Premier League. I wrote:

In my opinion, Test cricket may be compared to the finest Scotch, fifty-overs a side to Indian Made Foreign Liquor, and 20–20 to the local hooch. The addict who cannot have the first or the second will make do with the last. The pleasures of the shortest game are intense but also wholly ephemeral. There is no time to savour delights offered in such a rushed and heady fashion. The medium form allows one to take in the booze more lesiurely. Here, a batsman can bat long enough to develop an innings, to play strokes other than the hoick over mid-wicket or mid on. Although a bowler is restricted to ten overs, sixty deliveries constitute a spell in a way in which four overs cannot – long enough at least to plan, and excecute, a dismissal. As compared to 20–20, 50–50 allows a greater exposure to the varieties and subtleties of the game. After spending a whole day at the cricket one can, as it were, remember individual sips of the drink that one has consumed. On the other hand, after a 20–20 game all one remembers is that one got drunk, and one's side won, or lost.

But proper cricket can only be Test cricket. Spread out over five days, the game unfolds as in an epic drama. No restrictions are placed on anyone. The bowler can bowl forty overs at a stretch; the batsman plays on until he gets out. Even the fielder has greater opportunities to display his wares. He can (as in limited-overs cricket) dive to his left at cover point to stop a boundary; and he can also (unlike in limited-overs cricket) dive to his right to take a low catch at short leg. In this long, leisurely, civilised form of the game, a villain is allowed to redeem himself, a hero to reveal his flaws, a team to show reserves of character one could have scarcely thought it possessed. As with the finest Scotch, one savours every sip; and yet, as with the finest Scotch, the whole is infinitely greater than the parts.

My screed against T20 cricket was read by a literary scholar in Nagpur named Nadeem Khan. He sent me a splendidly polemical letter of support, the choicest bits of which I have plucked out below:

> I have a visceral dislike for this format of the game. I suspect it marks me out as an old fogey; I imagine, the shepherds who played it with a rag-ball and a stout stick would have had as much disdain for gloves and pads and boxes as the glove guys had for the helmets and chest guards. Life moves on, and so does cricket. The cricket of the sixties has just a few of us relics left to hear it croak, and all of us are in our sixties too. The society that spawned that cricket and the set of values that went with it gurgles piteously.
>
> My bile (as yours too) has been trained to rise against gents who want to call themselves Knight Riders and Warriors and Super Kings and Royals and Dare Devils. The names alone tell you that the offering is going to be sleaze and muck – faux thrills, faux skills, faux loyalties, faux highs and faux lows, except when millions are lost and won. But I guess that is faux money too, won and lost by faux human beings.
>
> The orange wigs, the baying crowds, the ostrich-buttocked cheer girls, napkins-peeping-out-of-pockets, the macho vulgarities of the players, maybe they go well with soccer, I don't know. The game of cricket is important to me not only because that was where all my pocket-money went. It is important because it has become powerful enough to determine the texture of the society in which my children grow and choose their dreams.

My article excoriating T20 was also read by a sports economist at the University of Michigan named Stefan Szymanski. He wrote saying he was soon to visit Bangalore, and would like to meet. He turned out to be a very personable fellow, who was in India to advise on the scheduling of the matches of the Indian Premier League. He himself taught in a business school, and wondered if, as a historian, I resisted the coming of the new. Perhaps if I went to a few IPL matches I might have a more open mind? At the end of the lunch (for which I paid, since it was my city) he took out a bottle of single malt Scotch whisky, which he handed over to me. I didn't have the heart to tell Professor Szymanski that I didn't drink myself; my analogy being based on academic knowledge rather than first-hand experience.

As a member of the Karnataka State Cricket Association I have a complimentary ticket for every match played in the Chinnaswamy Stadium. But I have never been to an IPL match there, not when my FUCC mate B Akhil was playing for Royal Challengers Bangalore, not when an old college friend, now the CEO of the global liquor conglomerate Diageo, invited me to his private box for an IPL final in which RCB (owned by Diageo) were one of the teams. In the twelve years that the Indian Premier League has been on, the only time I have been tempted to use my KSCA Member's Pass was when Jacques Kallis played a season or two for the Royal Challengers. In the event, my detestation for the IPL overcame my admiration for Kallis, so I never went at all.

I do watch international T20 matches on the television though, especially if no Test matches are on at the same time. And sometimes what I see can charm and move me. In 2014, when the World T20 Championship was being played in Bangladesh, I didn't follow any of the early matches. But then I read that this was the last chance for two Sri Lankan masters I greatly admired to win an ICC Trophy. These were Mahela Jayawardene and Kumar Sangakkara. Mahela and Kumar had grown up on stories of Sri Lanka's epic win in the 1996 World Cup. Fifteen years later, they were in the eleven that played, and lost, a World Cup final in Mumbai.

I admired Mahela and Kumar as cricketers, and as human beings. I also knew that they were close, on and off the field; they were, as the Indian saying goes, 'fast friends'. Their bonding, personal and sporting, recalled that of the Australians Miller and Lindwall, the West Indians Walsh and Ambrose, the Indians Gavaskar and Viswanath. So when Sri Lanka reached the final of the 2014 World T20 Championship I sat down in front of the television to watch. India batted first, and posted a modest total. Two early wickets gave them a sniff, until the Old Firm came together and took charge. Mahela then threw his wicket away with a careless, unnecessary, stroke, holing out at mid-wicket. He walked off, muttering to himself, then turned around and held up his bat to Sangakkara, in a touching gesture of apology and contrition. When his friend took Sri Lanka home on his own, Mahela was the first to rush onto the ground to greet him.

An addict needs his fix; if the cricketing equivalent of single malt Scotch and IMFL are not in stock, then the local hooch will have to do.

V

One of my favourite cricketing stories comes from the 1956 Australian tour of England. The former England opening bats- man Len Hutton was in the press box, as was the former Australian googly bowler, Arthur Mailey. During one of the matches, news came in that Hutton had been granted a knight- hood by the Queen. Mailey went up to him, shook his hand, and said in a whisper loud enough for everyone to hear, 'Congratulations, Sir Leonard. But I hope next time it is a bowler. The last bowler to be knighted was Sir Francis Drake.'

The remark brilliantly captured the social prejudice against bowlers, a prejudice so deep that even the British monarchy shared it. The batsmen Jack Hobbs and Don Bradman had been knighted prior to Hutton. The batting all-rounders Frank Worrell and Garry Sobers were to be knighted after him. It was ages later, in 1990, that Sir Richard Hadlee finally joined Sir Francis Drake.

Cricket is a game whose myths and stories have always favoured batsmen. It is batsmen who make the headlines; batsmen who get to be captain; batsmen who the spectators flock to see. The dominance of batsmen is cricket's one universal law. In the second half of the nineteenth century, no English sportsman was better known than W G Grace. Through much of the twentieth century, Don Bradman was the greatest living Australian. And Indian sport's first superstar was Sunil Gavaskar. All, of course, were batsmen.

The changes in the structure of the game since I first began following it have only consolidated the hegemony of batsmen in cricket. The covering of wickets has helped them enormously. No longer have they to contend with pitches made more difficult by dust or rain. The bats themselves have become better and stronger; even mishits nowadays go for six. The coming of one-day cricket has further tilted the scales in their favour. A batsman can play for fifty overs, but the bowler can bowl only for ten.

That I myself dreamt – or fantasised – about having a bat in hand was a product of this wider tendency to glorify batsmen and batsmanship. That I was always woken up before I got to the crease was also indicative – I had to be denied the prize. (Though this was probably just as well; my captain hadn't put me down at number ten or eleven without a reason.) It is significant that not one of the cricketing dreams of my youth had me in the role of a bowler, fielder, or wicketkeeper.

I stopped playing cricket altogether in my mid-twenties. By the time I was in my mid-thirties I had stopped dreaming about the game too. For the next decade most of my dreams were about libraries and archives, until one night the game came back to me once more. I was now in my mid-forties; and due to give a lecture in New Delhi, on a new research theme I had never spoken about in public before. The night before my talk I had a dream, a cricketing dream. This featured an India–England match, where, at one stage, Anil Kumble was bowling to Alec Stewart. The batsman played for the googly – Kumble's stock delivery – but the ball held its line, took the outside edge, and was caught low down to his right at slip by Rahul Dravid. As soon as the catch was safely held I woke up.

When it came to my professional anxieties I did not call batsmen to mind in my sleep. Rather, I sought succour in the deeds of a bowler, who happened to be from my own home state (as, indeed, was his slip fielder). In the event – helped no doubt by the calm brought about by the dream – my lecture went swimmingly.

This Kumble–Dravid dream occurred in 2002. Since then, the game I love most has not figured in my sleep. Nowadays, my dreams tend to be about the woods and fields of the Dehradun of my youth (woods and fields since claimed by homes and offices). However, on the days when I cannot easily go to sleep – days that come with greater regularity as one advances into the sixties – I will put myself to rest by visualising the two greatest and most gifted bowlers of my time.

These are Shane Warne and Wasim Akram. So, if I am awake at night, I think first of Warne, his short, slow run-up, the sudden whirl of the wrists with those strong shoulders propelling the ball, which dips and turns to the right to catch the edge or else goes straight on and has the batsman lbw. Or I think of Akram, running in fast and fluid, left-arm over with the new ball, an inswinger taking middle stump, or left-arm round with the old ball, reverse swinging from leg to off to have the hapless batsman caught at slip.

To explain why I so admire Warne and Akram, I need to tell one more Arthur Mailey story. During the 1930 Australian tour of England, the home side picked the young and untried wrist-spinner, Ian Peebles. In between Tests, the debutant asked Mailey for advice on how to disguise his googly. The lesson asked for was given, whereupon some Australian critics accused Mailey of being unpatriotic. Mailey answered, 'Spin bowling is an art. And art is international.'

Swing bowling is an art too. And its acknowledged modern master is Pakistan's Wasim Akram. Some years ago, I was watching an India–Pakistan match at the ground, in the pavilion. Akram came down from the commentary box, and, as he did, Zaheer Khan (who was sitting out the match with an injury) rushed to be at his side. As Akram spoke with friends and fans, Zaheer stood silently, looking at his hero with sheepish adoration. On that occasion they did not exchange words, but we do know that at other meetings Akram advised Zaheer on changes of pace, reverse swing, when to shift from over the wicket to round the wicket, and other special features of the swing bowler's art. For this he has been chastised by xenophobic Pakistanis (just as Mailey was by parochial Australians). But Akram has carried on teaching Indians (and Kiwis and Australians, and Sri Lankans and Bangladeshis) regardless.

As a boy, I harboured foolish fantasies about becoming a batsman. Now, I would rather restore the place of bowlers in the history and imagination of cricket. Until I was in my thirties, I always wanted my country to win. Now, I only want a good match. That is why, when I seek to put myself to sleep these days, I think of the sublime beauties of Shane Warne's leg-break and Wasim Akram's late inswing. That neither of these bowlers is an Indian, that one of them is, in fact, a Pakistani, that both are considerably *younger* than me, are not, one thinks, entirely coincidental.

The chauvinisms of generation and nation I have left behind me. The partisanship towards bowlers and Test cricket I shall retain until the end of my days. And when FUCC plays BUCC in the KSCA's First Division League, or when Karnataka plays Mumbai in the Ranji Trophy, I leave no one in any doubt about which side I want to win.